THE UNIVERSAL JEW

THE
UNIVERSAL
JEW

MASCULINITY,
MODERNITY,
AND THE
ZIONIST
MOMENT

MIKHAL DEKEL

NORTHWESTERN UNIVERSITY PRESS
EVANSTON, ILLINOIS

Northwestern University Press
www.nupress.northwestern.edu

Printed in the United States of America

10 9 8 7 6 5 4 3 2 1

"Parade of the Fallen," from *No Rattling of Sabers: An Anthology of Israeli War Poetry,*
translated by Esther Raizen, reprinted by permission of the Center for Middle Eastern
Studies at the University of Texas at Austin.

Library of Congress Cataloging-in-Publication Data
Dekel, Mikhal, 1965–
      The universal Jew : masculinity, modernity, and the Zionist moment / Mikhal
    Dekel.
          p. cm.
      Includes bibliographical references and index.
      ISBN 978-0-8101-2717-3 (pbk. : alk. paper)
      1. Jewish literature—19th century—History and criticism. 2. Jewish literature—
    20th century—History and criticism. 3. Hebrew literature, Modern—History and
    criticism. 4. Zionism in literature. 5. Masculinity in literature. 6. Gender identity in
    literature. 7. Jews—Identity. 8. Eliot, George, 1819–1880. Daniel Deronda. 9. Herzl,
    Theodor, 1860–1904. Altneuland. I. Title.
    PN842.D45 2010
    809.88924—dc22

                                                                          2010028928

To my mother, Zipora Dekel

CONTENTS

ACKNOWLEDGMENTS

This book began as my dissertation at Columbia University and has been long in the making. Both individually and as a pair, Zionism and gender are highly embattled and politicized topics; they are also, for me, deeply personal, and as such defied, at times, critical evaluation. I could not have worked through the various permutations and challenges of this book without the knowledge, critique, wisdom, and support of numerous mentors, fellow doctoral students, colleagues, and friends. Dan Miron, whose brilliance in all things literary drew me to Columbia in the first place, was its earliest, most demanding, and most instructive reader. Nicholas Dames, who uniquely combines copious amounts of geniality and smarts, helped shape my early understanding of Eliot. Hannan Hever, a friend and exacting reader to this day, repeatedly sharpened my political understanding of texts. Eve Sedgwick infused me with a theoretical framework and academic boldness; her absence from our world still feels so raw. To these and other early readers at Columbia and CUNY, including Patricia Williams, Hamid Dabashi, Avi Matalon, Marlene Clark, and Karen Lindo, my book owes its early shape.

Other friends and colleagues have been essential interlocutors. Nick Pappas explicated Nietzsche and more than once helped me break out of intellectual impasses. Josh Wilner taught me how to read closely. My beloved CCNY colleagues, Elizabeth Mazzola and Geraldine Murphy, generously commented on various chapters of the book. Several grant-giving institutions—the Foundation for Jewish Culture, the Andrew W. Mellon Foundation, the GSUC Center for the Humanities, the CCNY Office of the Dean of Humanities, and the PSC-CUNY—have provided me with much-needed time and money to complete this book.

Finally, there are a number of people without whom this book would not have seen the light of day: Nancy Miller, who came into my life and this project rather late but has since helped and inspired me in crucial and numerous tangible and intangible ways; Salar Abdoh, my dear, dear friend; Sharon Dekel, sister and constant interlocutor; Andrew Parker and Vivian Liska: astute and generous readers; Lynn Dion, my wizardly scholarly editor; Henry Carrigan Jr. and Heather Antti of Northwestern University Press; and, of course, Amir and Daniel Halfon, who give the deepest meaning to my life and make everything in it possible.

The Universal Jew

Introduction: Man-Jew-Woman

*After the terror of the bloody atrocities a moment of calm
followed for baiter and baited to catch their breath. Meanwhile
the Jewish refugees, with the very funds collected for their
immigration, are being—"repatriated"! But the Western
Jews have again learned to suffer the cry, "hep! hep!" as their
brothers in the old days. The eruption of blazing indignation
over the shame to which they were subjected has turned to a
rain of ashes, gradually covering the glowing soil. Shut your
eyes and hide your head like an ostrich—there is to be no
lasting peace unless in the fleeting intervals of relaxation you
apply a remedy more thoroughgoing than those palliatives to
which our hapless people have been turning for 2000 years. This
is the kernel of the problem, as we see it: the Jews comprise a
distinctive element among the nations under which they dwell,
and as such can neither assimilate nor be readily digested by
any nation. Hence the solution lies in finding a means of so
readjusting this exclusive element to the family of nations, that
the basis of the Jewish question will be permanently removed
. . . The great ideas of the eighteenth and nineteenth centuries
have not passed us by without leaving a trace. We feel not only
as Jews; we feel as men. As men, we, too, would fain live and be
a nation like the others.*

—LEO PINSKER, *AUTOEMANCIPATION* (1882)

*Descendants of the Sodomites, so numerous that we may apply
to them that other verse of Genesis: "If a man can number
the dust of the earth, then shall thy seed also be numbered,"
have established themselves throughout the entire world; they
have had access to every profession and pass so easily into*

the most exclusive clubs that, whenever a Sodomite fails to
secure election, the blackballs are, for the most part, cast by
other Sodomites, who are anxious to penalize sodomy, having
inherited the falsehood that enabled their ancestors to escape
from the accursed city. It is possible that they may return there
one day. Certainly they form in every land an Oriental colony,
cultured, musical, malicious, which has certain charming
qualities and intolerable defects . . . but I have thought
it as well to utter here a provisional warning against the
lamentable error of proposing, just as people have encouraged
a Zionist movement, to create a Sodomist movement and to
rebuild Sodom. For, no sooner had they arrived there than
the Sodomites would leave the town so as not to have the
appearance of belonging to it, would take wives, keep mistresses
in other cities where they would find, incidentally, every
diversion that appealed to them. They would repair to Sodom
only on days of supreme necessity, when their own town was
empty, at those seasons when hunger drives the wolf from the
woods; in other words, everything would go on very much as it
does today in London, Berlin, Rome, Petrograd or Paris.

—MARCEL PROUST, SODOM AND GOMORRAH IN
IN SEARCH OF LOST TIME (1921–22)

"Coming Out" as a Jewish Nation

For Proust, the social position of closeted gays and assimilated Jews, at
once liminal and prominent within Christian fin-de-siècle Europe, is not
merely tolerable but ineluctable. It is the place that Swann inhabits, as do
Marcel and his younger brother Robert, all of whom descend from Jewish
lineage, are baptized as Catholics, and maintain fabulous social positions
and various open secrets. It is the end of the nineteenth century, the beginning of the twentieth. Jews have been naturalized or assimilated to
various degrees in both Western and Eastern Europe for a century or
more. If the "Jewish Question," as Steven B. Smith (1997:1) writes, is "the
most vivid form of the question of the Other with which modernity and
liberal [European] society labored to come to terms," then the semi-open
Jewish closet that Proust imagines and inhabits is a kind of solution; it is
a place where the Enlightenment fantasy of equal rights is both mocked
and masked, allowed to perpetuate in its basic assumptions through a

kind of "don't ask, don't tell" mentality that Proust's irony both exposes and sanctifies. It is a place strained, bent, and rendered hardly habitable by the late nineteenth-century rise of European nationalisms and the attendant dramas of Dreyfus in the West and violent pogroms in the East. Yet the antithetical scenario—coming out of the Jewish closet into an openly Jewish nation—is for Proust a useless solution as a Jewish state will appeal only in the face of calamity. On days of calm, both Jews and Sodomites (who are often interchangeable in fin-de-siècle discourse) will disperse among the large European cities—"form[ing] in every land an Oriental colony, cultured, musical, malicious, which has certain charming qualities and intolerable defects"—keeping half-secret and half-Christian identities in "London, Berlin, Rome, Petrograd or Paris."

Proust thus forewarns us against the national phantasm: the possibility of turning a half-closeted minority into an open majority. He warns us against the appeal and also the effectiveness of a Jewish/Sodomite nation in which one will be able to come out as a Jew/Sodomite within a monolithic community of Jews/Sodomites. He lambastes the possibility of the nation operating as an island of absolute transparency, where inner and outer Jewish/homosexual identities converge in an undivided self; the structural binary division of Jew/Christian, homosexual/heterosexual, minority/majority, he suggests rather, is so ingrained in culture that it will outlive any normalizing politics of nation.

Proust was wrong, however, in imagining the nation as a lucid, transparent haven of monolithic identity, one that can easily be relinquished when the wolf has gone back to the woods. That much we know from the nation's dissection by postmodern and postcolonial critics: Anderson, Žižek, Lloyd, Berlant, Gourgouris, to mention just a few, who by now have shown the nation to be an incoherent, heterogeneous institution organized largely around a collective fantasy, an intricate dream-language that through mostly unconscious processes ties members to each other and to the experience of nationality. Gourgouris has called this the nation's "dream-work": those intangible elements that constitute the "nationalizing experience," the "historically specific national fantasy [around which] the experience of nationality is woven" (1996:28). This dream-work is present from the nation's very foundation, *particularly* at its very foundation, when the nation is just an idea, an imagined community that, in Zionism's case, is still unmoored in a territorial claim. And it is through the dream imagery that emerges at what I call here the "Zionist moment"—roughly around the end of the nineteenth century—that the nation propels a restructuring of terms, a reshuffling of the inner/

outer, minority/majority oppositions that Proust sanctifies into something else, something new, a hybrid identity of sorts. This reshuffling, the process through which a minority group becomes "majoritized" or "nationalized" and disparate individuals become a "people" occurs, as theorists of nation building have shown, in the aesthetic, imaginary, and symbolic realm no less—perhaps more—than in the realm of outright political or legal struggle. Or to put it more precisely: it is in the imaginary that both the production and the reception of the ideological and political take place. The overarching ambition of this book is to examine this process in the particular case of Zionism, to delineate the coming out and coming-into-being moment of the Jewish nation as it unfolds in late nineteenth- and early twentieth-century Europe, to examine the terms and the techniques through which, imaginatively, *this* minority begins to imagine itself as a majority.

Jews/Men

If Proust gives us the structuring taxonomy of European culture in the form of hierarchically organized binary definitions—Christian/Jewish, heterosexual/homosexual, majority/minority, open/secret, et cetera—for early Zionists these binary pairs are encapsulated in the binary terms Man/Jew: *We feel not only as Jews; we feel as men.*

But what is the meaning of "Jews" here? What is the meaning of "men"? A simple sentence, but deceptively so, for each of these terms evokes its own genealogy and associative register, and each comes under increasing definitional pressure at the turn of the nineteenth century. "What, then, is the Jew if he is nothing that a man can be?" Otto Weininger asks in his 1903 best-seller *Geschlecht und Charakter* (published in English as *Sex and Character* in 1906). In Weininger's text, which by now needs little exposition, the "Jew," like the "woman," is positioned as the antithesis to "Man." Because Jews are heteronomous in the strict Kantian sense, namely, unfree and dependent on others, because they are not stable and autonomous subjects but vacuous entities—"they have no intrinsic standard of value—nothing in their own soul by which to judge of the worthiness of any particular object"; they are "nothing in themselves" and therefore "can become everything"—they lack the qualities of Man and therefore of citizen:

> Citizenship is an un-Jewish thing, and there has never been
> and never will be a true Jewish State. The State involves the

aggregation of individual aims, the formation of and obedience to self-imposed laws; and the symbol of the State, if nothing more, is its head chosen by free election . . . Rousseau's
much despised theory of the conscious co-operation of individuals to form a State deserves more attention than it now
receives . . . The true conception of the State is foreign to the
Jew, because he, like the woman, is wanting in personality; his
failure to grasp the idea of true society is due to his lack of free
intelligible ego. Like women, Jews tend to adhere together, but
they do not associate as free independent individuals mutually
respecting each other. (Weininger 1906:187–88)

For Weininger, as Slavoj Žižek has argued, the distinction between
Man and Jew/Woman is thus grounded in the very ontological difference between subject and object, active spirit and passive matter
(1994:97). The Jew is not *precisely* like Woman: while "the woman is
material which passively assumes any form impressed upon it," the
Jew "is not dominated by others but submits himself to them"; while
Woman is pure receptivity, in the Jew "there is a definite aggressive-
ness," a force that discharges from within and is not only received from
without; therefore, the essential trait of "being-nothing and becoming-
all-things differs in the two." Woman receives her value from Man, is
constituted by Man, while the Jew is intrinsically "gifted." Nonetheless,
like Woman, the "Jew" is construed by Weininger as that which is not
Man: "Man has no object outside himself; he lives for nothing else; he
is far removed from being the slave of his wishes, of his abilities, of his
necessities; he stands far above social ethics; he is alone." The Jew by
contrast is immersed in "Jewish solidarity," "matchmaking," "family,"
and "sexuality"—all of which are contra to "free, self-governing individuals" who are able to choose between virtue and vice "in the Aryan
fashion" (Weininger 1906).

It is easy to reduce *Sex and Character* to the sum of the antifeminist and anti-Semitic prejudices of Weininger's historical moment. More
precisely, it is easy as well as historically accurate to read Weininger's
effeminization of the Jew in the way that Anne McClintock (1997) and
others have read the effeminization of the Bengali man: as the product
of colonialism/Aryanism. The masculinity of empire, as McClintock has
shown, was articulated in the first instance through a symbolic feminization of the colonized, amply contained in Thomas Macaulay's famous
observations: "During many ages [the Bengali] has been trampled upon

by men of bolder and hardy deeds. Courage, independence, veracity, are qualities to which his constitution and his situation are equally unfavourable" (cited in Roselli 1980:122). Likewise for Weininger, the masculine identity and coherence of Aryan culture is sealed by its opposition to the effeminate Jew.

Yet what is lost in such a reading of *Sex and Character* as the perverse expression of circumscribed Aryan anxieties is a sense of the work's astounding popularity beyond Aryan culture, in the first decades of the twentieth century, across Europe and the United States and among a great diversity of people, including Sigmund Freud, who called *Sex and Character* "remarkable" and its author "highly gifted but sexually deranged" (quoted in Le Rider [1993:168]). Žižek attributes this popularity to the "effect of recognition" that was triggered by Weininger's works. "It was," Žižek writes, "as if he 'called by name' all that the 'official' discourse silently presupposed, not daring to pronounce it publicly" (1994:97). This official "discourse" was not solely the cultural product of the nationalist wave that had washed over Europe since the 1880s but, more significantly, and despite Weininger's supposed anti-Enlightenment agenda, of Enlightenment thought itself.

Notwithstanding his perverted interpretation of Kantian morality, Weininger by his own admission draws the image of Man as autonomous, self-governing subject directly from Kant, the foremost Enlightenment philosopher, and from Rousseau, whose notion of the "social contract" hinges on the supposition of a self-willed individual subject. It is to this image that Weininger opposes Jews and women. Yet as Horkheimer and Adorno have further shown in their *Dialectic of Enlightenment* (1972), such opposition was inherent already in the Enlightenment project itself, which invariably represented the ideal of self-liberation as a dialectic whose "uncivilized" half was linked to the Jews. If the Enlightenment ideal of self-liberation was a reincarnation of the story of Oedipus, who time and again was destined to wrestle with the forces that threatened his still-fragile individuality, on a societal level, the sacrifice upon which Western civilization fell back in its attempt to free itself was intimately tied to the abjection of the Jews (1972:168–228). Indeed, Weininger stresses that the "Jew" is not a person or a race but a label, an eternal "platonic type" representing a set of abjected qualities opposite or even potentially internal to Man.

Both postmodern and nationalist scholars of Jewish history have presented accounts similar to those of Adorno and Horkheimer. Over and above the commonplace assessment that individual Jews were the legal beneficiaries of Enlightenment rhetoric and ideals (the status of their group identity is, of course, more questionable[1]), these scholars have shown that within the political rhetoric of Enlightenment "sameness," the "Jew" as such represented an unassimilable difference. Though the Enlightenment marks the beginning of the legal emancipation of European Jews, sociologist Zygmunt Bauman has claimed that "Allosemitism"—the practice of setting the Jews apart from all others—had in fact increased in direct correlation to the abolition of legal and visible differences (1991:145). Culturally, Bauman argues, Jews were positioned not as subjects but as by-product of the Enlightenment, as that which must be (symbolically and materially) expunged on route to the liberation and autonomy of *Man* (1991:168–228).

Autoemancipation (Pinsker 1882/1944), one of the earliest articulations of the Zionist idea, is an attempt to shift this binary opposition between Man and Jew in part by reenacting both sides of the dialectic of Enlightenment thinking within the identity of a Jewish national subject. "The great ideas of the eighteenth and nineteenth centuries have not passed us by without leaving a trace," Pinsker writes. With the exclusion of its Revisionist or Rightist margins, early mainstream Zionist discourse, as Hannan Hever (2002:43) and others have shown, was essentially liberal, deploying the language of French liberalism in preference to the language of blood kinship of the German Volk. Early Zionist demands for national particularity are couched in broad universal language—the right to be "a nation like all nations," the right to honor, the right to dignity, freedom, and autonomy—and not in claims to Jewish particularity. These will come later, in post-1967 Israel. What is locatable in the early Zionist period, perhaps its most poignant pedagogical aim, is the psycho-political redefinition of the Jew as an autonomous, concrete universal subject, as *Man*. This, of course, is not an aim unique to Zionism; the very morphology of "nation," as Gourgouris writes, "exemplifies the predicament of the Enlightenment insofar as it bears its central paradox: it is at once particular and universal" (1996:5). Yet if for European culture, the "Jew" par excellence represented the contra-Enlightenment—that which is psychically invested with nonuniversalizable particularity and inherent heteronomy—then the Zionist reshuffling of terms demanded a particularly elastic brand of intellectual, emotional, and political acrobatics and demands today a particularly rigorous and complex analysis.

Lack of National Affiliation as Moral Sickness

How then is the quest for a universal/Jewish self-identity negotiated at the late nineteenth-century Zionist moment when the "Jew" as such represents the essence of nonuniversality in the very thought upon which it is drawing? Often through a discourse of self-critique that mimics the very logic of Enlightenment dialectic. In this vein, Pinsker depicts the "Jewish people" as the nonhuman Other within the world of European nations:

> After the Jewish people had yielded up their existence as an actual state, as a political entity, they could nevertheless not submit to a total destruction—they did not cease to exist spiritually as a nation. The world saw in this people the uncanny form of one of the dead walking among the living. The ghostlike apparition of a people without unity or organization, without land or another bond of union, no longer alive, and yet moving about among the living—this eerie form scarcely paralleled in history, unlike anything that preceded or followed it, could not fail to make a strange, peculiar impression upon the imagination of the nations. And if the fear of ghosts is something inborn, and has a certain justification in the psychic life of humanity, what wonder that it asserted itself powerfully at the sight of this dead and yet living nation? Fear of the Jewish ghost has been handed down and strengthened for generations and centuries . . . Judeophobia is a form of demonopathy. (1944:77–78)

Pinsker thus lays down the basis for an ambivalent Zionist discourse that is at once critical of Gentile victimization of Jews yet lays the blame for victimhood on the Jews themselves. And like Weininger, the critique of the latter is rooted in the heteronomous condition of Jews:

> Since conditions are and must remain such as we have described them, we shall forever continue to be what we have been and are, *parasites,* who are a burden to the rest of the population, and can never secure their favor . . . What a pitiful figure do we cut! We do not count as a nation among the other nations, and we have no voice in the council of the peoples, *even in affairs which concern us.* Our fatherland is the other man's country; our unity—dispersion, *our solidarity—the gen-*

eral hostility to us, our weapon—humility, our defense—flight,
our individuality—adaptability, our future—tomorrow. What a
contemptible role for a people which once had its Maccabees!
. . . What a difference between Past and Present! (1944:87, 93,
95; my emphases)

The diachronically aligned Man/Jew of Enlightenment thought is
thus replaced within the Zionist paradigm with a synchronic opposition between past and present, between the Maccabees, leaders of the
Jewish revolt against the Hellenic establishment, who become associated
with solidarity, individuality, autonomy, and action, and modern Jews,
aligned with humility, reaction, and survival. "Man" is locatable in pre-
modern Jewish civilization; "Jew" is projected onto modern Jews whose
moral existence is reduced to the tactics of self-preservation:

> Seeking to maintain our material existence, we were con-
> strained too often to forget our moral dignity. We did not see
> that on account of tactics unworthy of us, which we were forced
> to adopt, we sank still lower in the eyes of our opponents, that
> we were only the more exposed to humiliating contempt and
> outlawry, which have finally become our baleful heritage. In
> the wide, wide world there was no place for us. We prayed only
> for a little place anywhere to lay our weary head to rest; and
> so, by lessening our claims, we gradually lessened our dignity
> as well. (85)

Pinsker walks a tightrope here between irony—"He must be blind indeed who will assert that the Jews are not *the chosen people,* the people
chosen for universal hatred" (79)—and "objective" description of the
modern Jewish condition. Mostly, like Weininger, he is straight-faced.
To the extent that Kant's standard of morality, the Categorical Imperative, is the law of an autonomous will, Pinsker, like Weininger, locates
Diaspora Jews outside its prerogative. Like the Enlightenment philoso-
phers, he deems the self-governing moral ego to be at the center of his
concept of nation and citizenship; because the Jews are parasitic and
heteronomous—that is, either willingly (Weininger) or forced (Pinsker)
into submitting themselves to others—they are incapable of perform-
ing the duty of a potential citizen. Because they are under the control
of others—"man" but also their tribe and family (Weininger), their host
nations (Pinsker)—and because, given this subordinated position, they

must act out of self-preservation, which is a motive extraneous to duty itself, the Jews' actions, even if law-abiding, do not have moral worth or moral dignity. Though Pinsker's rationale is that a self-governing Jewish state—"We need nothing but a large piece of land for our poor brothers" (94)—will necessarily bring with it moral dignity, his essay often follows a reverse logic, one much closer to Weininger's, suggesting that a change in Jewish "character" is necessary to bring about the state. Both Weininger and Pinsker qualify the essentialist nature of these claims (Pinsker deems Jewish flaws to be a consequence of their environment; Weininger declares his claims as nonessentialist so that the "Platonic" definition of the "Jew" can potentially apply even to an Aryan); yet both writers define heteronomy as an ingrained Jewish "quality" that must be lifted before any external change may occur.

Pinsker in particular distinguishes between freedom—"the ability to act with sufficient resources and power to make one's desires effective" (Berlin 2000) and autonomy, concerning the independence of the desiring subject and the authenticity of the desires and values that move him to act in the first place. In order to be able to organize politically and seek freedom—that is, desire to be free—the Jews must first achieve personal autonomy:

> The strongest fact . . . to prevent the Jews from striving after an independent national existence is the fact that they do not feel the need for such an existence . . . In a sick man, the absence of desire for food and drink is a very serious symptom. It is not always possible to cure him of this ominous loss of appetite . . . The Jews are in the unhappy condition of such a patient. (77)

Thus, not only anti-Jewish hatred (which Pinsker calls Judeophobia) but also the disinterest of Jews in autonomous national life is depicted as a terminal illness. Yet if this can be overcome, the national solution will heal both diseases, eliminating Judeophobia and constituting the Jew as a living, healthy, manly desiring subject:

> In unity and in serried ranks we once accomplished an orderly departure from Egypt, to escape from shameful slavery, and conquer the fatherland. Now we wander as fugitives and exiles with the foot of the ruffianly boor upon our necks, death in our hearts, without a Moses for our leader, without a promise of land *which we are to conquer by our own might*. (95)

> It [thus] is our bounden duty to devote all our remaining
> moral force to re-establish ourselves as a living nation, so that
> we may finally assume a more fitting and dignified role. (90)

> If we seriously desire that, we must first of all extricate our-
> selves from the old yoke, and rise manfully to our full height.
> (97)

Lack of National Standing as "Unmanly"

Early Zionist discourse, stating as its explicit aim the liberation of Man
in Jew, is thus predicated on a distinction and a hierarchy similar to that
of Enlightenment as well as Weiningerian thought. How must we read
this proximity? For the most part, Zionism's anti-Semitism had evaded
critical attention until the emergence of postcolonial and new historical
thought, which in conjunction with an increasingly critical stance toward Israel and Zionism made such analysis possible. If, as David Lloyd
(1997) has argued, the West has generally distinguished between "good"
and "bad" nationalism, pre-1967 Israel, particularly in its socialist manifestation, was cautiously labeled as good or progressive both internally
(by its Jewish citizens) and externally (by many who were not its direct
opponents). Indeed, while thinkers from Rousseau to Benedict Anderson have celebrated the nation as the most universally legitimate political entity and a propellant of modernity, non-Western postcolonial
nations have increasingly been viewed as atavistic, violent, as solvents
of modernity.[2] But where does Zionism fall? For its critics in the West,
particularly since 1967, Israel is increasingly falling under the latter
category, and for this reason some aspects of its identity have increasingly been examined in relation to its "colonized" past. Daniel Boyarin
(1997), for example, has read the works of Theodor Herzl, founder of
the political Zionist movement, to support his reading of Zionist masculinity as the internalization of the Aryan masculine ideal:

> Pre-emancipation Jewishness in eastern Europe (and tradi-
> tional Jewish identity in general)—it could be argued—was
> formed via an abjection of the *goy*, as Ivan, a creature stereo-
> typed as violent, aggressive, coarse, drunk, and given to such
> nonsense as dueling, seeking honor in war, and falling in ro-
> mantic "love"—all referred to as *goyim naches*. For those Jews, it
> was abjection of "manliness"—itself, of course, a stereotype—

that produced their identity. In the colonial/postcolonial moment, the stereotyped other becomes the object of desire, of
introjection rather than abjection, and it is the stereotyped self
that is abjected. (Boyarin 1997:304)

To a not inconsiderable extent, the project of these Zionists
(known as political Zionists) was to transform Jewish men into
the type of male that they admired, namely, the ideal "Aryan"
male. (Boyarin 1997:277)

Boyarin's argument and the readings he presents in its support are
cogent but limited.[3] A rejection/introjection, before/after model predicated on the substitution of one stable identity (Jew) for another (Gentile) cannot account for the hybridic nature of either, nor for the ambivalent and complex position of Jews in Europe; nor can such a model account for the radical break that the advent of Zionism represents. What
I mean is that at the Zionist moment in the late nineteenth century, a
host of texts, pamphlets, stories, images, and so on, begin to form a new
national imaginary—the network of fantasies, icons, and dreams that, as
Cornelius Castoriadis and later Žižek have argued, make up the "reality"
of a particular historical nation—which is not merely reactive to Europe. It is through this network that national "feelings" arise, that an image of a unified national "people" is delineated, that a vision of "citizen"
emerges. Early Zionist texts like Pinsker's and Herzl's are in this sense
speech acts that performatively *enact* the nation, and convey a meaning
in excess of any literal interpretation. An account of the turn to Zionism
that is predicated on seamless continuity (with either a monadic Jewish
national identity or with "Aryan masculinity") and does not theorize this
"lens" through which, from this point on, later texts and situations will
be read, necessarily obscures the vision not only of lovers but also of
enemies of Zionism. And it is for this reason that Michel Foucault has
insisted on genealogical readings that return to the fracture or foundation—the "point zero"—of discourses and institutions. As he writes (in
relation to the invention of "madness"):

We must try to return, in history, to that zero point in the
course of madness at which madness is an undifferentiated
experience, a not yet divided experience of division itself. We
must describe, from the start of its trajectory, that "other form"
which relegates Reason and Madness to one side or the other

of its action as things henceforth external, deaf to all exchange, and as though dead to one another. (2001:xi)

Imperfect Hindsight: Seeing Early Zionism Through a Modern Lens

To capture that "other form," that psycho-ideological shift after which a Jewish national subject will become constituted and forever distinct—not only from Europe but also from "Jews-as-subjects-of-other-nation"—requires, I think, a different terrain of interrogation and a different tool set from those that have tended to characterize the work of most nationalist *and* postnationalist scholars of Zionism, one that accounts for the discontinuity, the radical break that a nation and a new nationalist discourse constitute. Because early Zionist texts like *Autoemancipation* do not ultimately depict a preexistent identity but rather *create* and *disseminate* a consciousness that can be called "national" and an image of a national subject that did not exist prior to their inscription in and by these texts, their function as "speech acts" warrants an analysis not only or even primarily of what they say but of what they do and how they do it. A colonial/postcolonial model that depicts the Zionist moment as one in which identity x is flatly exchanged for identity y in essence ignores, or at any rate fails to account for, not only this *performativity* but also the radical *contingency* of the moment of subject formation. It does not account, for example, for the fact that at the foundational moment, identity, to the extent that it is indeed the subject's "new" identity, is assumed imaginatively—that is, before the subject has become a subject and from a relative position of powerlessness. Once we do account for these, we are led, for example, to pose a question not unlike one which in relationship to women has been posed by feminists for several decades now: Is a masochistically construed Jewish self-image really only an internalization and endorsement of an oppressed subject's sense of worthlessness? "Or," as Eve Sedgwick has asked, "may not this self-representation stand in some more oblique, or even oppositional, relation to her political experience of oppression?" (Sedgwick 1985:6). Might not, in other words, the use to which Zionist writers put the stereotypical image of the Diaspora Jew serve, at its foundational moment, a purpose other than a pure abjection of Jewish identity and its substitution with Aryan masculinity?

Indeed, because the nation, as Benedict Anderson has brilliantly intuited, is closer in its morphology to family than it is to ideology, because it taps into deeply seated dreams, traumas and repetitions of traumas,

external and internal stereotyping, and the interlinking between all of
these factors, it can neither be rendered through the indigenous knowledge of its members nor yet through binary, preconceived theoretical
paradigms. "The radical contingency of its terrain," as Gourgouris writes,
demands a more ambivalent mode of interrogation. For if we accept that
the nation is a social imaginary institution, we must also accept that its
dream-language, like any dream-language, is greatly more multifarious
and opaque than any temptingly simple and neat line of inquiry—one
that draws a straight, neat line from past to present—allows. For a theory
that allows for the radical ambivalence at the heart of the "nation" to be
interrogated, I then turn to a different school of postcolonial, postnational thought, one that zeroes in on the national's morphology, on the
aesthetic, political, and emotional strategies through which the "nation-
thing," as Zizek has called it, is articulated. I refer here specifically to the
works of Benedict Anderson, Lauren Berlant, Slavoj Žiźek, and Stathis
Gourgouris, among others who have interrogated the various dreams
and fantasies of various nationalities.

That a nationalist historian of Zionism is already working from *within*
this social imaginary is self-evident; yet a theoretically rigid anti-Zionist
critic may be equally blinded by consciously or unconsciously ignoring
the force and scope of the Zionist imaginary. Who then holds the grid to
the interpretation of a national dream? Certainly not the dreamer. For
if the best metaphor for the nation is family, it is clear enough how, to
the extent that the interrogating subject is contained within the nation's
imaginary, the nation, like the family, will always remain partially outside her purview: this, no matter how far removed or even rationally
opposed the inquiring subject is from the nation's central ideology or
logic. Gourgouris astutely captures this predicament in musing on his
own relationship to his native Greece:

> In my attempt to ground this interrogation of Greek national
> culture within a more or less concrete social-historical con-
> tingency and not rely on some prefabricated theory or some
> ethnically indigenous knowledge, I discovered that no precise
> *situation* of contingency was ever possible. My link to the en-
> tity "modern Greece" was, at one level, bound to a precisely
> specified necessity. At the same time, paradoxically within and
> by virtue of this necessity, I also found "myself" exterior to
> the logic of this entity, the Neohellenic *logos*. This became the
> primary level of understanding *Greece* as a social-imaginary

signification, in the sense that it remained stubbornly beyond
reach. (1996:5)

The nation, then, constitutes its members as citizens through their
inscription in a shared social imaginary whose totality is at the same
time outside their grasp; it is perhaps that the nation *appears* transparent
and knowable only to its most zealous members or to its opponents. This
does not mean that one who stands outside the purview of a nation's
social imaginary is not implicated by *a* national imaginary, by *some* national imaginary (even, and perhaps to a greater degree because of its
supposed absence, in the "postnational" West). Indeed, one of the most
glaring limitations of postnational critique has been that there *is cur-
rently no place outside the "nation,"* any nation, with its specific set of
exclusions, fantasies, privileges, and permitted/unpermitted discourse,
from which to launch an "objective" critique of the nation as such.

This problem of subject position in relation to the nation became clear
to me with the Israeli bombardment of Gaza in January 2009. While
nearly everyone I knew outside Israel followed the magnitude of Israeli
military violence with responses that veered from perplexity to revulsion, nearly everyone (though not *all*) inside Israel—its mainstream media and Jewish inhabitants at any rate—felt it fully justified and necessary. It was telling, indeed shocking, to compare the responses of two
otherwise very similar acquaintances (in terms of class, profession, family background) living inside and outside the nation's border. The latter
could not see *any* logic or purpose to Israeli actions and was appalled by
their repercussions; the former, a distinguished and committed doctor
who intensely labors on behalf of humanity every single day of his life,
considered this extreme violence on behalf of the state a perfectly legitimate and effective act of self-defense. Notwithstanding the complex
and dangerous impasse that the Israeli occupation has now reached, it
was, I thought, a demonstration of the working of the paranoia-driven
national imaginary at its extremist and most absurd instantiation.

Yet at the same time, a call to boycott Israeli academic and cultural
institutions in response to Gaza, sent to me over the Internet, seemed
also blind, not necessarily because of the actual call for boycott (which is
unfair to individual academics but could arguably yield some necessary
results in the region) but because of the letter's language, which depicted
Israel/Palestine through a clear-cut, binary framework of colonizer/
indigenous people (calling the Israeli assault on Gaza "one of the most
brutal uses of state power in both this century *and the last*"; emphasis

mine). This characterization seemed to me so descriptively inadequate that despite the fact that I found myself entirely outside the *logos* of the nation and utterly opposed to the Gaza operation, I could not bring myself to sign the petition. It is only from a safe distance, I thought, that one can imagine another nation as perfectly legible, as a perfectly transparent and interpretable text.

The Social Imaginary of Early Zionism

Foundational Zionist discourse at the late nineteenth and early twentieth centuries produced not only the national imaginary but a self-understanding in the realm of imagination and fiction. Contemporaneous as it was with psychoanalysis (Freud and Theodor Herzl met and frequented overlapping Viennese circles; Freud even reports dreaming about Herzl[4]), this discourse self-reflexively locates Zionist individual and group identity formation in the psychic power of images and the unconscious. There are numerous instances of this recognition, perhaps most powerfully demonstrated in the reading of the prominent Hebrew essayist Ahad Ha'am ("One of the People," the nom de plume of Asher Ginzburg) of the image of Moses. Moses for Ahad Ha'am stands as a symbol for Zionist revival first and foremost in his role as *Prophet*, one who by his very nature transcends the present; yet he also represents—as he does for Pinsker—absolute autonomy and absolute agency:

> [The Prophet] sees facts as they are, not through a haze of personal presuppositions; and he tells the truth as he sees it, without regard to the consequences. He tells the truth not because he wants to tell the truth, nor because he has convinced himself that he is in duty bound to tell the truth, but because he "can no other." Truth-telling is the law of his nature . . . Secondly, the Prophet is an extremist. His ideal fills his whole heart and mind; it is the whole purpose of his life and its empire must be absolute. The world of actuality must be remodeled to conform with the ideal world of his inner vision. ("Moshe" [1904] in Ahad Ha'am 1970:105)

To the extent that the modern Jewish condition is marked for Pinsker, Herzl, and even Ahad Ha'am by heteronomy and diffusion of identity, Moses is thus heralded as the embodiment of the autonomous, impenetrable self. Yet even as Moses embodies this idealized identity for the emerging national community Ahad Ha'am stresses again and again that his value lies strictly in the *realm of the symbolic:*

> The hero who lives on through the ages is not the hero as he was in his lifetime, but a creation of the popular imagination, which produces what the people wants and likes; and it is this imaginary creation, not the short-lived actuality, that influences mankind for hundreds or thousands of years. So too, when learned men rummage in the dust of ancient books and manuscripts to reconstruct the lives and personalities of historical figures as they actually were. The scholars think that they are ruining their eyesight in the cause of historical truth; but it seems to me that they over-rate the value of their discoveries, and overlook the simple fact that not every truth of archeology is also a truth of history. The truths of history are concerned only with the forces that have influenced the collective life of humanity. A man, even an imaginary man, who has left his mark on human life is a historical force, and his existence is a fact of history . . . Goethe's Werther, for example, though a creature of fiction, had sufficient influence in his time to cause suicides . . . What does it matter to history whether the source of this influence was once a walking and talking biped, or was never anything but a creature of the imagination labeled with the name of some actual man? In both cases, his existence is an indisputable fact of history, because he has helped *make* history.

On the threshold of Jewish history the figure of Moses, the greatest of our national heroes, stands like a pillar of light. As I read the Haggadah, on Passover eve, his image hovers over me and lifts me to a higher plane, where all the doubts and questions that have been raised about Moses do not trouble me in the least. Did Moses really exist? . . . Questions there are plenty; but I wave them aside with a short and simple answer. This Moses—I say to the erudite questioners—this man of antiquity, whose existence and character you are investigating, is no concern to anybody but learned antiquarians like yourselves. We have another Moses of our own, whose image has been enshrined in the hearts of the Jewish people for centuries, and who has never ceased to influence our national life from the earliest times to the present day . . . Even if you succeeded in proving beyond all doubt that the man Moses never existed,

or that the actual Moses was different from our picture of him,
that would not in the slightest degree affect the historical reality of the ideal Moses—the Moses who not only led us for forty
years in the wilderness of Sinai, but has led us for thousands of
years in all the wildernesses in which we have wandered since
the Exodus. (1970:101)

Lambasting contemporaneous scholars of the *Wissenschaft des Judentums* for their incessant scientific obsession with the historical Moses (an
obsession to which Freud's *Moses and Monotheism* was also a response[5]),
Ahad Ha'am hails the unquantifiable, immeasurable value of symbolic
power for the cohesion of national identity. It is of course against their
"scientific" attempts to contest Moses's Jewish origins that Ahad Ha'am
is subtly arguing, stressing instead the symbolic power of the imaginary
Moses for generations of Jews. In this evocation of the Moses *image* over
and against nineteenth-century revisionist readings of the Bible, and also,
parenthetically, over and against Jewish prohibition against symboliza-
tion, Ahad Ha'am not only elaborates on the nonpositivistic nature of
nation as a social imaginary but also evokes an image whose inner contradictions and otherness are part of its idolatrous power for modern
fin-de-siècle Jewish readers.

What is perhaps most radical in this work, however, is its inscription of the national "people" as at once prior/external to and constituted/
embodied by the Moses image: "This ideal figure is the creation of the
Jewish spirit; and the creator creates in his own image. It is in figures
such as this that the spirit of a people embodies its own deepest aspirations" (1970:100). So the traumatic, questionable origin of the historical
Moses, like the traumatic, questionable origin of the Jewish nation as an
autonomous entity, is erased though the repeated generation of meaning
over decades and centuries around the ideal figure, not around the Bible
or positivistic rabbinical texts. It is Moses's fictionality that enables generations of Jews, including, by his own admission, the writer himself, to
project their dreams onto the image; and yet concurrently, in the effects
that it imposes on history, the Moses figure transcends its own fictionality. In extending the story of Moses to the present, Ahad Ha'am unifies
the disparate existences of Jews in Europe and elsewhere under the sign
of "wildernesses" and, as Pinsker does in *Autoemancipation,* projects
back to his readers an image of a unified people, the presumption of an
uncontested "we."

It is this essentially imaginary core at the heart of the nation, of any
nation that has escaped most readers of Zionism, whether nationalist,

post-Zionist, or even anti-Zionist.[6] My mode of interrogation deviates from nationalist as well as current postnationalist readings of Zionism in two ways. First, fully cognizant of the limitations of historical inquiry, it reaches back to "point zero" of the Zionist idea in an attempt to isolate and avoid that which is never fully avoidable: the projection of the present into the past. Second, and I cannot stress this point enough, I am in full agreement with Gourgouris that the force, the desire, the aggression associated with the nation demands that we explore its formation as a social imaginary institution; that the nation is in essence an imaginary, fantastical formation, always *elsewhere* from its precise geographical location or explicit ideology. "A nation cannot be read as a text; even if it were to make sense, we would distrust it" (Gourgouris 1996:30); in this sense, though my reading is grounded in texts—unquestionably the primary source for the dissemination of early Zionist consciousness across Eastern and Western Europe—they are decidedly nonliteral. Rather, I seek to explore nation formation through the effects, psychic traces, and fantasies that are iconically and symbolically inscribed *in* and *by* foundational national texts. The focus on "by" implies attention to the reception and performativity of images, and to the ways that they collide with, trespass, broaden, and substitute for readers' fantasies; it is in this specific interplay between text and reader, I argue, that the process of nationalization occurs and readers are inscribed as citizens at the Zionist moment.

Early national texts—even if they are produced in disparate geographical locations—can thus never be read in isolation from each other nor from an imagined, implied, or historical reader; rather, these texts constitute the fabric upon which a national imaginary begins to be inscribed at *a specific historical moment*. Indeed, a national imaginary is particular and historical (Ahad Ha'am's representation of Moses's "eternal" value, for example, is a condition of the fin-de-siècle Zionist moment, corresponding to the "Real" in the everyday sense of the word; this merging of reality and the imaginary anyone living in Israel/Palestine knows perfectly). Yet the nation, as those same people also know perfectly well, is concurrently and essentially unintelligible, the interpretation of its dream-content, as in any dream-content, always deferred and beyond reach.

The "Jewish Ghost" as Holy Ghost

I would like to return here by way of example to additional associative paths marked by Pinsker's seemingly disparaging image of the Diasporic

"Jewish ghost." Pinsker, as we have seen, uses it to conjure up an image of the Jews as a spiritual essence without a material body, continually haunting the European nations. Sociologist Zygmunt Bauman has used a similar yet markedly distinct image, the "living fossil," to describe the particular and peculiar position of Jews vis-à-vis the Christian imagination: "Having overstayed their time and outlived their mission" (to give birth to Christ and Christianity), Bauman writes, in the eyes of Christian Europe the Jews "continued to haunt the world as living fossils" (1991:146). A living-dead ghost, however, taps into a much deeper well of associations than that of the inanimate trace of a long extinguished organism. Over and above its overt function in *Autoemancipation* to connote the "abnormal" position of Jews within European culture, the image of the ghost radiates in several directions, evoking not only (and not only negatively) the inhumanity of Jews but also the spiritual quality of Judaism as well as the Holy Ghost and Hamlet's ghost: that which needs to be avenged and that which mediates between God and believer. Tragedy and Christianity are thus brought, across the bar of Jewish prohibition, into the fold of the Zionist imaginary.

Indeed, if the national imaginary constitutes a dream-language, then formative Zionist texts constitute its "dream-content"—the condensed, censored, and circumscribed dream material that, through the process of interpretation, becomes linked to the numerous associative paths that Freud had called dream thoughts. *Jews as ghosts:* in the process of condensation and displacement that makes up dreaming, a mass of dream thoughts is distilled into this single image. To read it as a pure internalization or mirroring of anti-Jewish stereotypes is thus to miss the complexity and breadth of the Zionist dream. Indeed, it is through this image that Jewish past and future are temporally conflated into what Benedict Anderson (1983) has called the nation's permanent present tense; it is through this image that a potential conflict between the Jewish religion and the Jewish nation-state is resolved when the spiritual ghost (religion) is imagined as a pipeline to the modern nation; and it is through this decidedly Christian image that traces of Christian doctrine are incorporated into the Jewish national dream as well.

Unlike Bauman, who locates the impulse to castigate the Jew as Other directly and predominantly in Christianity's need to deny its own origins, Pinsker, like other nationalist writers, hardly gives Christianity a nod. To the degree that Christianity is explicitly permitted into Zionist discourse, it is always in the form of decontextualized and often minimized Christian anti-Semitism ("[The Jews] are said to have crucified Jesus, to have drunk the blood of Christians," Pinsker writes briefly[7]). This investment in minimizing the Christian effect on Jewish life and disregarding completely their mutual implication makes sense, of course, for a separatist national political discourse. Zionism thus displaces the story of European history as the history of Christianity with the modern narrative of nations in which, through the equalizing paradigm that parcels Europe into nations, the Jews are conceived as one "nation" among many. What are repressed, of course, are the Christian undercurrents of the nation paradigm itself, the Christian roots of Rousseau's civil religion and "universal" contract politics, the Christian undertones of the "universal" subject as such. For Rousseau, a civil religion whose essence is the centralized power of the state and the dutiful obedience of its citizens is needed exactly for the political organization of the dispersed Christians who lack in tribal or ethnic unity. Pinsker too presents a similar lament about the dispersion of the Jews, their lack of unity, their misguided and pluralistic identification with their numerous, respective host nations. Hence the image of the "Jewish ghost"—the idolatrical icon of the spiritual, personified ghost iterated in the New Testament as the "Spirit of Truth" (John 14:15–18), that which in the Holy Trinity helps Christians obey God and reach communion with one another and with the Father—transported into the Zionist imaginary as that which links the dispersed Jewish people as well as their past and present "national" state.

I am not suggesting here that early Zionism consciously embedded Christian doctrine into its mythology; but I am suggesting that if we begin to look at *Autoemancipation* first and foremost as a *performative* text, a text aimed at imaginatively constituting a national "people," we see that it does so not only with a reference to normative Jewish texts and common Jewish heritage (the Maccabees) but with idolatrous Christian imagery. For the image of persons as ghosts is much closer, in this regard, to the Christian Holy Spirit than to *Ruakh ha-kodesh*, the nonanthropomorphic spirit of God found frequently in Midrashic and Talmudic literature. In its attempt to seamlessly transition Judaism from religion to nation, in its attempt to universalize itself (and is there a purely "universal" space that is completely outside the domain of Christianity?), early Zionist writings thus make implicit use of those idolatrous symbols that have been explicitly tabooed in Jewish law and culture. It is exactly through its treading back and forth in forbidden waters and conjuring up a Christian image against the bar of Jewish prohibition that the dream image of a (secular) Jewish nation is projected onto would-be readers/citizens.

Reading the Zionist Moment

The Zionist imaginary thus constitutes a dream made up of "dream-thoughts" that are repressed from its official ideology. These associative links lead to Christianity, but also to European culture at large, on whose soil Jewish national thought emerges and consolidates itself. That nationalist accounts of Zionism would downplay—and in fact have downplayed—its negotiation with the European imagination is self-evident. Yet even a postnationalist account such as Jacqueline Rose's recent *The Question of Zion* (2005) traces a relatively simple narrative of Zionism from *within* its narrow Jewish context, namely, Zionism as a hard-headed, atavistic response to the "Jewish problem." Not unlike nationalist historians, Rose identifies a stable and clearly delineated Zionist subject—in her case, a slightly demented child who nonetheless possesses a few redeeming qualities—and an equally stable, objective, and antinationalist European subject, who is also the implicit addressee of her book. The assumption of the stability and autonomy of both these subjects is misguided on several counts, not the least of which is the morally shaky ground of Western antinationalism, based as it is, as Lloyd (1997) has shown, in the West's deep antipathy toward the anticolonial movements that its own "good" nationalism had inadvertently propelled. Indeed, as postcolonial scholars have often lamented, in its worry that the progressive history of the nation has dangerously swayed off course in twentieth-century nationalisms, the West seems to have "forgotten" its own atavistic past and so projected it on "regressive" nationalisms elsewhere (Gandhi 1998:107). This, of course, has a particular irony in the case of the Jews who, as even our cursive summary has shown, have played an ambivalent yet decidedly crucial role in the construction of "good" enlightened Western nationalism. Which is not, not at all, to dismiss the dangers of Israeli nationalism, nor its capacity for murderous violence, nor, as we have also seen, the imprint of Europe on its national imaginary.

Gourgouris identifies a similar problematic, though in profoundly different ways, in the mutual implication of Europe, Greece, and India:

> Both [Greece and India] are burdened with a classical past, a similar trap for the nationalist phantasm: modern malaise to be overcome and ancient glory to be regained. And in both cases, though in decidedly different ways, the trap is fed by Europe's own self-serving and autoscopic investment—*self serving because autoscopic.* This is the great historical and institutional

co-incidence of Philhellenism and Orientalism, Sanskrit and Greek being philology's bread and butter. In this respect, if the story of India is the paradigmatic condition of the colonialist imaginary, then the story of Greece is the paradigmatic condition *in* the imaginary. (1996:6)

Judaism, at once an insider and an outsider of Europe, occupies an even more ambivalent position in the European colonialist imaginary than Greece and/or India. For if classical Hellenic culture has been designated the origin of a European history that culminates in the nation-state, Judaism in turn is imagined as the origin prior to the origin, as that which has been eclipsed and repressed but which nonetheless has retained its presence. "In the course of its self-definition," Bauman writes, Christian Europe

marked the Jews as, above all, an oddity—the uncanny, mind-boggling and spine chilling incongruity that rebelled against the divine order of the universe. Many varieties of logical incoherence—indeed, all unresolved contradictions swept under the carpet in the orderly home of the Christian Church—converged in the image of the Jew laboriously constructed by Christian thought and practice in the process of their self-assertion. There were in the image of the Jews the motifs, mutually exclusive though already loaded with the most awesome ambivalence, of parricide and infanticide: the Jews were the venerable ancestors of Christianity, who however refused to withdraw and to pass away once Christianity was born and took over. (1998:146)

Judaism then, is mirrored by Europe's "autoscopic investment" but at the same time cast outside its field of vision, replaced exactly by the Hellenic ideal as the precedent to Christian culture. "They hardly know that Christ was a Jew," George Eliot laments about her fellow Englishmen in an 1876 letter to Harriet Beecher Stowe. "And I find men, educated, supposing that Christ spoke Greek."[8] In its formation story, modern Europe thus identifies with and appropriates ancient Greece as the idealized foundation of its historical narrative (a narrative whose autonomy and coherence is guaranteed by this idealized origin) while Judaism is in turn cast in the role of the abjected mother, the *real,* material origin that must always be denied.

Both modern Greece and Israel then (and Pinsker's text is paradigmatic here) are attempts at domestication, normalization, and containment of an idealization/abjection. Both sever ancient Greece/Judaism
from European history and European history from modern Greece/
Israel; but that does not mean that they are in turn severed from Europe's autoscopic gaze. Nor can either Philhellenism or Zionism sever
its self-imagining from Europe. For as Gourgouris notes, the refracted
mirroring of Europe will inevitably arise behind the effort to trace *any*
national imaginary, which is not to dismiss the long and relatively autonomous history of Jewish life, nor to regard the nation-state strictly
as a European import; yet it is to acknowledge that the process of nationalization of Judaism required an implicit negotiation with European
history and with the position of the "Jew" within its framework, a cunning procedure through which this framework is both internalized and
redefined vis-à-vis a "nationalized" narrative of Jewish history that in its
explicit accords glosses over two thousand years of Jewish life in Christian Europe. It is the desire to inscribe the "Jew" as a modern, universal,
"majority" post-Jewish subject, to undo, within an inscribed geographical space, the Enlightenment's binary opposition between Jew and Man
that are at the core of the foundational Zionist dream.

The "Jewish Ghost" as Hamlet's Ghost

One of the ways in this book in which I show early Zionist culture universalizing Jewish history is in the reshaping of the reader's understanding of the Jewish condition as *tragedy*. Tragedy: not in the vernacular
but in the classical sense, a world determined by fate, suffering, and the
tragic hero.[9] *Autoemancipation* is emblematic of this shift, not only in
linking Jewish suffering to the ancient sin of desertion of the homeland,
but also in evoking a powerful allusion to Hamlet's ghost—reconfigured
as the Jewish ghost—whose call for revenge and action is broadcast to
Pinsker's readers. The ghost who is said to torment the Gentile nations is
thus positioned within the context of the work to torment another: the
imagined male national subject-in-becoming who is Pinsker's implicit
addressee. Indeed, as the tone of *Autoemancipation* shifts from "objective" description of the dismal condition of the Jews to direct address, a
rhetoric of anger and an indirect call for action arise:

> The wretches! They reproach the eagle who once soared to
> heaven and recognized the Divinity, because he cannot rise

high in air when his wings are clipped! But even with wings
clipped we have remained on a level with the great peoples of
civilization. Grant us the happiness of independence, allow us
to be sole masters of our fate, give us a bit of land, grant us only
what you granted the Serbians and the Roumanians, the ad-
vantage of free national existence, and then dare to pass judgment upon us. At present we still live under the oppression of
the evils you have inflicted on us. What we lack is not genius,
but self-respect, and the consciousness of human dignity of
which you have robbed us. (86)

Even as he is casting the Jews as living ghosts and lamenting Jewish
passivity and heteronomy, Pinsker addresses an imagined "we" that encompasses the writer and imagined like-minded readers, who are constituted vis-à-vis an "enemy" at once known and unspecified (anti-Semites?
Western civilization at large?). In this, *Autoemancipation* performs what
it urges the Jews to do: first, via the image of the ghostly Jewish nation
that links the biblical past with the European present, it vertically consolidates an image of a "people" who are horizontally dispersed; second,
it conjures up the presence of potential male citizens in the image of an
implicit *tragic* addressee: a conflicted, deliberative Jewish Hamlet, cur-
rently unable to act against the offenses inflicted on his "nation" or the
"people," yet nonetheless, like prince Hamlet, potentially primed to "rise
up to [his] manly height" and exact revenge on their behalf.

Through this mobilization of universal (Christian/tragic) cultural
traces, and more specifically through its evocation of images like that
of the tragic male hero, which resonate universally, early Zionist discourse masks over Jewish otherness, pushing the limits of Jewish cultural discourse and the boundaries between Jew and Man. To be read
accurately, however, this gesture should be perceived not only in relationship to Jewish history and the structural overturning of the Jewish
condition in Europe but also to modernity at large, the modernity which
Hobsbawm (1990:14) and others have argued is the core of the process
of nationalization.

Enlightenment, Modernity, and the Advent of Zionism

In Adorno and Horkheimer's account, as well as that of Bauman, the
problematic of Enlightenment and the related problematic of the "Jew"
within the Enlightenment had reached its spectacular crisis with the

peak of modernity at the late nineteenth century. "It is now," Georg Simmel writes in 1908, "no longer a question of being a free individual but of being such and such a determinable and noninterchangeable individual . . . the tendency pervades the whole of modern life: the individual in search of himself, as if he did not yet possess himself, with no certain foothold except himself."[10] This pan-European vision of modernity and individual identity becomes most dramatically and cruelly personified, as Jacques Le Rider has demonstrated, in the insoluble identity crisis of modernized European Jews (1993:165–83). In Western Europe, a century-long assimilation process halted by anti-Semitic backlash produced a new type of Jewish individual: one who could not fully claim a European identity, nor yet return to the traditional Jewish life from which he has been permanently severed. In the Russian Pale, where nearly half of Europe's Jewish population lived, a series of pogroms in the 1880s and the beginning of the twentieth century dampened assimilatory hopes to an even greater degree. Yet concurrently, modernity had thrust thousands of young East European Jews away from a long-established religious tradition, education, and family life and in search of a new identity whose essence and inspiration were intensely debated. It is the plot of the young Jewish man "in search of himself" that propels the modern Hebrew bildungsroman from the mid-nineteenth century on. And it is in this sense that Pinsker's image of the Jewish ghost connotes yet a third meaning: that of a vacuous, ungrounded identity, seeking anchorage, an image of modernity itself.

Thus, even if the Jew had once symbolized that which is external to the Enlightenment project, by the late nineteenth century the Jew had come to symbolize the problematic *in* the Enlightenment: autonomy turned into isolation, freedom into nonidentity. It is in this sense that the Jewish nation functioned as a mitigating, compensatory force: both as agent of modernity and a force against its relentless tide.[11] If alienation from the self and from other Jews constitutes the modern Jewish condition, Pinsker imagines the common goal of nation building as a unifying and curative effort.

And yet—and here Zionism's turn to tragedy, in the spirit of Nietzsche and Schopenhauer, is a distinct feature of its modernity—in early Zionist fiction Zionism is rarely presented as a strong and simple solvent of the problematic of modern identity crisis or as an idealized antithesis of the modern condition; rather, it *represents* national belonging as ambivalence, not a desire to belong as much as a *struggle,* a tragic, fated destiny. Indeed, by the time *Autoemancipation* was published, the Enlightenment project of political and social emancipation of the individual had given way to critiques by Schopenhauer and Nietzsche of individual liberation and agency, critiques that impacted early Zionist discourse directly. And though *Autoemancipation* places Kant's Enlightenment ideals of personal autonomy and agency at the heart of its project, Zionist writers writing only two decades later would portray these ideals' inevitable decline. Rarely are the fictional characters of these works—written by young male writers for young male readers—happily autonomous and strong willed; more often than not, these protagonists' plots follow the path of what Raymond Williams (1966) has called "liberal tragedies," their quest for individual liberation and agency crushed against a tide of inner and outer obstacles. In these works, the nation emerges not as a chosen liberating solution but a destiny born out of the shattering of all other forms of individual happiness. Indeed, images of "tragic" male protagonists with their ambivalent and often failed relationship to the liberating project and to the "people" play a central role in the Zionist imaginary at its foundational moment. It is around these images, as I argue later in my book, that the experience of nationality is in fact woven.

"Woman" and Early Zionism

Given that Zionism, as we have seen, universalizes the image of the "nationalized" Jewish man, effects a shift in the binary terms Man/Jew and places the figure of tragic male sacrifice at the heart of its social imaginary; given that for the most part it was the opposition of Jewish *man*—not woman—with "Man" that had dominated "enlightened" European culture; given that, as Anne McClintock has argued, *all* nationalisms have "typically sprung from masculinized memory, masculinized humiliation and masculinized hope" (1997:261); and given that, as Israeli feminists have demonstrated, the creation of the nation-state had for the most part—even in its socialist manifestations—resulted in, or at any case did not at all end, the marginalization of women (including women writers) within the public sphere and their circumscription in metaphorical roles (predominantly as mothers): what is the position and function of Woman at the transient, tentative "Zionist moment"?

Nationalist discourse, as Partha Chatterjee has shown, is "a discourse *about* women; women do not speak [there]" (2001:154; emphasis mine). Indeed, at the Zionist moment, early Zionist discourse was produced predominantly by men, about men, and for men, yet the position of women vis-à-vis this discourse—both historic and symbolic—has not been subject to much analysis. Gender and nation has been on the agenda of scholars of nationalisms only in the past two or three decades. Indeed, more than perhaps any other domain, the nation had for the longest time proven to be immune to the kind of gender-based interrogation to which other institutions have been subjected by feminist academics over the past four decades. For the canonical theorists of nation (a lineage that extends from Ernest Renan to Ernest Gellner, Eric Hobsbawm and Benedict Anderson), gender categories and gendered knowledge had traditionally been viewed as adding absolutely nothing to the enigmatic question of the nation's morphology. For contemporary postcolonial critics, on the other hand, gender categories have come to permeate *everything* in the vicinity of the nation-form: From symbolic constructions of nation as family, to the feminization of the land to be conquered and defended, to the nation's dual relationship to time—at once nostalgic and progressive—which Anderson outlined and McClintock (1997) gendered. In Chatterjee's classic work on Indian nationalism, he demonstrates how in its discourse, women become associated with interiority, spirituality, and authentic national identity and men with modernity and progress; McClintock (1997) generalizes this model to nationalisms at large, demonstrating how an affirmation of traditional gender roles works to naturalize the nation and how the nation works to naturalize rigid and traditional gender roles. That the relationship between gender and nation has led to such extreme theoretical nodes of understanding—connoting either everything or nothing—speaks precisely to the high stakes, to both the blindness and the defensiveness that the nation propels. The psychological pull of the national fantasy—for men and women—is so great that feminists require the heaviest ammunition, the most all-encompassing theories to work through the layers of resistance put up by the experience of national belonging.

If in his universalization through and in foundational national discourse, Jew is substituted with Man, Man also comes to symbolize (Hu)man, blurring gender differences under the sign of uniform citizenship. It is in this sense that, as Gayatri Spivak (1988:306) has observed, the figure of woman disappears exactly *in* the process of postcolonial/national, male subject formation (though in what way Woman "existed" prior to nation has not been sufficiently analyzed).

Yet *how* does woman appear/disappear at Zionism's point zero? That from the Enlightenment on, the liberation of Jews and women had taken a somewhat similar route, that at the turn of the century both the "woman question" and the "Jewish question" had reached monumental urgency, that the fin-de-siècle crisis of identity was closely associated with question of gendered identities—these have been the subject of ample scholarly investigation. For Weininger, as we have seen, Jews and women are almost (though not entirely) interchangeable as the abject contrast to Man; for Freud, women and Jews are understood under a single sign— that of castration—which denotes their relative or partial value in rela- tion to Man. If Zionism then is a quest to shift this paradigm, to assert Jewish difference for the purpose of reducing Jewish difference, to obliter- ate (Gentile) Man from the discourse of Jewish identity, what becomes of Woman? Is Woman to Nation, to paraphrase Barbara Johnson's paraphras- ing of Sherry Ortner's famous dictum, as ground is to figure (1998:17)?

This book consists of three detailed readings of early Zionist works— by George Eliot, Theodor Herzl, and fin-de-siècle Hebrew writers (Bialik, Brenner, Berdyczewski)—each of which ends up with the national male figure at its center and the figure of woman at its periphery or altogether absent. Each presents the male subject as dramatically altered at the end of its narrative, and each redefines the meaning of masculinity and femi- ninity in a new imagined national "space." Yet each work or cluster of works also offers a slightly different analysis of how it ends there. And in each there are also traces and loose narrative threads that suggest that the effort to redefine, contain, and normalize gender arrangements within the emergent national framework has been nothing less than a struggle.

Perhaps the most serious analysis of this question at the Zionist mo- ment is taken up in George Eliot's *Daniel Deronda,* which offers a paral- lel exploration of the "Jewish question" and the "women question" in the late nineteenth century. A lengthy double-plotted bildungsroman, it works through the problem of subject formation for Daniel Deronda and Gwendolyn Harleth—the Jew and the woman—whose plots converge at the beginning of the novel and radically diverge by its end: while the Deronda plotline leads to Zionism and marriage, with Deronda's wife (Mira Cohen) representing Eliot's version of the bourgeois Jewish "angel in the house," Gwendolyn's plot ends (in contrast both to Deronda's nar- rative and to Eliot's previous novels) without comfort or closure. Having failed not only at achieving a measure of independence *but also* at be- ing subsumed in marriage and the patriarchal family, Gwendolyn's plot remains unresolved within the terms of the novel and the possibilities that it envisions for women. Unresolved also is the short yet powerful plotline of the Alcharisi, Deronda's icy, acerbic mother, the cosmopoli- tan artistic genius who has denied not only religious and national ties to the Jews but the maternal ties to her own son. The Alcharisi is presented by Eliot as nothing less than the enemy of Zionism: that which *refuses* to be assimilated into the Jewish nation or any other national discourse. Against Eliot's vision of a Jewish nation created by male bonds and male tradition, Woman is defensively pitted as the symbol of radical individualism and a decadent Europeanism that will resolutely remain outside the Jewish national fold.

Though Chatterjee's/McClintock's model fits certain aspects of Zionist nationalism, I'd like to suggest that at Zionism's foundational moment, a paradigm of nation and gender arises that symbolically positions woman not as the "interior" or "spiritual" core of the nation, not as the "mothers" of the nation, nor yet as its victims in need of protection, but as that which remains outside its fold. Woman at the Zionist moment is associated, I argue, with radical individuation, with the nonnationalist assimilatory route or, alternatively, as she does for Weininger, with prenation, presubject matter. In either capacity, Woman represents the threat to the integrity and insularity of the nation, that which needs to be repeatedly interrogated and integrated, coerced or seduced into national belonging. It is precisely because Woman is positioned at the edge of the nation that the drama of subject construction and membership, of acceptance, exclusion, critique, and rejection is played around her figure at the Zionist moment. Woman, I argue in the body of this book, represents in the early national imaginary the liminal place between membership and nonmembership that later will be occupied by Palestinian Israeli citizens. At the Zionist moment—prior to the encounter with the native Palestinian and after the disappearance of the "Gentile" as Other—woman is imagined as the potentially unassimilatable force at the edge of the nation.

Eliot provides perhaps the most clear-cut demonstration of woman's extraneous position vis-à-vis the nation, but other examples abound: the literary apologia by the fin-de-siècle Zionist writer and critic David Frishman addressed to an imaginary worldly woman ("You, whose entire life was spent in the gorgeous museums, among the most beautiful treasures of the large cities . . . you bent your pretty red lips in disdain at the sight of the 'paintings' and 'sculptures' of the people of Israel" (1893/1968); the image of Rahil in Yosef Hayyim Brenner's *Ba-khoref* (*In Winter*) (1904/1978), a story of the unrequited love of a young, secularizing Jewish man for a beautiful, cold, assimilated girl, headed to Belgium with her virile fiancé; even in Theodor Herzl's *Altneuland* (1902/2000), a didactic and idealized portrayal of both nation and marriage, we hear that the protagonist's wife, Sarah, "used to belong to the opposition."

Just as Herzl's supporter and most famous speechwriter, Max Nordau, publically lashed out against Nora's famous door slam in Ibsen's *A Doll's House,* Herzl displayed a similar anxiety about women's independence. Upholding a fantasy about the absorption of women within a "revised," non-European patriarchal model, Zionism is for Herzl, as it was for Eliot and Nordau, a normalizing politics, not only as it pertains to the "Jewish question" but also to the "woman question." For the resolutely *non*bourgeois East European Zionist writers and thinkers, a vision of perfect patriarchy is rarely entertained. Yet woman—either as liberated (or "loose") or as nonhuman other—is likewise imagined as a threat to the integrity of the (barely integrated) male subject and the nation of men as a whole.

Such anxiety around the loyalty of Woman to nation is to a degree a feature of all postcolonial struggles, which Fanon in his famous "we must first of all conquer the women" (1963:37–38) had brilliantly, if uncritically, captured. Yet in the Zionist case, the particular circumstances that made nineteenth-century Jewish women generally less susceptible to anti-Semitism and more likely, in the upper echelons of even Orthodox Jewish society, to have received a degree of education in European languages and culture (in contrast to the traditional Jewish education that was reserved for men only), combined to make women more likely to be Europeanized and less likely to embrace the national cause.[12] The Zionist moment, moreover, was particularly situated and greatly affected by the fin-de-siècle crisis of identity which, as Le Rider (1993) and others have demonstrated, greatly revolved around the negotiation and questioning of feminine and masculine identities. A century after the beginning of the industrial revolution and the entrance of women into the marketplace (especially the artistic marketplace), the "feminization of culture" was a theme treated—in a variety of ways—by the majority of fin-de-siècle writers (Le Rider 1993:101–26); indeed, one need not turn to Fanon's colonized Algeria in order to locate anxieties around women's autonomy and sexuality and around shifting gender roles, nor to identify the relationship between these anxieties and anxieties over the integrity of "nation" in, say, Bram Stoker's *Dracula.* Nietzsche, Freud, Schopenhauer, Dostoyevsky, Lawrence, George Eliot, Simmel, Weininger—at the Zionist moment, there is hardly a writer who does not in some way write as a defense against Woman.

Against the image of Woman as a corrosive or threatening entity, early Zionist discourse does not, however, set the hypervirile, violent ultramasculine Man. For while, as Boyarin (1997) and Gluzman (2007) have convincingly argued, Zionism emerges as a response to the feminization of Jews in European culture, it also responds—and this is a big "also"—to the *overmasculinization* and rigid, gendered hierarchies of traditional Jewish life. Indeed, as the Zionist bildungsroman appears at the late nineteenth century, depicting the experience of the young Jewish man who has deserted religious life for the prospects of an uncertain modernity, the rejection of, even the revulsion toward the patriarchal model of traditional Jewish life emerges as a repeated theme. Often, it is a failed heterosexual erotic relationship that will lead a male protagonist to the bosom of the nation. More than an upholder of patriarchy, the Universal Jew, the Man of Jewish nationalism, emerges as a lone *tragic figure:* a bearer not of "ordinary" Jewish suffering but a Hamlet, an Oedipus—a mute, lone figure, at once autonomous and controlled by the Gods (and/or by the state and the people). It is this figure, whose origin can be traced to the Zionist moment, which in the later statehood works investigated in chapter 8 will appear as the dead or dying soldier, sacrificed on behalf of (an often cynical and uncaring) nation-state. A unifying and appealing figure, drawing pity and empathy, the tragic male figure serves in the imaginary to coalesce the "feel" of the national community and mask over fractures, dissension, and gender differences. Indeed, the tragedy at the center of the Zionist national imaginary appears as a form of seduction, organizing the gaze of both male and female citizens around the tragic male figure. It is through its mechanisms that Woman—the imagined Other of nation—is brought into the national fold.

It is for this reason, I think, that it is hardly possible to argue that by virtue of women's exclusion from the core of the national imaginary, by virtue of women's historical position as relative outsider to the Zionist project and by virtue of their imagination as rejecting, female members of the nation have generally occupied a more consciously critical position vis-à-vis the nation than men. Structural relations shifted quickly when, from the 1920s on, Zionism was translated into a politics on the ground and the Arab, much more than the Woman, became the Other, the fracturing element of the national imaginary. Moreover, the image of the tragic male figure and the corresponding understanding of Jewish history, including the tragic understanding of the Jewish-Arab conflict, continued to dominate the national imaginary, at least until the break marked by the 1982 (first) Lebanon war. It is perhaps not coincidental that an explicitly female form of internal dissent emerges exactly then— in the form of the "Four Mothers" and "Women in Black" groups, which have continued their activities since.

Perhaps the most poignant demonstration of the ambivalent position of Woman vis-à-vis the nation is embodied in Hannah Arendt's relationship to Zionism. Arendt, who supported the Zionist idea and called for the politicization of the Jews, later became profoundly and vocally critical of Zionist politics.[13] Rational and painfully clear-sighted in her anticipation of Arab rejection of the State of Israel, she called for the constitution of a federation of states, among whom Israel would be one. Standing firmly outside the national logos, she maintained her critical position even in her coverage (for the *New Yorker*) of the Eichmann trial. To Gershom Scholem's accusation that she did not particularly "love the Jewish people" Arendt replied:

> What confuses you is that my arguments and my approach are different from what you are used to; in other words, the trouble is that I am independent. By this I mean, on the one hand, that I do not belong to any organization and always speak only for myself, and on the other hand, that I have great confidence in Lessing's *selbstdenken*, for which, I think, no ideology, no public opinion and no "convictions" can ever be a substitute. (1978:470)

It is Arendt's appeal to *selbstdenken*—think for yourself—that had made her, in the eyes of her followers, the paragon of critical and individual integrity. Yet it is precisely her radical individualism: her belief that one *can* inhabit a space from which one may think only for oneself and that "identity" can and should be transcended that has made her the subject of critique by poststructuralists and feminists as well. At the end, moreover, even Arendt was not immune to the specter of male heroism. By all accounts, she was overcome with joy at the Israeli military victory in the Six Day War, writing variously to Karl Jaspers that the Israelis had done a wonderful job, that she liked Moshe Dayan (then the defense minister) a lot, and that Nasser should be hanged instantly. A friend described her as behaving like a "war bride" (Pitterberg 2007).

PART I

JEWISH MEN,
UNIVERSAL WOMEN:
NOVEL, NATION,
AND CREATION IN
DANIEL DERONDA

CHAPTER 1

Jews, Modernity, and the End of the European Bildungsroman

The Deronda Problem

Daniel Deronda is widely known as a flawed novel. Many readers, from Eliot's affronted contemporaries to F. R. Leavis in his notorious attempt at amputating the novel's "bad half"[1] to twentieth-century structuralist and social critics, have tried to explain why the novel ultimately fails its readers; why Eliot, whose genius by the time of its conception was beyond reproach, would produce a work that many, not only anti-Semites or fervent lovers of realism, find didactic and strange.

One of the most spirited and compelling explanations is Franco Moretti's. Moretti ends *The Way of the World*—his prodigious study of the European bildungsroman—with Eliot's *Daniel Deronda* and *Felix Holt,* arguing that the failure of these works ("indeed, terrible novels") is tied to the failure of their genre, the bildungsroman, as "the symbolic form of its age" (1987:200): that Eliot had chosen for these novels a form that was already extinct. If the bildungsroman, which thrived from the late eighteenth to the late nineteenth century, centers on the individual young hero whose symbolic attributes—mobility, interiority, individuality, dynamism, and restlessness—were the symbols of an earlier age, in Deronda and Felix, Moretti writes, "the contrary historical process becomes legible: the sacrifice of individuality typical of the 'age of the masses.'" In Deronda and Felix, "we can no longer see two men dedicated to their ideals, but the first functionaries of abstract beliefs" (Moretti 1987:227). It was not Eliot who was at fault here, but the material and ideological conditions of her times:

> When the new psychology started to dismantle the unified image of the individual; when the social sciences turned to "synchrony" and "classification," thereby shattering the synthetic

> perception of history . . . when in ideology after ideology the in-
> dividual figured simply as part of the whole—then the century
> of the bildungsroman was truly at an end. (Moretti 1987:228)

Indeed, the 1870s saw not only the emergence of new disciplines and discourses of classification, including anthropology and sexology, but also a host of new collectivist nationalisms and an increasingly intense focus on the "nation question" abroad as well as in England. Between 1871 and 1891 alone, Eric Hobsbawm writes, the number of newspapers describing themselves as "national" or "nationalist" rose in England from one to thirty-three (1990:105). But what has *Deronda* changed, *really*? For even the hero of the classic bildungsroman, says Wilhelm Meister, serves as a "part of a whole" in the sense that he belongs, even signifies a place, a language, a *nation*. Indeed, if the bildungsroman, according to Moretti, is an attempt to solve "the dilemma coterminous with modern bourgeois civilization—the conflict between the ideal of *self determination* and the equally imperious demands of *socialization*" (1987:15)—then it assumes the existence of an a priori spatial entity into which its hero may (or may not) be socialized. A place of origin may be an obstacle to be transcended; this does not mean, however, that it has ceased to exist in the mind of writer, character, and reader. If history always leads its hero beyond his place of origin, beyond the borders of his village, his city, even his nation, this hero must nevertheless belong *somewhere*. In this regard, the bildungsroman is a national form per se; the certainty of place of origin and national roots is so ingrained that it can be "forgotten" altogether.

But the relationship between individual and collective identity in the classic bildungsroman is nonetheless distinct from the one presented in the *Deronda* plotline, as it is deeply rooted in pre-1880s conceptions of liberal citizenship. Particularly in Britain, the philosophical core of liberalism stemmed from its stress on individual "negative" liberty, which John Stuart Mill defined as the individual's "capacity for self-directed choice, free from internal or external constraints of a psychological or physical nature" (Bellamy 1992:22). Though Mill recognized that people are largely formed by their environment and history, the desire to transcend these circumstances in order to pursue one's unique life trajectory remained an ideal goal. Mill, after all, grounded his ideas of liberty in his own bildungsroman: the story of his strict education in the hands of his behaviorist father and his rebellion against its imprint thereafter (23). "Negative liberty," the lifting of obstacles like tradition and class so that the individual could develop according to his own inward nature, is the operating principle of the bildungsroman, a principle that no longer holds true for Daniel Deronda's formation.

We must remember that *Deronda* contains, nonetheless, a fierce representative of negative liberty in the character of the Alcharisi, Daniel's monstrous mother, the Orthodox Jewish girl turned European opera star. "I wanted to live a large life, with freedom to do what everyone else did, and be carried along in a great current": this is how she justifies the abandonment of her son. If, as part of his liberal program, Mill asserts that "genius should be allowed to *unfold* freely," the Alcharisi embodies just that, relinquishing even the bonds of motherhood for the sake of her musical gifts. Her caricaturing aside, she comes closest, in fact, to Mill's ideal of an autonomous, self-willed individual in whom eccentricity is a mark of strength.[2] We will come back to the Alcharisi later.

Deronda's own story is diametrically opposed to his mother's. Though it is possible to read him as embodying the liberal ethos at the beginning of the novel—or perhaps as a sign of its capacity for decline, since he lacks self-will and "desire[s] nothing too strongly"—in the novel's latter half he comes to represent its antithesis. He seeks not to be free from group affiliation, but to join and embrace it. As such, his plotline marks a shift in British liberal thought, from individualism to collectivism, from pragmatism to idealism, from "negative" to "positive" liberty, a shift that is directly reflected in his transformation from reflective youth to executor of national ideals. Though his mother, the Alcharisi, had sought to eliminate the supposed obstacles to his happiness and freedom—his Jewish parentage, his middle-class roots—by arranging for his aristocratic upbringing, the novel is a record of her failure. Its year of publication, after all, is 1876, a time when even Mill himself begins to focus in his writings not only on the removal of obstacles hindering liberty but on the creation of conditions for fostering it. Isaiah Berlin has read these conditions as fostering "positive liberty": the wish of the individual or the collective to be his own master, to be a subject, not an object. In *On Liberty,* Mill dubs this desire "pagan self assertion," yet deems it to be "one of the elements of human worth" (1955:66). And with the new nationalisms of the 1880s, with their stress on self-definition separateness (Hobsbawm 1990:101), we find the idea of positive liberty echoed in various intellectual quarters, Eliot's included:

> An individual man, to be harmoniously great, must belong to
> a nation . . . If not in actual existence yet existing in the past, in
> memory, as a departed, invisible, beloved ideal, once a reality,

and perhaps to be restored. A common humanity is not yet
enough to feed the rich blood of various activity which makes
a complete man. (1879/1994:150)

Eliot's words, taken from "The Modern Hep! Hep! Hep!," refer specifically to the Jews who, without a nation, "may be in danger of lapsing
into a cosmopolitan indifference equivalent to cynicism, and of missing
that inward identification with the nationality around them"; but they
are also directed at the British themselves, whose national definition
after a century of empire building she views as increasingly diffused.
Such ideas were, of course, shared by many writers in the last quarter
of the nineteenth century, from T. H. Lawrence to Bram Stoker (Williams 1983:102). Most notably, they are present in the writings of T. H.
Green (1836–1882), who followed Mill as the theorist of British liberalism. In Green's thought, which is replete with theological overtones, the
individual can only realize himself within the context of society. If for
Mill society was in some conflict with individuation, for Green, society or community is always its foreground. Accordingly, the pursuit of
the common good is derived from national feelings. *"Patria,"* he wrote,
in language that Eliot echoes, "is an organization of a people to whom
the individual feels bound by the ties derived from a common dwelling place and its associations, from common memories, traditions and
customs, and from the common ways of feeling and thinking which a
common language and still more a common literature embodies" (Bellamy 1992:37–38).

What *Deronda* has changed, then, is not the association of novel and
nation, but the level of visibility that is given to the nation. The nation
does not replace the individual; it becomes the necessary condition for
the possession of individuality. In this thought, the individual does not
simply figure, as Moretti writes, as a "part of the whole"; rather, national
belonging is figured as a prerequisite to the possession of individual
"character." Eliot stresses this point relentlessly: "To repeat: not only the
nobleness of a nation depends on the presence of a national consciousness, but also the nobleness of each individual citizen" (1879/1994:148).
Deronda, who begins the novel as one in danger of lapsing into a "cosmopolitan indifference" and ends as a Jewish nationalist and an idealized "complete man," is supposedly a case in point.

But as Moretti points out, Deronda's "perfection" is also his doom: as
a novelistic character he fails to convince or even to interest. It is not so
much his choice of Judaism as cause célèbre (though that is there too),

but the adequacy of national belonging as an end-all solution to the problem of subject formation that fractures the conventions of the bildungsroman. Indeed, for its hero to find permanent solace in a stable national *identity* is to contradict its very essence, an essence that lies, according to the young Georg Lukács, in "the inadequacy that is due to the soul's being wider and larger than the destinies that life has to offer it" (1971:56); an inadequacy that generates an interiority "not only fuller than before but also perennially dissatisfied and restless" (Moretti 1987:5). "The inner form of the novel," Lukács asserts, is "the process of the *problematic* individual's journeying towards *himself*" (1971:80). Can this journey lead a hero to discover and embrace the totality of a collective identity? The answer, according to Lukács, must be negative. For in the novel, which is, he writes, predicated on "the certainty of defeat," "the fullness of life . . . is revealed precisely through the manifold *failures* of [the hero's] struggle and search" (126; my emphasis). Indeed, if Deronda fails as novelistic hero, it is not only because he becomes remarkably adjusted and perennially *satisfied* through the narrative of national belonging, but because his "interiority" finds perfect meaning in external reality (the "life of practically energetic sentiment," as he calls it) and thus, in effect, ceases to exist. And not only interiority, but also "mobility" is halted in *Deronda*. Instead, as Moretti laments "The giddiness of mobility, of being swept by history's flow across the whole of society, has been anaesthetized by the superstitious expectation of monumental palingeneses" (200).

But let us backtrack for a moment to the golden age of the realist bildungsroman: *Whose* "interiority" are we talking about? *Whose* mobility, opportunities, restlessness? Could the bildungsroman hero be imagined as just anyone? Could we imagine this hero as an immigrant, a colonial subject, a Jew in late nineteenth-century Europe? *Deronda*, I think, calls for a more precise analysis of these questions. *It is,* I think, an analysis of these questions. For it isn't only the narrative of national belonging that disrupts Deronda's effectiveness as bildungsroman character but also the specific narrative of *Jewish* national belonging. In its failures and its successes as a novel, in those ideological pressures it explores and those that come to weigh down on it, *Deronda* is an analysis of exactly the problem of Jews and nationhood. What happens to the bildungsroman once a Jew is imagined as its hero, namely, once he is universalized? Why is the nation both the precondition and the solvent of individual identity? What are the definitional pressures that come to bear on the modern novelistic hero that Moretti and Lukács exalt once he is faced with the collapse of Enlightenment liberal "national" discourse and the rise of the "Jewish question"? True, as Moretti claims, *Deronda*'s rejection of restless interiority and tumultuous mobility marks the end of the bildungsroman as the symbol of its age; but it is equally true that in the late nineteenth century, these attributes lose their glamour precisely because they explicitly become linked to the Jews. Interiority and mobility, indeed modernity itself, that is, come to be increasingly associated with the condition of the modern, assimilated European Jew.

Jews and Liberal Discourse

During the eighteenth and nineteenth centuries, the compatibility of Jewish difference with liberal citizenship was the subject of intense discussions (Smith 1997:8). The answer, for the most part, was the shedding of Jewish particularity in return for national belonging. "Hellenized" Jews such as the actress Rachel Félix, Heinrich Heine, and Constance de Rothschild would even be read as symbolizing, for Matthew Arnold and others, a sort of "perfection" brought about by the containment of Hebraism within Hellenism, provided they transcended their immediate Jewish past (Cheyette 1993:21).

By the 1870s, however, Eliot and others reject assimilation as invariably leading to moral decline: "If [the Jews] drop that separateness which is made their reproach, they may be in danger of lapsing into a cosmopolitan indifference equivalent to cynicism" (1879/1994:156). *A cosmopolitan indifference* or moral decadence is seemingly what plagues the prenationalized Deronda, whom the narrator describes as "a contemplative rather than an active ... human type" who is perpetually "questioning whether it were worthwhile to take part in the battle of the world" (17). Through this characterization, I will shortly show, Eliot constricts Deronda as an assimilated Jew from the very beginning of the novel. Yet as I will also show, this characterization, which marks Deronda's Jewishness in a late nineteenth-century novel, could have applied a couple of decades earlier just about to any protagonist. Lukács uses Eliot's exact words—"a contemplative rather than active" human type—to describe the prototypical protagonist of the novel of "Romantic Disillusionment" (1971:210); Moretti, for whom Deronda's Jewishness holds little importance, reads the prenational Deronda explicitly as "a member of the same family as the Beautiful Soul and Frédéric Moreau, social parasitism included" (1987:224).

In her questioning of the moral soundness of Jewish assimilation, Eliot voices and largely prefigures the assumptions of early Zionism. The triple notion that "a common humanity" was not enough to feed an individual man, that feelings of national belonging were essential for individual and common good, and that Jews could never satisfactorily feed on the "common memories, traditions and customs" of their respective "host" nations began gaining momentum among a growing minority of Jews in the 1880s and 1890s, mostly in Eastern Europe. In 1882, following a series of highly publicized pogroms, a Jewish-Russian physician and essayist named Leo Pinsker would publish *Autoemancipation,* a work that would become the basic text and ideological summation of the Zionist idea:

> The essence of the problem, as we see it, lies in the fact that, in the midst of the nations among whom the Jews reside, they form a distinctive element, which cannot be assimilated, which cannot be readily digested by any nation. Hence the problem is to find means of so adjusting the relations of this executive element to the whole body of the nations that there shall never be any further basis for the Jewish question. (181–82)

Among West European Zionists, Eliot's assertion that individual "character" is predicated on national belonging is even more faithfully echoed. After all, Eliot and (particularly West European) early Zionists alike were fed by similar intellectual sources: on the one hand, the liberal imagination of Mill and Locke; on the other, the conservative, antidecadent, anticosmopolitan, and nationalist spirit of the late nineteenth century.[3] Thus the fin-de-siècle critic Max Nordau addresses the first Zionist Congress in 1897 with language almost identical to that of Eliot: "Man needs a *heimat* (native soil), a community he can call his own; otherwise, he becomes unbalanced (*haltlos*), with all the consequences for body and mind this entails."[4]

Eliot, like Nordau, conveys the necessity of national affinity in the language of sickness and health:

> It is certainly worth considering whether an expatriated, denationalized race, used for ages to live among antipathetic populations, must not inevitably lack some conditions of nobleness ... Unquestionably, the Jews, having been more than any other race exposed to the adverse moral influences of alienism, must, both in individuals and in groups, have suffered some moral degradation ... Why, our own countrymen who take to living

abroad without purpose or function to keep up their sense
of fellowship in the affairs of their own land are rarely good
specimens of moral healthiness. (1879/1994:156)

In setting her critique of empire and the moral degeneracy of British expatriates as a metaphor for Jewish "alienism," Eliot wishes to universalize the "cosmopolitan indifference" that in the late nineteenth century is
deemed an inborn "Jewish" trait; yet such metaphorical relationship positions the Jews as aliens (or expatriates) *within* Europe, a position that
is further strengthened by Eliot's direct appeal to her readers regarding
"our own countrymen." In this way, an intimacy between author and
reader is conjured up on the basis of assumed national ties from which
British Jewish citizens, the subject of the essay, are excluded.

This notwithstanding, Eliot's (and Nordau's) critique of Jewish "moral
degradation," as the above passages demonstrate, shared a profoundly
similar language with the critique of British moral decline at the late
nineteenth century. Both were couched in the language of Victorian
character discourse that is already evident in Mill's works. Samuel Smiles,
"the high priest of Victorian 'character,' " organized this discourse in his
books on *Character* (1871) and *Duty* (1880) around a cluster of virtues—
self-culture, self-control, prudence, honesty, integrity, temperance, so-
briety, energy, industry, independence, manliness, and duty[5]—all of
which come under threat with uncontrollable British expansionism and
a bankrupt aristocracy (represented in the novel by Mallinger Grandcourt).[6] Among other things, what *Deronda* teaches us is how much the
critique that was aimed at the Jews at the late nineteenth century owed to
Victorian liberal discourse on character formation—but also how much
of the anxiety around British expansionism and moral/national decline
was projected onto the Jews.

Jewish nationalism, then, is presented in *Deronda* as a way out of both
the Jewish and the British predicament: a way to transcend the character
flaws propelled by the cosmopolitan Jewish condition and unruly British expansionism. Yet in shedding these flaws—interiority, ambivalence,
multiplicity, passivity—Deronda ceases to be a literary "character" altogether. This is the essence of his failure.

Deronda and Victorian Discourse of Character

That the traits that are symbolized by the bildungsroman's hero several
decades earlier are under attack in *Deronda* is evident from the start.

Not only does the prenational Deronda, despite his flaws, come closer than any other novelistic character to embodying the Victorian character ideal—his maturity and self-mastery are referred to throughout, particularly by Sir Hugo Mallinger, who anoints him his most trusted advisor and would-be son—but Deronda's female nemesis, the beautiful and uncontrollable Gwendolen Harleth, is on the defense from the beginning. If Gwendolen is defined, from the novel's first scene, by the seething casino where she is first spotted by Deronda, the loss and shame that quickly amass there trigger the series of endless humiliations she suffers by the plot. The casino, a microcosm of cosmopolitan, glamorous, fast-paced modernity, one where Gwendolen's hopes rise and fall at the turn of the wheel, is quickly and efficiently negated. We will return to Gwendolen later. For now it is sufficient to note that we are meant to understand Deronda, from the beginning of the novel, as stable, prudent, and "good," the upholder of moral order, the antithesis of the worlds represented by the casino, by Gwendolen, by modernity as Lukács and Moretti define it.

And yet, prudent and in control and "good" as he is, Deronda suffers, the narrator tells us, from "an apparent indefiniteness in his sentiments . . . which threaten[s] to hinder any persistent course of action." He lacks, as far as Smiles's categories go, in energy, independence, and manliness. Only with the "discovery" of his religious and national roots will Deronda supposedly reach his full fruition as a truly ideal Victorian character, representing manliness and duty as well as honesty and integrity. Indeed, it was Eliot's great perversion—positioning Sir Grandcourt, a landed British aristocrat, as the symbol for lewd and degenerate Victorian masculinity, and a nationalist Jew, Deronda, as the best of Victorian culture. This must have been at least one of the reasons for the novel's dismissal by the general British public and its popularity (excluding its Zionist conclusion) among the Jews.

Like "The Modern Hep! Hep! Hep!," *Deronda* therefore contains an implicit critique of Victorian culture. The England depicted in the novel's first half does not offer any of its young characters (including Rex, Gwendolen, and Deronda) the kind of environment that is needed for "character" formation. Rex will leave for the colonies, and Deronda, as we know, will opt for a nationalism that is a mixture of religion, law, and moral life. This solution to Deronda's maturation problem could conceivably be read as Eliot's universally applicable model for the salvation of modern Britain, with Deronda himself as its symbol.[7] Yet precisely because Deronda's maturation is linked to his transformation from an English gentleman to a self-proclaimed Jew, his nationalism loses its universal appeal and his character ceases to be interpretable through the lens of Victorian character discourse. This is one of the reasons why Deronda's character was unimaginable to Eliot's contemporaries. As one reader wrote:

> When a young man of English training and Eton and University education, and, up to manhood, of assumed English birth, so obliging also as to entertain Christian sympathies, finishes off with his wedding in a Jewish synagogue, on the discovery that his father was a Jew, the most confiding reader leaves off with a sense of bewilderment and affront.[8]

Except for the character of the Jewish composer Klesmer, whose status as artistic genius makes him less dependent on his environment, the possession of a universalizable moral character among British Jews is presented in the novel as an impossibility. As such, Eliot is careful to set Deronda apart not only from that flawed specimen of Victorian masculinity—Sir Mallinger Grandcourt—but also from the novel's Jewish male characters. It is Deronda, after all, who already in the very first scene of the novel reclaims a pawned necklace from a highly recognizable Jewish usurer.

Eliot fashions her Jewish characters: the petty merchants and pawnbrokers—Ezra Cohen and his family and the "various queer-looking Israelites not altogether without guile" (1995:336)—according to all the stereotypes of her time. Indeed, if "The Modern Hep! Hep! Hep!" is an attack on late nineteenth-century anti-Semitism, it also contains a taxonomy of the alleged vices of the Jews. Likewise in *Deronda,* Eliot deploys this readily available taxonomy to harp again and again on the Cohens' looks, their talk, their greediness:

> Not that there was anything very repulsive about [Mrs. Cohen]: the worst that could be said was that she had that look of having made her toilet with little water, and by twilight, which is common to unyouthful people of her class, and of having presumably slept in her large earrings, if not in her rings and necklace. (387)

Or:

> "I should like to look at the silver clasps in the window," said Deronda; "the large ones, please, in the corner there."

> "They are only three guineas, sir," [Mrs. Cohen] said, encouragingly.
>
> "First-rate workmanship, sir—worth twice the money; only I got 'em a bargain from Cologne," said [Ezra Cohen], parenthetically, from a distance. (389)

Indeed, stereotypical, banal portraitures. Jews as usurers, Jews as small, exploitive merchants, as symbols and operators of the marketplace and the degraded sphere of exchange—these were highly popular images in nineteenth-century liberal and socialist discourse, which became, as Catherine Gallagher has shown, increasingly hostile toward groups that seemed to represent a realm of exchange divorced from production: "traders in general but especially costermongers in works like Mayhew's *London Labour and the London Poor,* prostitutes in the works of Mayhew, Acton, W. R. Greg and others, and Jews in the works of almost everybody" (Gallagher 1986:43).

By positioning the Cohens as small traders in the international market, where production and exchange are so clearly divorced ("First rate workmanship, sir—worth twice the money; only I got em a bargain from Cologne"), Eliot thus appeals to readers' most readily available images of Jews. And the alternative images of Deronda's devout yet dictatorial grandfather and the messianic Mordecai are more esoteric than inviting. Only in Deronda, in whom, as we have shown, a cluster of Victorian "character" traits converge, could a reader have potentially found a positive figure of identification. Indeed, it was Deronda's image that won Eliot unanimous praise in Jewish publications across Europe, even from those who explicitly shunned her nationalistic ideas.[9]

Yet aside from these readers, Deronda's reception as character was chilly at best; Deronda was deemed, by most, an aesthetic failure. Had Eliot tried too hard to create a positive Jewish character? This was probably true; but in any event, she could not have succeeded. The definitional pressures around the construction of a Jewish male character at the late nineteenth century were too great, and despite her best efforts at constructing Deronda counter to popular anti-Semitic images, Eliot could not extricate herself from the web of associations surrounding the Jews. Deronda's character, it seems, became too entangled in these pressures to cohere. He appears at once too good and too vague, a caricature of virtue. Indeed, if as Moretti claims, Deronda fails as a character because he is a mere receptacle of abstract ideas, this failure has less to do with the ideas Deronda stands for (Jewish nationalism) than with the ideas that come to bear on his characterization (racial stereotypes). For though Deronda's Jewish origin is unbeknownst to him or to the readers as the beginning of the novel, it was on Eliot's mind all along. Deronda is conceived as a Jew, and as such, his character appears as simultaneously praised and diminished, resulting from the very beginning of the novel in the paranoid construction of, well, the assimilated Jew.

Deronda and Racial Discourse on Jews

There are many signs in the novel's first half that mark Deronda as a racial "other." His "piercing gaze," for example, is alluded to already on the first page. In this famous casino scene we encounter our two protagonists: a gambling Gwendolen Harleth and a staring Daniel Deronda. The inward debate raised in Deronda by Gwendolen's intricate beauty, we are told, "gave to his eyes a growing expression of scrutiny," while Gwendolen had "the darting sense that he was measuring her and looking down on her as an inferior, *that he was of a very different quality from the human dross around her*" (1995:5; my emphasis). Deronda's gaze, the narrator tells us, "seemed to have acted as an evil eye" on Gwendolen. She describes him as "the dark-haired young man with the dreadful expression." When they meet again, Deronda stares at Gwendolen with "his usual directness of gaze—a large-eyed gravity, innocent of any intention" (332). Universalizing this marker, the narrator tells us that "his eyes had a peculiarity which had drawn *many men* into trouble; they were of a dark yet mild intensity." Yet the eyes and the gaze are made specific by their contrast with the pale motionlessness of the quintessential English subject, Sir Mallinger Grandcourt:

> Deronda, turning to look straight at Grandcourt . . . might have been a subject for those old painters who liked contrast of temperament. There was a calm intensity of life and richness of tint in his face that on a sudden gaze from him was rather startling . . . Grandcourt himself felt an irritation, which he did not show except by a slight movement of the eyelids. (162)

It ought to go without saying that the same intense gaze characterizes all Jewish men in the novel: the pawnbroker who scrutinizes Gwendolen's jewels (Gwendolen herself compares Deronda's scrutiny and valuation of her to the pawnbroker's inspection of her jewels); Klesmer's "grand frowns"; Kalonymos's "examining look"; and finally, the detailed description of the physiognomy of the quintessential Jewish man, Mordecai Cohen, which echoes the repeated references to Deronda's eyes and face. Mordecai is said to have

> a finely typical Jewish face, wrought into intensity of expression apparently by a strenuous eager experience in which all the satisfaction had been indirect and far-off, and perhaps by some bodily suffering also, which involved that absence of ease in the present. The features were clear-cut, not large; the brow not high but broad, and fully defined by the crisp, black hair. It might never have been a particularly handsome face, but it must always have been forcible; and now with its dark, far-off gaze, and yellow pallor in relief on the gloom of the backward shop, one might have imagined one's self coming upon it in some past prison of the Inquisition, which a mob had suddenly burst open. (386)

Late nineteenth-century Europe produced plenty of books on the Jewish body, character, habits, and gaze. Francis Galton, the founder of *Eugenics,* saw the "cold, scanning gaze" of the Jew as a sign of Jewish difference and potential pathology.[10] German-Jewish physicians like Moses Julius Gutmann wrote of the "melancholy, pained expression" associated with the Jew (Gilman 1991:64, 69). Indeed, it is by their intense, pained gaze that the two "very Jewish" characters—Kalonymos and Mordecai— are introduced into the novel's plot.

Likewise, Deronda's dark physiognomy is repeatedly contrasted in the first half of the novel with the fair-skinned complexion and reddish-blond hair of Mallinger Grandcourt, who contrary to the intensity and striking bodily presence of the Jewish male characters, showed "not a trace of self-consciousness or anxiety" (111). The narrator, it should be noted, has no kind words for Grandcourt, whose "long narrow gray eyes expressed nothing but indifference" (111); he is surely the image of aristocratic perversity and despotism. Nonetheless, and in contrast with Deronda, according to the physiognomic grid of the novel, he "looked like an heir."

Then there are Deronda's character defects: his indeterminacy, his dependence on the opinion of others, his lack of resolve—all features attributed to the "Jewish psyche" in late nineteenth-century literature. These characteristics are discussed in three very long paragraphs, immediately before Deronda's first encounter with the Jewish synagogue:

It happens that the very vividness of his impressions had often made him the more enigmatic to his friends and had contributed to an apparent indefiniteness in his sentiments. His
early-wakened sensibility and reflectiveness had developed
into a many-sided sympathy, which threatened to hinder any
persistent course of action: as soon as he took any antagonism,
though only in thought, he seemed to himself like the Sabine
warriors in the memorable story—with nothing to meet his
spear but flesh of his flesh, and objects that he loved. His imagination had so wrought itself to the habit of seeing things as
they probably appeared to others, that a strong partisanship,
unless it were against an immediate oppression, had become
an insincerity for him. (364)

This "subdued fervour of sympathy, an activity of imagination in behalf of others," as Moretti notes, are the same ones that marked Eliot's
much-beloved Dorothea Brooke (1987:224), yet attributed to the male
Deronda the identification with others gets linked with a lack of resolve
and a skewed masculinity. Deronda is aligned with the Sabines, whose
attempt to avenge the Romans' rape of their wives and daughters was
thwarted by the women themselves. The narrator here alludes not only
to Deronda's indetermination but also to a lack of manliness and a tendency for self-flagellation that were frequently attributed to Jewish men
(Gilman 1991). No wonder, then, that in the first half of the novel he is
depicted mostly at home, blushing in the company of women and girls.

Deronda's overidentification with others, the narrator tells us, amounts
to a diminished sense of self; "roaming [in social life] like a disembodied
spirit," young Deronda falls into a "meditative numbness," "gliding farther and farther away from [the] life of practically energetic sentiment"
(365) and refusing to participate in the battle of life. Though fatigue and
passivity plague both Deronda and Grandcourt, and though in some re-
spects they are depicted as suffering from the ennui and ethical paralysis
that are common to fin-de-siècle characters, Eliot takes great pains to
distinguish Deronda's condition from that of Grandcourt, whose aristocratic version of *alienism* is depicted as an excessiveness of his masculine
traits: complete autonomy turned detachment; complete control over the
body turned into lifelessness; power and authority turned into sadism.
Deronda's indifference and melancholy, his particular *alienism,* can be
read from the beginning of the novel as specifically Jewish. Not only, as
the Sabine analogy suggests, is it synonymous with his effeminacy, but it

is moreover a consequence of his metaphorical and literal homelessness, his "wandering energy," the lack of a "fixed local habitation" into which he can stir his "vague social passion."

Deronda even contains, as Jacob Press (1997) has noted, an implicit reference to Daniel's memory of his own circumcision:

> Daniel . . . straining to discern something in that early twilight, had a dim sense of having been kissed very much, and surrounded by thin, cloudy, scented drapery, till his fingers caught in something hard, which hurt him, and he began to cry. (Eliot 1876:165)

Prior to the retrieval of this memory, "life was delightful to the *lad*" (note the quintessential English word "lad" that refers to life *before*). "He had not lived with other boys" and was oblivious to his difference. "But at this moment among the rose-petals," the narrator writes, Deronda was making "a first acquaintance" with "griefs" and "shame" ("deep blush"). He resolves to never admit "the sore that had opened in him" (171) and, for the first time, rebukes his adoptive father's attempts to display his beauty "in an embroidered Holland blouse which set off the rich coloring of his head and throat" before an admiring "small party of gentlemen." Indeed, Deronda's plot alludes to Deronda's corporeal difference early on. Yet this difference is instantly masked by an alternative explanation for Deronda's isolation: at thirteen, he overhears his tutor speak of illegitimate children of priests and concludes that he is Sir Hugo's illegitimate son.

Signs of Deronda's "Jewishness" are thus present in the text all along. Yet it is equally true that all the characteristics of "the Jew," all the signs that we have thus far delineated, act as double signs. Even circumcision in itself is not a reliable signifier, as many Victorian babies, particularly of the higher classes, were circumcised (Press 1997:167). Deronda's penis, whether circumcised or not, cannot therefore be anything but an ambivalent signifier, which further allows a double reading of Deronda as a British gentleman *or* as a Jew. But it is also true that it is precisely the doubleness of meaning in Deronda's identity signs in the first half of the novel that marks him as a closeted Jew and potential assimilate. As in Proust's characterization of Swann in *À la recherche du temps perdu,* Eliot's shift between covert and overt narrative practices around Deronda's body and character simulates the social act of identifying an assimilated Jew among aristocrats. And the very ambivalence of the sign, like the repeated references to Deronda's dark complexion in contradiction to Gwendolen's and Grandcourt's whiteness—a complexion that could nevertheless be attributed to a Spaniard or an Italian—triggers in readers and interpreters, modes of understanding that are neither wholly conscious nor binary. Nineteenth-century audiences may or may not have discerned Deronda's physique and mental state as particularly Jewish. May have, because the medical, racial, and popular signs for "identifying" a Jew are all present from the beginning of the novel. May not have, because these signs (even circumcision) are not only masked and connotative of multiple meanings, but could be attributed to anyone.

Indeed, Deronda's "Jewish" traits apply to many young heroes of the nineteenth-century novel, from Julien Sorel to Frédéric Moreau. His symptoms—his indecisiveness, his lack of resolve, his "alienism"—*could* have been interpreted as universal a decade or two earlier. They *are* the novelistic symptoms of modernity. Yet unlike the characteristics of Julian Sorel or Dorothea Brooke, Deronda's symptoms are presented, as we have seen, not only as a *problem* but as a *Jewish problem*. Only a couple of decades later, Otto Weininger would write that "the uncertain facial expression of the Jew is the physiognomic correlate of an inner multiplicity,"[11] echoing (though not consciously) Deronda's characterization as a young man suffering from "a reflectiveness that threatened to nullify all differences" (365). And by offering Jewish nation building as a cure for Deronda's symptoms (his newly aroused interest in Judaism, the narrator tells us, is "an effectual remedy for ennui"), Eliot further associates those symptoms with Jewish particularity. Indeed, Deronda's vocation as a Jewish nationalist will indeed cure Deronda of this "multiplicity"; it will also transform it, or its cause—"alienism"—from a pan-European modernist symptom into a "Jewish symptom."

What I have so far attempted to demonstrate is Eliot's difficulty, indeed the impossibility, of constructing a male Jewish bildungsroman hero in the late nineteenth century. Another way of saying this is as follows: Victorian discourse on national culture and on character grounded in nationality could not contain the idea of a Jewish subject. In order to have "character," late Victorian discourse demanded that one have a national affiliation. But for Deronda to have a national affiliation, he would have to shed Jewish particularity, which in turn would be perceived as leading to alienism. The only way of achieving excellence of character must lead Deronda outside the borders of British national culture. His story, therefore, becomes a narrative of "passing": having been constructed as closeted Jew in the first half of the novel, he later secretly acknowledges, and finally openly embraces, his identity of origin.

Reading *Deronda* as a Passing Novel

Cynthia Chase (1978) has sardonically characterized the circular logic of *Deronda* as symptomatic of the novel's skewed causality: A reading of the novel as "present causes of past effects" (that is, because Deronda is now a Jew, he must have felt alienated from his aristocratic home, must have been attracted to the Jews, and finally must have become a Jewish nationalist) triumphs over the conventional reading of a realist novel as the "history of effects of causes" (that is, because Deronda was in search of a cause, and because he met Mirah and Mordecai, he discovered his long-lost Jewish identity and became a Jewish nationalist). But this is skewed historical logic only if we read *Deronda* as a realist bildungsroman, which it isn't. American narratives of identity and passing, most notably Nella Larsen's *Passing* (1929/1997), are often structured around such reverse logic: the hero, rediscovering her identity, reads the trajectory of her entire life in light of this discovery and return. This, as we have seen, is how Eliot constructed Deronda's story as well. But thinking about the nineteenth-century European novel as the psychological journey of a universal subject rather than the American journey toward an "identity" makes it strange to think of Deronda as a "passing novel."

As in many passing narratives, midway in the plot comes a moment of recognition, which sheds clear light on the hitherto covert identity of the "outed" member. In *Deronda*, Daniel is spotted as Jew by a fellow Jew, and from this point on, reading the plot backward as "present causes of past effects," his Jewishness is revealed as an open secret: the reader discovers that the signs were always there.

This scene of recognition takes place when Deronda travels to Frankfurt on the business of Sir Mallinger and inexplicably wanders into an Orthodox synagogue in the Jewish ghetto. Following the prayer services, an elderly Jew—Kalonymos—stares at Deronda and asks for his origin: "What is your parentage—your mother's family—her maiden name?" The revealing question, accompanied by Kalonymos's gaze, directs the reader's awareness to the possibility of Daniel's Jewish origin. Yet this cognitive process does not materialize in our hero himself, whose affect is depicted in great detail here: he averts his gaze when his eyes meet the old man's—"an undesirable chance with unknown persons and a reason for Deronda for not looking again." The touch of the man's hand, making "an abrupt sort of claim," is described as "an unpleasant sensation" to which Deronda has "a strongly resistant feeling." With his answer—"I am an Englishman"—to the questioning of his maternal lineage, Deronda performs a subtle act of passing, of which only the reader and Kalonymos are cognizant. The latter continues to "look at him dubiously . . . then just lift[s] his hat and turn[s] away—whether under a sense of having been mistaken or of *having been repulsed*" (my emphasis). Deronda, rushing away from the scene, experiences a strong "inward shrieking." He conceals the incident from his English family and continues to secretly explore his Jewish identity until it is fully affirmed and disclosed. When recalling this scene, some four hundred pages later, the elderly man makes it clear that in *his* eyes, Deronda was consciously and deliberately passing all along: "'A sin, a sin!' said Kalonymos, putting up his hand and closing his eyes in disgust. 'A robbery of our people'" (1995:660).

Yet Eliot goes beyond conceptualizing identity and belonging as a psychological/sentimental category. In Deronda's uncanny connection to the Jews, in the repeated evocation of Deronda's physical resemblance to his grandfather, and, most formidably, in the narrative of Mordecai's transmission of an organic Jewish past to Deronda, Eliot evokes a national heritage that is passed genetically, if unconsciously, between generations of men. Like other Victorians, most notably Herbert Spencer and George Henry Lewes, she strongly believed in the hereditary transmission of qualities. She believed, increasingly as the century progressed, that the key to social evolution lay in physiology (Shuttleworth 1984:281) and that inherited qualities were the basis of moral advancement in history (Haight 1969:415). Yet if in her previous works heredity is always in a dynamic interplay with the environment—what, after all, is the bildungsroman, Eliot's included, if not the exploration of the effects of a character's environment, his education, and particular life history upon his inherited constitution—Deronda's characterization marks a significant shift. Here Eliot imagines not only a character defined by race but a national consciousness transmitted through heredity, a process that Mordecai calls, utilizing a common metaphor for the heredity of qualities, "a way of printing on the body." As the novel progresses, Deronda is imagined, by Mordecai and by Eliot herself, as nothing else but the bodily matter on which the national message will be inscribed. Mordecai, we are told, imagines the existence of this body much before his subsequent meeting with Deronda:

> [Mordecai's] imagination had constructed another man who would be something more ample than the second soul bestowed, according to the notion of the Cabbalists, to help the insufficient first—who would be a booming human life, ready to incorporate all that was worthiest in an existence whose visible, palpable part was burning itself fast away. His inward need for the conception of this expanded, prolonged self was reflected as an outward necessity. The thoughts of his heart (that ancient phrase best shadows the truth) seemed to him too precious, too closely interwoven with the growth of things not to have a farther destiny. And the more beautiful, the stronger, the more executive self took shape in his mind, he loved it beforehand with an affection half identifying, half contemplative and grateful. (473)

Why Eliot chooses Kabbalah, a rather marginal doctrine in Jewish tradition, as the ground for Mordecai's prophecy and Daniel's Judaism, has been the subject of much speculation. Among the explanations offered are those that are centered on Eliot's fantasies about the transmission of her own works to potential (loving) readers and her dream of her own monumental rebirth (Gallagher 1986). Eliot's death, which was rapidly nearing, must have drawn her to visions of palingeneses as well. Yet in substituting the historical narrative of the bildungsroman with ideas of Kabbalistic reincarnation of souls, Eliot does more than articulate a private fantasy. For it is crucial to remember that Deronda emerges, via this Kabbalistic vision of reincarnation, out of the dead Mordecai's esoteric and visionary legacy, in the form of *modern national subject,* and that in conceiving Deronda, the new masculine citizen-ideal of the Jews, as an extension of the decrepit yet learned Mordecai, Eliot endows Deronda with a mythic prehistory that is profoundly compatible with the mythical origins of the modern nation. The kind of double history that Deronda's story presents—the vision of his nationalism as simultaneously a newly discovered ideal *and* an ancient calling—is precisely, as thinkers from Ernest Renan to Benedict Anderson have taught us, at the bottom of national mythmaking.[12] The nation, as Gourgouris has shown, is *the* social form, "in the age of Enlightenment (the age of disenchantment/demystification, as Horkheimer and Adorno would say) that evolves a new way of producing myth" (1996:15). Every work of nation building involves an occlusion of origins: a historical birth but also an

ancestral essence. It is no wonder, then, that Kabbalistic thought was infused into the nationalism of many assimilated West European Zionists,
most famously that of Gershom Scholem. This mythic logic of the nation
appears, in fact, in the very first lines of *Deronda:*

> Men can do nothing without the make-believe of a beginning
> . . . [but] no retrospect will take us to the true beginning; and
> whether our prologue be in heaven or on earth, it is but a frac-
> tion of that all-presupposing fact with which our story sets
> out. (7)

In this conscious articulation of the contingency of origins, Eliot appears to undermine the logic of national origins no less than she embraces it. But we can also read this statement to mean the exact opposite.
That "made-up" beginning is one's biological birth; Deronda as subject
begins not with his biological birth (which, as we will see, is rendered
meaningless by his own mother) but with the prehistory of his "people."
In "The Modern Hep! Hep! Hep!" Eliot states this clearly:

> Every Jew should be conscious that he is one of a multitude
> possessing common objects of piety in the immortal achieve-
> ments and immortal sorrows of ancestors who have transmitted
> to them a physical and mental type strong enough, eminent
> enough in faculties, pregnant enough with peculiar promise,
> to constitute a new beneficent individuality among the nations
> and, by confuting the traditions of scorn, nobly avenge the
> wrongs done to their Fathers. (1879/1994:164)

It is out of this "consciousness," as transmitted by Mordecai, that Deronda
emerges as a Jewish national subject; he emerges unaffected by everything in the plot that has been his "environment": his upbringing in the
home of Sir Mallinger, his childhood friends, and his years of British
education. To the extent that these had shaped him, they have done
so negatively: his detachment from them is the source of his "alienism"
and pain.

Deronda's Transformation

What, then, does Deronda's turn into a modern Jewish national subject
mean? Nothing, according to some. As Jacob Press summarizes: "Deronda

willingly divests himself of the identity category of 'Christian,' declares his 'identification' with the Jews—and that is where his transformation stops . . . Eliot articulates a vision of separatism that replicates that from which it has separated" (1997:324–25).

Yet whether he is read through the lens of Victorian discourse on character or through racial/national discourse on the Jews, Deronda does not "[replicate] that from which it has [been] separated" but undergoes profound change. In the first half of the novel, as we have seen, he is imagined as a *flawed* Victorian gentleman and, through countless signifiers, as an assimilated Jew. As such, Deronda is characterized, however poorly and didactically, by melancholy and indecisiveness, an enlarged interiority that cannot find an external ideal onto which to project itself. Ironically, it is only once he has become a Jew and a nationalist that Deronda comes to possess energy, duty, industry, and manliness—all of the characteristics of the Victorian masculine ideal.

By closing the gap between an inflated, confused "interiority" and a newly meaningful reality, Deronda sheds his Jewish particularity and becomes "every man." He also emerges from the state of the degenerate assimilated Jew, as a "normalized" subject: his thoughts are substituted by actions, his indecisiveness by a proclaimed aim, his "meditative numbness" with a "practically energetic sentiment," his loneliness by marriage to the angelic Jewess Mirah Cohen.

And it is only once he has reached this state that he becomes, at last, a desirable partner for the English Gwendolen Harleth. Grandcourt, the perverse embodiment of Victorian masculinity, is dead, murdered by the woman who had been its primary victim. A newly humbled Gwendolen now readies to marry Deronda, who at last combines manliness with his previously feminine attributes of empathy and care. But it is too late. For as the novel makes clear, though Deronda has become in many ways a Victorian character ideal, he is a Victorian no more. In their last encounter, Gwendolen will receive not a marriage proposal but a confession of Deronda's Jewishness.

> "A *Jew*!" Gwendolen exclaimed, in a low tone of amazement, with an utterly frustrated look, as if some confusing potion were creeping through her system.
>
>   Deronda coloured and did not speak, while Gwendolen, with her eyes fixed on the floor, was struggling to find her way in the dark by the aid of various reminiscences. She seemed at last to have arrived at some judgment, for she looked up at

Deronda again and said . . . "What difference need that have
made?"

"It has made a great difference to me that I have known it,"
said Deronda, emphatically, but he could not go on easily—the
distance between her ideas and his acted *like a difference of
native language,* making him uncertain what force his words
would carry. (801–2; my emphasis)

In her inability to contain the fact of Deronda's Jewishness (feeling
it as "a confusing potion creeping through her," a shock to the body),
Gwendolen demonstrates the limits of what Bryan Cheyette has called
"the false universalism of a materialist rationalism" (1993:21). Indeed,
Deronda's transformation is depicted as stretching beyond the liberal
imagination of Gwendolen or any other of the English characters in the
novel. But this does not much matter to the newly resolute Deronda.
If at the beginning of the novel, as we have shown, he is presented as
an alien in his own home, by the end of the novel, it is he who reads
himself as a foreigner, as one speaking a different "native language" than
Gwendolen. Indeed, Deronda emerges by the end of the novel not only
as a mature subject, but a speaker of a distinct foreign language (as he
had been secretly studying Hebrew)[13] and a non-European national. For
both of these reasons, he will decidedly fit the conventions of the bildungsroman no more.

In place of "interiority" and "mobility," in place of the negative liberty
on which the bildungsroman is predicated, Deronda procures, by his
own testament, "something better than freedom": a *duteous* bond that
his experience had been preparing him to accept gladly. The national
consciousness, which, as we have seen, is imagined as mythically transmitted, is finally communicated in the language of rational choice and
character attributes. Eliot articulates a similar logic of boundedness by
choice at the end of "The Modern Hep! Hep! Hep!," where, after enu-
merating the attributes and history of the Jewish nation, she ends with
the duty of the individual man:

> There is a sense in which the worthy child of a nation that has
> brought forth illustrious prophets, high and unique among the
> poets of the world, is bound by their visions.
> Is bound?
> Yes, for the effective bond of human action is feeling, and
> the worthy child of a people . . . feels his kinship with the glo-

ries and the sorrows, the degradation and the possible renova-
tion of his *national family.* (1879/1994:165)

In this triple emphasis on involuntary bond, the discourse of character,
and the language of feeling, Eliot anticipates, as we will see, a portrait of
national belonging that will emerge in many Zionist nationalistic works.
It is the willing acceptance of the *duteous bond* between the worthy child
and the nation, Deronda's absolute submission to Mordecai and to "his
people": this more than any other quality will define the nationalized
Deronda vis-à-vis his previous self. In contrast with the (fierce yet hopeless) battle against submission waged by Gwendolen and the Alcharisi
(which we will discuss in the following pages) Deronda embraces submission to a higher power "gladly" and by choice. In this play between
voluntary and involuntary submission as the basis for the cathecting of
citizen to nation, as in the fetishizing of the strength and beauty of the
emergent Jewish national male subject, Eliot foregrounds the most po-
tent characteristics of masculinity and citizenship to emerge and dominate Zionist and Israeli discourse in the decades to come. Ironically, it
is her emphasis on the family as the grounding metaphor for the nation
that will prove highly problematic. For in *Deronda,* as elsewhere in Zionist literature that will follow it, the family is anything but a realm of
kinship and love.

CHAPTER 2

On Woman and Nation in
the Late Nineteenth Century

*It is as if all the life I have chosen to live, all thoughts, all
will, forsook me and left me alone in the spots of memory,
and I can't get away: My pain seems to keep me there. My
childhood—all my girlhood—the day of my marriage—the day
of my father's death—there seems to be nothing since.*

For the speaker of these words, Deronda's mother Leonora Charisi, a.k.a.
the Alcharisi and Princess Halm-Eberstein, the clutch of collective identity comes down like a curse; the curse is the curse of the father and the
"spots of memory" that he inhabits and controls. The father is the executor of her reunion with Deronda—"I have been forced to obey my dead
father. I have been forced to tell you that you are a Jew, and deliver to
you what he commanded me to deliver"—though by the point she has
entered the plot, this reunion is necessary to making Deronda a Jew only
in the formal sense.

   Both plotlines of mother and son involve, therefore, a narrative of
passing and return; in both stories, the past wills and controls the present. Yet if Deronda embraces this past to the extent that he embodies its
modern reincarnation, if he makes the preservation of this past his life's
calling, the Alcharisi, while acknowledging its power to control her ("I
can't get away") fights it with all her strength. Compare the fluid merging
imagery surrounding Deronda's "return" to Judaism—"a divine influx in
the darkness"—with the Alcharisi's: "A power laying hold of me—that
is clutching me now." It is her father's ghost who has returned both to
punish the wayward daughter and, through her negation, to reclaim
Deronda, the male heir of his spiritual inheritance. This "return" will
erase the Alcharisi and her legacy of radical individualism from Deronda's story, though not, I think, from the plot as a whole.

At the end of the novel the Alcharisi is all but defeated: "It is as if all the life *I have chosen to live,* all thoughts, *all will,* forsook me." Having been "the greatest lyric artist in Europe" (639), she loses her voice, her fame, and her artistic genius. And yet, in rejecting Deronda's filial overtures ("I am your mother. But you can have no love for me"), in reducing his spiritual transformation to earthly desire ("You are in love with a Jewess!"), in refusing to return to her identity of origin and choosing defeat instead ("I cannot myself love the people I have never loved—is it not enough that I lost the life I did love?"), she comes to embody everything that is rejected by the Mordecai-Deronda plot.

Indeed, in her brief appearance in the text, the Alcharisi represents all the possibilities, for women and for Jews, that at the end are rejected by the plot. Eliot designates her as the one character in the novel who refutes the primacy of all biological origins ("I was not like a brute, obliged to go with my own herd") and unapologetically legislates herself as an individual, autonomous, identity-less subject. In her steadfast belief that she is the author of her own destiny, the Alcharisi embodies the universal liberal subject to its radical extreme; in her conviction that by sending her son to live among aristocrats she will produce a British gentleman, she is the truest believer in nurture over nature, environment over heredity. These are the beliefs, as we have seen, that are rejected outright by Eliot in *Deronda* and elsewhere.[1]

Admittedly, the Alcharisi is ridiculous: too extreme to be believable, too marginal for the reader to care about her fate. And yet her words stick. How many characters in the English novel, after all, deliver in the name of female freedom a tirade against motherhood with such cold conviction? How many are portrayed as aloof and detached when faced with a pleading son? Then there is Gwendolen. Though infinitely more complex a character than the Alcharisi, her story nevertheless echoes the latter's: the boundless ambition, the iron will, the desire to transcend a place of origin, the wish to become a world-renowned artist. Here are the classic bildungsroman heroines whose loss Moretti decries. It is they, not Deronda, who attempt to break their ties with "a reality that is heterogeneous in itself and meaningless to the individual"; they who embody "mobility, individuality, dynamism and restlessness" (Moretti 1987:5); they who desire to live "the fullness of life"; and it is they who will suffer by the novel's end "the certainty of defeat" (Lukács 1971:200). *I wanted to live a large life, with freedom to do what everyone else did, and be carried along in a great current* (630): so declares the Alcharisi, articulating Gwendolen's half-conscious desires. In the Alcharisi's stress on freedom, the great current of history, the similitude to "everyone else," she is indeed precisely the bildungsroman heroine who, as Moretti laments, has been written out of the history of the European novel by the nationalist/collectivist narrative.

Yet it is no longer possible, as Moretti argues and the Deronda's plotline demonstrates, to transcend one's origins at the late nineteenth century in the way that the Alcharisi had done earlier in the century. And it is also no longer possible because the very desperate attempt to erase her Jewishness now contains what it means to be read as "Jewish." Her defiance of national and religious belonging, her cosmopolitanism and internationalism, her artistic bent, *her lack of identity*—all these define her, in the Proustian sense, exactly as *a Jew* in the late nineteenth century.

Deronda's World as Colonial Space

Anthony Trollope's *The Prime Minister,* published in the same year as *Deronda,* is a case in point. Trollope portrays a Britain that, though liberal enough to have placed a converted Jew at its helm, nevertheless pounds away incessantly at his difference. This is seemingly untrue for the Alcharisi, who contrary to Trollope's Daubeny, reports on nothing but love and admiration from her European fans. Yet we must also remember that in *Deronda's* present, presumably the time in which Eliot was writing it, the Alcharisi's career is all but over. Even if Eliot meant us to understand her as the beneficiary of the liberalism and tolerance of the first and middle part of the nineteenth century, in 1876 and in the decades that followed it, English readers would have invariably read the Alcharisi through her racial difference. They would have heard, as we now do, all the nuances in Gwendolen's reference to "that little Jewess" (the Jewish actress Rachel) and also in the defensive complaint of the Alcharisi's father about those "Jewish women [who] are thought of by the Christian world as ware to make public singers and actresses of" (631).

A common humanity is not yet enough to feed the rich blood of various activity which makes a complete man: in *Deronda,* the "wide world" is read by Eliot, like the Alcharisi's father, as explicitly Christian. As such, the Alcharisi's decisive break with Judaism (including her conversion into Christianity) is understood by them not as a transparent and unproblematic integration into a secular, international "wide world" but a betrayal of a minority religious/national identity for a majority one. They read the Alcharisi's actions *politically,* as an act of passing within a field of power and contest akin to that of a colonial space.

In his interrogation of the contest between colonized and colonizer, Fanon (1963) stresses the position that colonial women occupy: treading between the two spheres and representing in their very bodies the threat of loss of native identity and assimilation into the colonizer's world. A similar analysis, I think, is in part at least offered by *Deronda*. For Fanon, as McClintock (1997) has shown, women serve through restrictions on marital or sexual relations as the boundary of the group's identity; as such, the fear and battle against women's transgression to the side of the colonizer is not so much the threat of women's autonomy but the fear of women's sexualization by one *outside the group*. It is such a fear that *Deronda* raises in conjunction to both its female Jewish characters (and singers): the Alcharisi, whose father's prohibition is explicitly directed at her sexualization by non-Jews ("he hated that Jewish women should be thought of by the Christian world as a sort of ware to make public singers and actresses of") and the young Mirah Cohen, Deronda's future bride, whose half-explained past, the narrator suggests, included public display and forced prostitution. Mirah's marriage to Deronda and her decision to no longer sing in public thus represents a victory of sorts for the nationalist plot in a way that the Alcharisi's defiance does not. If, as Fanon writes, the attempt to dismantle the colonial paradigm and replace it with an autonomous national identity begins with a war over women (1963:35–38), that war in *Deronda* is both won and lost.

Jewish Women and the End of the Age of Individualism

Yet it is not only the Alcharisi's desire to easily transcend an ethnic or religious identity or her crossing to the other side that is presented critically in the novel but her wish to surpass the limits of a female identity as well. Indeed, if Marian Evans's transformation into George Eliot had spurred one of the most triumphant literary careers of the nineteenth century, so, we are told, did Leonora Charisi's turn into the Alcharisi: "You wondered what I was. I was no princess then. No princess in this tame life that I live now. I was a great singer, and I acted as well as I sang. All the rest were poor beside me. Men followed me from one country to another. *I was living a myriad of lives in one*" (635; my emphasis). Yet with all her momentous desire to live "a large life," her world, which we enter only at the end of the novel, has clamped down on her quite harshly: she has lost her voice, her career, and her freedom only to be subsumed into a conventional life and a marriage. A similar fate, as Gallagher has shown, awaited Eliot, who shortly after *Deronda*'s completion ceased to write, married at the age of sixty-one for the first time, and died within a year. The possibility of a female genius creating not only like a man, but *as* a man, is deemed by Eliot at the end of her life not only impossible but passé, a laughable, condemnable fancy. Thus, by the end of the novel, the Alcharisi's options are either to return to her patriarchal Jewish lineage, crushed between her father's ghost and his namesake grandson, or to return to her later marriage. Similarly, the name George Eliot will be changed to Mrs. John Cross. Both will have lost their voice: the Alcharisi, we are told, has literally lost it; Eliot will cease to write. And both will have lost their audiences: the Alcharisi thrust into the far Russian wastelands; Eliot suffering from a considerable damage to her reputation caused by the negative reception of *Deronda*. Perhaps foreshadowing her own fate, Eliot will portray the Alcharisi as dying. She herself would die soon after.

Nowhere in Eliot's novels are women's unbridled ambition and desire for independence argued so forcefully and explicitly, but nowhere are they crushed so completely as in *Deronda*. The novel delivers a harsh, unequivocal condemnation of the Alcharisi and her fierce individualism. It also condemns, in a more complicated way, Gwendolen's desires, explored and ultimately crushed over hundreds of pages of gorgeous prose; having been brought down by her ambitious yet cruel marriage, Gwendolen herself comes to view her early desire for autonomy and success as childish vanity or worse: "I said I should be forsaken. I have been a cruel woman. And I am forsaken," she tells Deronda, who in turn instructs her to devote her energy and ambition to the common good (805). Indeed, the successful creation of Deronda as subject of and synecdoche for the Jewish nation is made possible exactly by the failure of Gwendolen and the Alcharisi's quest for "negative freedom," radical autonomy that denies even maternal and familial origins.

What relationship is set up by the novel between Gwendolen's and Deronda's desire? Does the Deronda plot subsume Gwendolen's? Susan Meyer has suggested that it does: Deronda's embrace of a collective ideal encompasses, consumes, and erases Gwendolen's "private" desire for individual freedom (1996:733). Indeed, at the end of the novel the narrator depicts Gwendolen as "outside history," feeling herself "reduced to a mere speck" when instead of a marriage proposal she is confronted with Deronda's political ideals:

> The world seemed getting larger round poor Gwendolen, and
> she more solitary and helpless in the midst . . . There comes

a terrible moment to many souls when the great movements
of the world, the larger destinies of mankind, which have lain
aloof in newspapers and other neglected reading, enter like
an earthquake into their own lives—when the slow urgency of
growing generations turns into the tread of an invading army
or the dire clash of civil war, and grey fathers know nothing to
seek for but the corpses of their blooming sons, and girls forget all vanity to make lint and bandages, which may serve for
the shattered limbs of their betrothed husbands. (803)

History, the narrator thus tells us, has entered Gwendolen's life like
an earthquake, and when history enters, all female vanity is forgotten
and care for wounded men begins. The novel does not make it clear,
however, if this is a lesson that the Alcharisi rejects and Gwendolen has
doubtfully learned. What we do know is that while at the beginning of
the novel, Deronda's and Gwendolen's fates appear equally problematic
(not only is Deronda presented as feminized, but Jewish and female protagonists serve as metaphors for one another: both need to create their
own destiny, as neither will inherit the house in which they were born),
by its ending they are worlds apart. Deronda will become fully grounded
in an idealized marriage, a nationality, and a vocation; Gwendolen will
emerge a penniless widow whose future is unknown.

Jewish Women and Late Nineteenth-Century European Culture

Why, might we ask, does a novel that will produce the first full-fledged
Zionist character, and one of the only somewhat positive (albeit flat)
Jewish characters in the English novel, also demand that its female characters (even ones who have remained within the bounds of the group)
give up any claim to autonomy and fame?

One answer is this: in *Deronda*, Eliot "sacrificed" her female characters in order to resurrect the embattled image of the Jewish man, an
image that she sought (though had not succeeded) to dignify through
its association with the national cause. Such a backlash against women's
independence is a common script at the nation-building stage. Chatterjee, for example, has documented how the "woman question," so central
to early and mid-nineteenth-century Bengal, disappears from the public
agenda with the advent of Indian nationalism later in the century. Wom-
en's politics, he explains, are folded at that point into "the binding and
overarching umbrella" of nationalist politics, which "subsumes other

and different political temporalities."[2] A similar backlash is noticeable in late nineteenth-century European culture where in such novels as Bram Stoker's *Dracula* anxieties over national boundaries pair up with the critique of fin-de-siècle "degeneration" to ridicule and contain images of the "emancipated" woman. Zionist rhetoric also intersected with this backlash in various ways, most directly through the figure of Max Nordau, who not only coined the term "degeneration" but was also the most famous personality to join the Jewish national cause. For Nordau, Zionism was not only the road leading to the political emancipation of the Jews but also to the utopian place where the patriarchal marriage and the nuclear family would be restored. (We will return to Nordau and *Dracula* in Part II.)

A nostalgic fantasy about an unproblematic return to patriarchal gender arrangements is written into virtually all nationalist scripts;[3] yet as Fanon, Chatterjee, and others have shown, the symbolic function of "woman" has importance for emergent nationalist cultures beyond it.[4] For the struggles between colonizer and colonized (or majority and minority cultures) are often waged over the treatment of women by colonized/minority men; it is the one issue that often comes to signify for the colonizer/majority the native man's absolute "barbarity" and otherness. These dynamics are not absent from *Deronda,* where the tirade against the treatment of Jewish women and girls by Jewish men is delivered, not surprisingly, by the Jewish woman herself:

> [My father] never comprehended me, or if he did, he only thought of fettering me into obedience. I was to be what he called "the Jewish woman" under the pain of his curse. I was to feel everything I did not feel, and believe everything I did not believe. I was to feel awe for a bit of parchment in the *mezuza* over the door; to dread lest a bit of butter should touch a bit of meat, to think it beautiful that men should bind the *tephillin* on them, and women not,—to adore the wisdom of such laws, however silly they might seem to me. I was to love the long prayers in the ugly synagogue, and the howling, and the gabbling, and the dreadful fasts, and the tiresome feasts, and my father's endless discoursing about Our People, which was a thunder without meaning in my ears. I was to care forever about what Israel had been; and I did not care at all. I cared for the wide world, and all that I could represent in it. I hated living under the shadow of my father's strictness . . . Such men turn

their wives and daughters into slaves. They would rule the world
if they could; but not ruling the world, they throw all the weight
of their will on the necks and souls of women. (630–31)

Michael Ragussis (1995) has convincingly demonstrated how the
Alcharisi's speech contains all the conventional arguments against Judaism that dominated nineteenth-century conversion literature. Indeed,
discourses of conversion, frequently aimed at women and girls, often
made Jewish male patriarchy and the repression of women the focus
of their argument. Jewish men, the Alcharisi protests, "would rule the
world if they could; but not ruling the world, they throw all the weight
of their will on the necks and souls of women." Eliot not only portrays
here Jewish male desire to block the private realm that women and family embody from the purview of the Gentile world but cleverly mobilizes widespread paranoia about Jewish world domination by placing
these fears, as much conversion literature had done, *in the mouth of a
Jew.* Deronda's mother is thus constructed not only as the antithesis and
harshest critic of Deronda's national ambitions but as the only explicitly
anti-Semitic character in the text.

The Distinct Fates of European Jewish Men and Women

Nonetheless, the Alcharisi's story: that of a girl for whom Jewish tradition and customs were oppressive and incomprehensible and in turn
escaped to Christian Europe had many historical and literary precedents
in the late nineteenth-century Jewish world. A traditional Jewish education for the most part was unavailable to women, who instead were
instructed in European languages and culture. Consequently and un-
intentionally, such girls became much more assimilated than boys and
much likelier to reject Jewish life in adulthood. Toward the turn of the
century, heated debates over Jewish women's education and concerns
over the plight of women and girls in traditional Jewish life were in fact
beginning to increasingly appear in Jewish presses. These debates, waged
mostly between men, question girls' exclusion from the traditional Jewish education system, an exclusion that inevitably leads to alienation and
at times to desertion of Jewish culture. The Alcharisi, who bluntly states
that Jewish customs were "thunder to [her] ears" is a case in point.

One such famous Alcharisi-like story that reverberated in Jewish
presses was the case of Mikhlina Aratin, daughter to a wealthy Hasidic
family, who on the eve of her arranged marriage to a Jewish scholar dis-

appeared into a nearby convent. When it became known that in place of a traditional education Mikhlina was offered a fine general education in European languages and culture, a debate over Jewish women's education was spurred. One commentator wrote in 1900:

> The same dedication that they show in educating their boys in the *Torah*, [Orthodox parents] show in educating their daughters in foreign schools . . . and they are proud of their girls' achievements in the secular studies in these schools . . . Their entire childhood they are left to do as they please and when it is time to marry them, then [the pious fathers] become strict and with a heavy hand they will fight their young daughters, using stick and whip, to force them into marrying a boy of their choosing. Reader, judge for yourself, if you possess a soul within you: sophisticated, educated girls, brought up in a foreign spirit, are forced to abandon their lives hitherto, their girlfriends and sometimes their boyfriends, and go marry righteous religious scholars. A chasm separates the girls and boys of Chassidic homes! Is it a wonder, then, that many of these virgins, knowing their fate, will reject it and find a refuge from their stern fathers in the convent?[5]

Or, on the stages of the European opera houses. The Alcharisi's story—her escape from a confining Jewish upbringing, her withdrawal from a marriage to a Jewish husband, her success on the European stage, her conversion—thus contains quite a bit of plausible historical truth. For despite her father's alleged strictness, as an English Jewish girl in the nineteenth century she most likely would have received a "general" education and relative access to European culture, and she would have also enjoyed, as she attests she did, a level of success and admiration that could not be paralleled for Jewish male performers. Jewish female artists like the Alcharisi in fact would have been embraced by Christian Europe much more readily than their male counterparts from as early as the middle ages. "From the onset a distinction must be drawn," writes the author of an 1898 study on the treatment of Jewish stage performers: "The Jewess enjoyed an extraordinary immunity from attack; she was as much lauded as the Jew was reviled. The stage Jewess was always beautiful, and was always intended to be love worthy" (Abrahams 1981:257). The pressures that would bear on Deronda's identity as assimilated Jewish man would therefore not bear equally on his artistic mother, making her more likely to stubbornly defend liberal assimilatory ideals and, given the novel's politics, raising the stakes against her.

The Alcharisi, whose post-Jewish life is virtually erased ("my girl-hood, my adolescence, my marriage—nothing exists since") is therefore punished by the plot for her unequivocal embrace of liberal ideals and for what is read by her father, as by traditional Jewish readers as well as by Eliot, as her transgression into Christian culture. Yet she refuses all identifications: she rejects her role as the "Jewish woman" on whose back the battle over conversion or nationalism is fought; she refuses nationalist and religious discourse and affiliation altogether, belittling her Christian affiliation as well and presenting her conversion as purely strategic. She flees Jewish life not for love (the common justification for women's passing in Jewish narratives like Sholom Aleichem's *Tevye and His Daughters*) but for the fulfillment of artistic genius. In justifying her actions to Deronda, the Alcharisi explicitly presents the denial of Jewish and maternal origin not as an act of passing into Christian culture but as the natural right of the self-creating artistic genius to flee a restrictive environment for the "wide world": "I had a right to be free. I had a right to seek my freedom from a bondage that I hated" (627, 630). She *continues* to speak, even as the basis for this language is eradicated by the late nineteenth-century plot, through the discourse of the "negative free-dom" of the liberal subject, appealing to natural rights and rejecting all identities, including those of wife and mother. Though she is punished and ridiculed by the plot (and relegated outside the domain of civilized Europe) she never returns to her Jewish home.

Refusal of Motherhood, Inassimilability into National Discourse

That the Alcharisi embodies absolute rebellion is important, particularly for a writer as ambivalent on women's issues as Eliot. For Jewish context aside, the set of problems that are embodied in the Alcharisi plot—the fissure between women's individualism and ambition and the proper functioning of society—have occupied Eliot at least as long as she was writing novels. In this sense, the Alcharisi plotline, as short and incom-plete as it is, exceeds the particular discussion of the Jews: "You do not know what it is like to have man's force of genius in you, and yet to suffer the slavery of being a girl," the Alcharisi proclaims, pointing to gender before Judaism as the greatest obstacle to her self-fulfillment. This lan-guage is exaggerated, but not profoundly different from a range of Eliot heroines—Maggie Tulliver, Dinah Morris, Dorothea Brooke, Gwendolen Harleth—and, of course, Eliot herself, who knew "what it is like" as she began her writing career while caring for an ailing father. The chain of identifications that leads from Dinah Morris to Gwendolen to the Alcharisi to Eliot herself cannot, I think, be overlooked here.

Indeed, the Alcharisi is not the first Eliot character to assume a male voice only to lose it later. Seventeen years earlier, *Adam Bede* begins with an eloquent fifty-page sermon by the Methodist preacher Dinah Morris, speaking in the name of a male God and in God's voice, only to end with a terse, stuttering explanation, delivered by Dinah's husband, Adam:

> Conference has forbid the women preaching and she's given it up, all but talking to the people a bit in their houses . . . Most o' the women do more harm nor good with their preaching—they've not got Dinah's gift nor her sperrit; and she's seen that, and she thought it right to set th' example o' submitting, for she's not held from other sorts o' teaching. And I agree with her, and approve o' what she did. (Eliot 1985/1869:583)

Such is the economy of *Adam Bede,* and such is Dinah's fate within this economy: to have willingly traded her voice for her husband's, her vocation for family, her oratory genius for love and marriage.

Deronda's gender economy, however, is altogether messier. Though the fantasy of blissful patriarchal marriage is made possible in the text in the image of the Deronda-Mirah dyad, a darker, more sinister vision of marriage—that of Gwendolen and Grandcourt—dominates the text. And though the desire of its female characters for absolute autonomy is shattered to the core, they nevertheless are not happily absorbed into the patriarchal family by "falling in love," not even with an offspring ("I did not want you," says the Alcharisi to her long-lost son; and Gwendolen's greatest fear, it is suggested, is to be impregnated by her husband). Unlike any other of Eliot's female characters, the Alcharisi does not internalize (not even slowly and painfully as Maggie Tulliver does) any "feminine" qualities: She does not embrace maternity, nor care for an insufferable mother-in-law, nor return to her familial origins. She may have lost the self-driving power and artistic fame that she had previously commanded, but she has hardly become a model for feminine values like caring and empathy.

Thus, *Daniel Deronda* represents a rejection not only of female autonomy (and autonomy altogether) but also of maternity as such. In part, Eliot implies, Deronda's abandonment by his mother should be understood as a consequence of her predicament as minority woman. In a racist society, as Fanon would argue almost a century later, the family ceases to be a locus of normality at the very moment that it comes into contact with the outside world.[6] As such it is possible, though the text only implicitly supports such a reading, to interpret the Alcharisi's decision to give away her son as a consequence of power and an example of how powerlessness disfigures the Jewish family. But this is only half the story. For Deronda's rejection by his mother also supports and advances the novel's nationalistic plot.

Indeed, the successful creation of Deronda as subject of and synecdoche for the Jewish nation is incumbent on the Alcharisi's failure at denying national and maternal roots. Eliot, as we have seen, sets the Alcharisi up as a character who had passed across several identity borders—race, class, religion, nationality, and gender lines, and who had orchestrated her son's passing as well. This in itself may register positively or negatively with a reader, depending on who is doing the reading and when. Yet by structurally tying the rejection of national/religious identity to the rejection of an offspring, the Alcharisi is positioned, so to speak, beyond the pale. Any sympathy the reader might have had for the Alcharisi's actions and motivations—certainly oppression suffered at the hands of a Jewish father would have elicited some—would stop at the point of the shocking act of abandonment of a child. We read her independence as egotism, her struggle for autonomy as betrayal, her artistic genius as frivolous. Indeed, by causally linking the abandonment of Daniel with the abandonment of Judaism, Eliot strengthens the coherence of Jewish identity and structures the Alcharisi story as a passing story, rather than the story of successful assimilation. It is precisely the Alcharisi's unrepentant *choice* to give up her child by design that dooms the act of passing as "unnatural." Deronda, having "returned," is set up as good and "natural"; she, having passed, is set up as bad and inauthentic.

The Alcharisi is not the first novelistic character to have given up a child, but her position is extreme. In many minority or passing narratives, female characters must give up motherhood or else contend with physical or mental separation from their child.[7] Yet even in the most troubling depiction of motherhood—say, Toni Morrison's *Beloved*—motherhood continues to stand as a powerful symbol of natural love and authentic origin ("motherland," *mamaloshen*). To the degree that mother-child ties are severed, this can be blamed on external oppression, not rational choice. Not so in *Deronda*. Having couched Deronda's abandonment in the story of his mother's enormous ambition, extreme individualism, and unequivocal rejection of origin, Eliot puts into question the *very idea* of maternal origin. The passing mother's self-justification ("What better could the most loving mother have done? I relieved you from the bondage of having been born a Jew") are heard by the readers, as they are heard by Deronda himself, as mere farce:

> Every woman is supposed to have the same set of motives, or else to be a monster. I am not a monster, but I have not felt exactly what other women feel—or say they feel, for fear of being thought unlike others. When you reproach me in your heart for sending you away from me, you mean that I ought to say I felt about you as other women feel about their children. I did *not* feel that. I was glad to be freed from you . . . I had not much affection to give you. I did not want affection. I had been stifled with it. I wanted to live out the life that was in me, and not to be hampered with other lives. (621)

As caricatured as the Alcharisi may be, her words leave a mark on the novel. Not only does she reject her son, but she organizes mother-child relations around experience, not nature. *I have not the foolish notion that you can love me merely because I am your mother, when you have never seen or heard of me all your life:* maternal bonds are denaturalized here as well as any bonds that are not grounded in shared experience; this goes against the grain not only of Deronda's romantic pull toward the Jews but also against the very logic of nationalities, which assume filial ties among unrelated individuals like Deronda and Mordecai. In this way, Eliot sets the reader up with two identities—the maternal and the Jewish—that are at once parallel and antithetical. The maternal is socially constructed, learned through mimicry and social pressure, and voluntary ("I have not felt exactly what other women feel—or say they feel, for fear of being thought unlike others"); Jewish identity, as evidenced by Deronda's uncanny transformation, is involuntary and divorced from experience. In the Frankfurt synagogue scene, where Deronda first encounters Judaism, he feels, we are told, an *immediate* emotional bond. His pull toward his Jewish origin is described as a merging with another: a prelinguistic, preimagistic "undifferentiated influx." Elsewhere, Eliot describes the nation as "family." Yet, as we have seen, the grounding or naturalness of national bonds in the naturalness of mother-child or familial relations is highly problematic in *Deronda*. Larsen's passing character Clare Kendry may be an orphan, but Daniel Deronda *has* a mother, whose absolute rejection of motherhood makes it impossible to neatly align his embrace of Judaism with the *naturalness* of maternal and familial bonds. The maternal is thus conceived through the Alcharisi plot not in metaphorical relationship to the nation but as its very antonym.

The Erasure of Women from National Discourse

Instead, Eliot imagines the passing of Jewish identity and history as an endless chain of men, duplicating each other over countless generations. Though Jewish identity is matrilineal, the Alcharisi's role in creating Deronda as a Jewish subject is mostly as his antithesis. She is the accidental womb that brought him into the world and soon after disappeared. Her departure, in this sense, clears the stage for male autogenesis; Mordecai Cohen succeeds in replacing her as the maker of Deronda's Jewishness and gives Deronda (re)birth within Jewish male genealogy. In sharp contrast with the harsh rejection of his own dying mother, Mordecai's "consumptive glance" as he gazes at Deronda, the narrator tells us, is that

> of the slowly dying mother's look when her one loved son visits her bedside, and the flickering power of gladness leaps out as she says, "My boy!"—for the sense of spiritual perpetuation in another resembles that maternal transference of self. (495)

Thus, the "maternal transference of self" becomes the organizing metaphor for Mordecai's relation to Deronda, even while Deronda's mother upholds a vision of herself as radically monadic and separate from her son. Mordecai thus comes to occupy the symbolic position of both mother *and* father (his family name—Cohen—means, among other things, that this name and the identity that it records passes through the father). He is depicted as conceiving the Jewish Deronda, but also as impregnating him with the old/new national heritage that will now become his. The maternal womb is turned superfluous in this vision of male parthenogenesis, and Deronda is now imagined as the womb into which Mordecai will pour the spiritual product that, as he hopes, will be the seed of a new nation:

> For many winters, while [Mordecai] had been conscious of an ebbing physical life, and a widening spiritual loneliness, all his passionate desire had concentrated itself in the yearning

for some young ear into which he could pour his mind as a testament [this invocation of the biblical testaments of course recalling Mary's spiritual fertilization—through the ear, as tradition has it], some soul kindred enough to accept the spiritual *product* of his own brief, painful life, as a mission to be executed. [He was] *yearning* for *transmission.* The *yearning* which had *panted upward* from out of overwhelming discouragements, had *grown* into a hope—the hope into a confident belief, which, instead of being checked by the clear conception he had of his *hastening decline,* took rather the intensity of expectant faith in a prophecy which has only brief space to get *fulfilled* in. (472)

And when Deronda appears, available to be impregnated with Mordecai's prophetic product, he is imagined as Mordecai's wife:

It has already begun, the marriage of our souls. It waits but the passing away of this body, and then they who are betrothed shall unite in a stricter bond, and what shall be mine shall be thine. (751)

Contemporary critics have focused on the strong homoerotic overtones of the Deronda-Mordecai plotline, a powerful spiritual and physical attraction between men (Press 1997). Yet the above descriptions symbolically resonate much wider than relations between two individual men. They evoke a merging of old and new: a fantasy (strongly homoerotic) of national renewal as it is projected onto a "beautiful," "strong," "executive," and modern male body; they allude to, as we have seen, Kabbalistic sources that strengthen the image of the nation as mythic and eternal and suggest a vision of palingeneses. Such erotic, male-centered Kabbalistic references have an additional importance here; whereas Judaism in general stresses, even celebrates, women's procreative role, Kabbalah enables Eliot to substitute women's parturition with parthenogenesis. Taken together with the Alcharisi's modern feminist sensibilities—namely, her self-willed rejection of maternity—the novel presents the birth of the nation as male autogenesis, a fantasy that will get its most spectacular secular articulation several years later in Nietzsche's neo-romantic writings.

Deronda's ending is simple enough: it leaves us, to borrow from Luce Irigaray, with Eliot's fantasy of "a fully constituted patrilineality," a "fan-

tasy of autogenesis or self-constitution [that] is effected through a denial
and cooptation of the female capacity for reproduction."[8] It also leaves us
with a denial of the possibility of absolute negative liberty in a space that
can be said to exist outside the national. If, as we have seen in our analysis of Deronda, "Jewish man" is constituted in this proto-Zionist novel as
a duteous, masculine, and autonomous subject through the narrative of
Jewish nationalism, the nonnationalized Jewish woman (as embodied in
the Alcharisi) and perhaps "woman" as such (Gwendolen) are deferred
by the end of the novel to what McClintock calls a "nowhere land beyond time and place" (1997:95).

To focus on this end alone, however, is to ignore the fact that most of
Eliot's contemporary readers (Gentiles *and* Jews) strongly rejected her
nationalist conclusion. It is also to ignore the hard work that the novel
undertakes, over hundreds of pages, to explore, probe, question, and finally defer its female characters' struggles around autonomy, individuality, and maternity. In its intense investigation of the Gwendolen plot, as
in its adamant characterization of the Alcharisi—a character so singular
that she deflects any attempt to eradicate her effect from the text—the
novel is, despite its decidedly antifeminist ending, a thorough *analysis* of
the nexus between feminism and nation. Eliot, as we know, never allows
her female characters to claim a collective identity and wage a political
struggle as "women." Thus their stories remain essentially distinct: the
stories of "the problematic *individual's* journeying towards" *herself.* Yet
in maintaining that women's formation narratives remain decidedly in-
dividualistic, she associates the "Jewish woman" in this late nineteenth-
century novel with "negative freedom" and the forsaken ideals of a liberal Europe, one that seemed but was not large enough to encompass
the Jews and other minorities, with women. Finally, to focus only on the
novel's female characters is also to ignore *Eliot's* own complex identifications in it—not with women but with Jewish men—a transgression
perhaps more significant and bolder than the Alcharisi's.

"Who Taught This Foreign Woman About the Ways and Lives of the Jews?": George Eliot and the Hebrew Renaissance

Cross-Cultural Transmission: Daniel Deronda and Early Zionist Culture

So far I have read *Deronda* as a text that marks certain aesthetic and po-litical shifts in European thought, a shift in which a neo-romantic kind of masculinity and nationality emerges, as well as a vision of women as residue of what has been left behind. Though in a completely differ-ent context, this shift and its attendant gender ramifications are echoed in much of early Zionist culture of the late nineteenth century; a case in point, in fact, is the story of *Deronda*'s translation into Hebrew and its reception in Zionist circles. It is a story that demonstrates not only Eliot's complicated position vis-à-vis the world of modern Hebrew let-ters but also the ambivalent position of women at large vis-à-vis the emergent national project. Eliot, as is well known, conceived the Zionist idea twenty years before the emergence of the Zionist political move-ment, and influenced emerging Zionists across Europe. She mastered, across the bar of Jewish prohibition, a textual tradition that was all but forbidden to women, delving into the Bible, medieval Hebrew poetry, the Kabbalah, and the study of the Hebrew language. In her case, writes *Deronda*'s translator, the prominent Hebrew critic and author David Frishman in 1893,

> it is not possible to mock women who demand education and know everything from buffalo's horns to nits, but when asked who was *Yehuda Halevi,* who was *Ebn Gbirol,* and who was *Moshe Ben Ezra,* stand like brutes who know nothing. Indeed George Eliot knows of all these important people and of the

wisdom of Israel, and at times she knows more than some of
the learned of Israel themselves.[1]

Indeed, Eliot had transgressed, and was allowed to transgress, the
conservative national and gender boundaries that she herself embraced.[2]
In effect she came to occupy the role of a (Jewish) male scholar. And
her novel's claim to fame, through its various German, Russian, and
Hebrew translations, extended far beyond British borders, spurring debates over Jewish nationalism worldwide. I end this part, therefore, with
a brief history of *Deronda*'s translation and reception, its function for the
newly emergent national culture, its place in the budding canon, and finally, with the perception of its main protagonist and author by Hebrew
readers.

Deronda's Reception

To write about *Deronda*'s translation from English to Hebrew in the
nineteenth century is to write about many things. It is a translation from
a lingua franca spoken and read by millions to an esoteric language read
by thousands and spoken by few. It is a transition from a Western European to a mostly Eastern European audience. It is a translation across
classes. As far as Jewish readership is concerned, it is a translation from
a generally assimilated Jewry to a generally less assimilated one. And it
is a translation from an audience of men and women to an audience that
consisted almost exclusively of men. As a rule, women were not traditionally educated and could and would not read Hebrew texts.[3]

Who, in the late 1800s, more than half a century before the creation
of a Hebrew-speaking nation-state and even before the foundation of
the Zionist movement, would read a novel in Hebrew? Well, not so few.
Secular Hebrew writings and translations into Hebrew have always existed; in every century, it seems there was *someone, somewhere,* who
was translating *something* into Hebrew: *Mystères de Paris,* say, or medical tracts, medieval Arabic poetry, even Mark Twain. Beginning in the
late eighteenth century with the *Haskalah*—the Jewish Enlightenment
movement that sought to modernize Jews and Jewish culture—there was
an even greater literary boom; that is when the first original Hebrew
novel appears. Yet it is only in the early 1890s, with the rise of anti-
Semitism across Western Europe and a fresh wave of pogroms in Russia,
that a nationalist cultural movement emerges; in the works of members
of this movement—*Khibat Zion,* or Hebrew Renaissance—we can today

identify the transition from minority to majority sensibilities and the emergence of "national consciousness": the incorporation of universal values into a particular literature, the transformation of "Jewish man" into "universal man," and a new Hebrew romanticism, centering on the individual male subject.

Who was operating in this cultural field? Men, almost exclusively. Men writing and men reading. Young Jewish men, traditionally educated, searching beyond their religious calling as they matured. Men between two worlds—tradition and modernity, the Jewish shtetl and the European city. Men who had read the *Gemara* and the *Mishnah* and were now reading Nietzsche. Men who had studied Hebrew in order to become proficient in the holy scriptures and now were dabbling with its vernacular, fictional uses. Men in search of a new, workable identity. Hebrew literature of the late nineteenth and early twentieth centuries is full of their autobiographies and short fiction.[4]

Gender and the Tradition of National Culture

To understand the symbolic and historical role that women occupy vis-à-vis this budding national/literary field is a complex undertaking. In many emergent postcolonial nationalisms, women are imagined as the gatekeepers of identity. In India, Radhakrishnan postulates,

> the nationalist subject straddles two regions or spaces, inter-
> nalizing Western epistemological modes at the outer or purely
> pragmatic level, and at the inner level maintaining a traditional
> identity that will not be influenced by the merely pragmatic na-
> ture of the outward change . . . The inner and inviolable sanc-
> tum of Indian identity had to do with home, spirituality, and the
> figure of Woman as representative of the true self. (1992:84)

Women as identity, men as symbols of reason, progress, and enlightenment; yet in the Jewish example, as the Alcharisi story so perfectly demonstrates, the opposite is true. It is women who for reasons both external (being less hindered by anti-Semitism) and internal (being excluded from traditional Jewish learning) represent "Western blueprints of reason, progress and enlightenment." Indeed, for all its fantastical qualities, the Alcharisi's story, as we have seen, contains quite a bit of historical accurateness. For in the nineteenth century even girls from Orthodox homes enjoyed relative access to European culture. In place of their brothers' Jewish education, they were often educated by tutors or in all girls schools in European languages and culture. Esther Solomon describes this phenomenon as a "curious combination of neglect and manifest permissiveness":

> The Traditional Jewish community actively encouraged wom-
> en's literacy not, of course, in the male ritual/study realm of
> Hebrew, but in Yiddish and European languages to bolster their
> capabilities as the prime breadwinners of the family while the
> men studied in yeshivas full time . . . Many women became,
> sometimes unwittingly and sometimes self-consciously, agents
> of enlightenment in their communities . . . This was an entirely
> unforeseen and ironic consequence of the effort to preserve a
> male monopoly on religious learning.[5]

Whether fleeing to a convent or to the European stages, women's greater access to European culture was a threat not only to the traditional Jewish way of life[6] but also to emergent nationalistic circles, which would ultimately both differentiate themselves from and seek to replace European culture. "To be a nation among all nations" meant, among other things, to own a culture and a literary canon that stood up to that of all (European) nations. Modern European culture, viewed as the backbone of the modern nation-state, would not be rejected outright, but on the contrary be incorporated into the world of Hebrew letters. Thus, if the national project called for a modernization of Jewish culture, then many Jewish women had what nationalist men now wanted: given their access to non-Jewish learning, which was now needed in the service of modern, particular/universal nationalism, women came to occupy a powerful and threatening position vis-à-vis the primarily male effort of creating a secular, national Jewish culture.

Within the world of modern Hebrew letters, women are therefore often imagined as the Europeanized judges of the emergent national literary canon. Consider, for example, the following passage by David Frishman, Eliot's translator and the most influential literary critic of his time, who addresses his "Letters Concerning Literature"—an apologia for the new Hebrew literature—to a worldly, sophisticated, Westernized woman:

> You, my friend, who always complained from your elevated
> and lofty place, shut your small, cute nose with your slender,

white fingers whenever I brought you to the poor and mean dwelling of our literature, so as to avoid the bad smell. You, whose entire life was spent in the gorgeous museums, among the most beautiful treasures of the large cities, who everyday saw the paintings and sculptures and literary works, you bent your pretty red lips in disdain at the sight of the "paintings" and "sculptures" of the people of Israel . . . You, whose entire life was spent reading the best poets of the universe's two halves, you could not understand how anyone could call by the name of literature the bag of tricks of our writers and authors. (1968: letter 4:40–41)

The ghost of a modern, assimilated woman figures in many works of the early national period. And anxiety about the quality and originality of the new Hebrew works is often tied to anxiety about the masculinity of their protagonist or first-person narrator. Late nineteenth-century Hebrew writers, who were later to be designated as the progenitors of the modern Hebrew canon, felt themselves not only at the margins of European letters but also (though increasingly less so) at the margins of both traditional Jewish communities and more assimilated ones.[7] Their self-representation, in works by Yosef Hayyim Brenner and Uri Gnessin, for example, is full of doubt and loathing. The lone Jewish nationalist, often a Hebrew writer and teacher, is portrayed as an undervalued prostitute: a poor young man, living on the meager wages of a disinterested patron and bitterly harboring unrequited love for an assimilated, Europeanized girl. In an exact reversal of Eliot's plot, where nationalism liberates the assimilated Deronda from the realms of exchange and prostitution, it is Hebrew cultural production that initially gets associated with dependence, prostitution, and deformed masculinity.[8]

With her sympathetic, proto-Zionist novel, her intense focus on Hebrew texts and Jewish history, and her absolute preference of Deronda over his Europeanized mother, Eliot did her share in resurrecting the image of the fallen Hebrew nationalist and lifting it above the modern, assimilated Jewish woman. Indeed, Frishman, who in 1893 translated *Deronda* into Hebrew, praises the extent of Eliot's Jewish learning, while contrasting her to women at large:

Most of all, we are amazed that Eliot knows the Jewish literature. She is proficient in phrases from the holy books and their judgments; she knows how to support her claims when

needed. Jewish history is always before her and she knows to
name Yehudah ha-Levi, Ibn Gbirol and Eben Ezra and their
likes. This time it isn't possible to mock women.[9]

Eliot is thus singled out above Jewish women "who demand education" but know little, and also above those worldly ladies with refined
noses who like the Alcharisi ignore all things Jewish. Indeed, Eliot's deep
interest in the literature that, as Frishman imagines, will be snubbed by
an assimilated Jewish woman had infused the flailing world of modern
Hebrew letters with pride. "These days," wrote one reader, "when Israel
is unwanted, days of hatred, envy and competition, like lightning [the
novel] brightens our night."[10]

Yet as the history of *Deronda*'s translation demonstrates, within the
world of Hebrew letters, Eliot herself became entangled in the same dynamics of gender and nation that I have so far been delineating. For
concurrent with the magnitude of her success in proto-Zionist circles,
she too, like her female protagonists, was destined to suffer the loss of
authorial agency and ultimate erasure from the narrative of both novel
and nation.

Deronda and Early Zionism

Many British and Western European Jews, like many other British and
Western Europeans, read *Deronda* as it was published, or very soon after. Many Eastern European Jews also read *Deronda* early on, in Russian
and German translations. Their responses were for the most part positive and sentimental. Across Europe, Jewish publications praised Eliot
for her unflinchingly sympathetic depiction of the Jews at a time of rising anti-Semitism, though numerous Western European Jews refrained
from, and even criticized the novel's support for a narrow, separatist
definition of Jewish identity.[11]

Several chapters of *Deronda* were also published in Hebrew by a
prominent British Jewish figure, Hayyim Guedella, in conjunction with
a plan to purchase parts of Palestine from the Turkish government in
return for the dismissal of large debts in Britain.[12] The excerpts, mostly
from the "Hand and Banner" chapter, appeared first in the *Jewish Chron-
icle* in London and later in various European Jewish publications. As
might be expected, Guedella's plan, and the excerpts from *Deronda*, did
not receive a warm reception in Britain. But even among traditionalists
and protonationalists in Eastern Europe, the direct intervention in the

"Jewish question" by a Western European female author evoked ambivalence and anxiety. Guedella's and Eliot's motives were questioned; one reader suggested that the author, who had "received a large payment" for *Daniel Deronda*, "should donate a tenth of her earnings to strengthen the settlements in Eretz Yisrael."[13] Another anonymous reader, identified as "a faithful son," wrote, likewise sarcastically, that

> even if Guedella will not be able to carry out his plans, still Miss Lewes wrote an essay about it. Did not the clever young woman receive a large sum for this [book]? And where there is no-one to save Israel, the young English woman will rise to its support. This girl will live to be a hundred and the novels she will write will be enough to pay for the redemption of the land.[14]

The aging Eliot is thus referred to as a "clever young woman" and as "Miss Lewes." While it is not clear where the "Miss Lewes" originated, its result, strangely echoing Eliot's own fears, is her identification not as George Henry Lewes's partner, but as his daughter. Or perhaps, Guedella's daughter. Guedella rose to Eliot's defense by pointing to the wide distribution of her novel and its far-reaching effect on readers. Yet it is the association of writing with the market—the use of writing to support the financial transaction of nation buying—that Guedella's opponents attack.

In their attacks, the metaphor of prostitution is central. One example is the contemptuous response of Yehiel Bril, editor of the Hebrew periodical *ha-Levanon,* who accused Guedella of using only selective parts of *Deronda* and editing them to suit his needs. Bril called for a full and accurate publication,

> in order to show the world how [Guedella] ruined this pleasant novel; how he twisted and destroyed it in order to attach it to his plan and capture the hearts of the sons of Israel; in order to show everyone that he did not copy the novel as it was written but selected from it only the phrases needed for his prostitution business.[15]

In a perfect symmetry, the assault on Guedella's plan to purchase Palestine from the Turkish government in cash, that is, to prostitute the Land of Israel, is transformed into an attack on Guedella's prostitution of Eliot's work. Bril's language is particularly strong: the word *shakhat,* meaning "ruined," also means (in a different spelling) "slaughtered." By prostituting Eliot's text for his own commercial purposes, Guedella has slaughtered the "pleasant novel." And this slaughter serves as symbol for the destruction and slaughter of the Holy Land.

And yet, by the mid-1880s, with the rise of anti-Semitism across Europe, the pogroms in Russia, and the consequent emergence of the Hebrew Renaissance movement, Guedella's nationalistic ideas and Eliot's version of Jewish nationalism grow increasingly popular. It was with the proponents of the nationalistic Khibat Zion (Lovers of Zion)—readers and writers of Hebrew prose—that *Deronda* resonated most strongly. They read *Deronda* as a novel of identity, as a passing novel whose modern hero had discovered his ancient roots. Unlike the British readership, Hebrew readers saw no logical problem with *Deronda*'s plot, or with its claim to realism. They read it naturally as a passing novel not simply because, as we will see, the Hebrew translation made the work more palatable for Jewish audiences, but also because Jewish narratives of passing, from the biblical story of Moses to the works of Sholem Aleichem and Heinrich Heine, were part of their cultural heritage. From a minority point of view, the story of *Daniel Deronda* was one of assimilation and its discontents, and that was a story well rehearsed.

For these men, Deronda became a kind of romantic hero, a figure of identification, a role model. One such enthusiast was Eliezer Ben Yehudah, a major force in the revival of Hebrew as a spoken language, who found in the novel support for his linguistic ideas years before they became commonplace. An 1889 biography tells of how he came across portions of *Deronda* in a Russian journal: "He read [them] with great love; their effect on him was strong and endowed him with hope and courage."[16] For such readers, still a small minority even among Eastern European Jewry, Eliot's novel was both a source of encouragement and a speech act, giving reality to hitherto half-formed ideas and incipient national feelings. And yet it is the *character* Deronda, not his female creator, who is repeatedly credited with pointing young male readers toward an imagined national and masculine identity. In another late nineteenth-century text—the autobiography of the son of a prominent Hasidic rabbi—the writer slips directly from book to character when he tells of "discovering German and Russian literature alongside Daniel Deronda, who turned our hearts to Eretz Yisrael."[17]

"Cultural politics," write David Lloyd and Paul Thomas, "which is profoundly pedagogical in its aims, turns upon an exemplary person

[Coleridge's "parson" or *persona exemplaris* and Wordsworth's poet] who comes to represent 'man in general'" (1998:6). To more than a few scattered protonationalists, such was Deronda's role. More than half a century before the creation of the State of Israel, and even before the creation of the political Zionist movement, a new national conscious-ness was informing the works of Hebrew Renaissance writers, who were themselves creating and shaping it. This was, in many ways, a shift from minority to majority consciousness. Writers of the Hebrew Renaissance were laboring to transform "Jewish man" into "universal man." A type of Hebrew romanticism, which placed the individual male subject at its center, was being born. Deronda, who fused a Western gentleman's edu-cation with traditional Jewish identity and texts, came to embody uni-versalism within national culture and thus a model of both citizenship and masculinity, the universal-particular male subject at the core of the liberal nation-state.

Masculinity was very much the issue here. And not only because Jew-ish nationalism was in part a response to the feminization of Jewish men in European culture, as it was, or because anti-Semitism was directed to a much greater extent at Jewish men than Jewish women, as it also was. These were, I want to stress, traditionally educated men writing for other traditionally educated men. They had emerged from and were now chal-lenging a patriarchal, male-centered Jewish tradition with very clearly defined gender roles. As in the classical tradition, Jewish thought has a long history of associating spirituality with men and materiality with women: men engage in the study of holy texts, women care for material needs. Zionism's critique of traditional Jewish life, of its lack of practical aims, its lack of grounding in the material nation and the land, in a ma-teriality hitherto associated with a degraded, female sphere, was in fact a critique of Jewish men. It was precisely the ideology of the nation that was disrupting and devaluing traditional Jewish gender categories and putting men on the defensive.

Deronda's Hebrew Translation

Despite its importance for the budding nationalist culture, *Deronda*'s translation into Hebrew took almost twenty years to appear. In 1885, a portion of John Cross's *George Eliot's Life* was translated into Hebrew by a Berlin-based writer, but the novel's first Hebrew installment, which was published serially, first appeared only in 1893. This delay was, in part, because Eliot's nationalistic vision preceded the Zionist movement

by two full decades: in 1876, the so-called founder of the Zionist movement, Theodor Herzl, was still quite unconcerned with Jewish issues. The
first Zionist Congress would convene only in 1897, and Hebrew would
become a spoken "national" language only several decades later. But this
is only a partial explanation, for readers of Hebrew and translations into
Hebrew, as we have seen, have always existed, and their numbers were
rapidly increasing in the late nineteenth and early twentieth centuries.
A small yet influential cultural sphere of publishing houses and literary
journals catering to a readership of thousands made translation projects
into Hebrew ever more viable and easy to disseminate.

   Deronda's translation was delayed, as the translator explains it, because of its hybrid nature:

> Because the first part of the story does not deal with Hebrew
> things alone but with life in general and the lives of aristo-
> crats and British families, translators were bound to retreat;
> they saw that this portion will be a burden to Hebrew readers
> who will run out of patience waiting for the additional parts.
> (1893:5)

   Frishman's "solution" to the novel's problem, mirroring in reverse
F. R. Leavis's famous proposal to cut the "Jewish half," was to condense
the Gwendolen part to the minimum that was necessary for the coherence of the plot. Indeed, if Leavis had planned (and failed) to "liberate"
Gwendolen Harleth from Daniel Deronda,[18] it was Daniel Deronda who
in actuality would be liberated from Gwendolen Harleth, and to a degree, from Eliot herself. The translator's guiding principle, it seems, was
to cut or trim chapters that deal strictly with Gwendolen or with "the
lives of aristocrats and British families" alone. Chapter 1, for example,
which portrays Deronda's first encounter with Gwendolen, is faithfully
recounted. Yet chapters 3 through 14, mostly detailing Gwendolen's past
and present predicament, are crammed in the Hebrew translation into
one medium-length chapter. Beginning with Book VI—"Revelations"—
the translation tracks the original more or less faithfully until the end,
with slight omissions of extended scenes that depict exchanges between
Gwendolen and Grandcourt. The translator also omitted most of the epi-
graphs, with the exception of those directly related to the Jews or quoted
from Heine, with whom most Hebrew readers were familiar. He omitted
the division into books and instead divided the novel into three untitled
parts. Many of the narrator's comments—for example, the meditation

on the need for a family home at the beginning of chapter 3—were truncated as well.

Frishman, who himself was a realist prose writer, an influential critic, and a trendsetter in the field of modern Hebrew letters, justified his interventions in a preface to the first installment:

> The first part [of *Deronda*] has wonderful imagery, strong logic based on theories of cause and effect and power relations, and may greatly enhance any human being; yet for the Hebrew reader—for him the translator felt obliged to shorten and change the first part as he saw fit, and by doing so did not omit a single thing from the story. (5)

Unlike Leavis, who veils a nationalistic motivation behind an aesthetic justification, Frishman claims that he has sacrificed aesthetic achievement for a nationalistic aim. Yet Frishman's appeal to the limited taste of the Hebrew reader is only partly convincing, since it was exactly the quest to transcend particularity and become a universal "human being" that was the pedagogical aim of the national project. Translation, as Ahad Ha'am had written, was "incorporation without assimilation" of foreign cultures into one's own,[19] and this was a reason to keep the first part and strengthen its bond with the second. The claim that the Hebrew reader of the 1890s disregards all things non-Jewish simply isn't true.

What is true is that *Deronda* is a long and winding and demanding read, particularly in half-biblical Hebrew. What is also true is that the English part involves a subversive and arrogant heroine whose morally ambiguous story line was less than palatable for the Hebrew (male) reader. Indeed, Frishman had cut many references to Gwendolen's cockiness, including much of the tantalizing exchange between her and Grandcourt during their courtship, stressing instead her deference to Deronda and Klesmer, her loyalty to her mother, and her unlucky fortune as a penniless widow. The very relations between Gwendolen and Grandcourt had lost their edge in the translation, with Grandcourt's passion described as "constant and calm" rather than the original "flickering" (chapter 15). It was not, I think, the reader's limitation that was the problem, but Gwendolen's contradictory, insolent, ambitious, and calculated nature; the second, fully translated half of *Deronda*, it should be noted, features not only "Hebrew things," but Gwendolen's, and the Alcharisi's, ultimate humbling. If translation always involves a loss, what is lost in the Hebrew translation is not only the complexity of Deronda's journey toward a Jewish identity but also the complexities of the female characters' formation narratives that are played out over hundreds of pages in Eliot's original work.

Yet the greatest confusion, it seems, was caused by Eliot's own gender-bending ambitions—to have assumed the role of a Jewish scholar and to have called for national renewal for the Jews before they themselves had fully articulated this desire. Frishman, as we have seen, took great liberties with Eliot's original creation, greater, perhaps, than he would have taken with a male writer. He cut not only chunks of the story line but many of the narrator's interventions, presumably Eliot's own authorial voice.[20] Yet he lavishes Eliot with the highest praise and reads her artistic achievement as nothing less than prophetic:

> Who taught this foreign woman about the ways and the lives of the Jews? How did this wonderful author know what other authors, including Hebrew authors, did not know? Where did the wisdom to know and judge the Jewish texts come from? Who planted in her the spirit of truth and prophecy? Who awakened her to prophesize our future and to call on us to return to Zion? The answer to these questions is: there is indeed a spirit in the human being! And when we read the book of Daniel Deronda we know: there is indeed a wonderful spirit in George Eliot, a spirit from above rises in her, and it has opened her large eyes to penetrate us and to know our dreams and our hidden secrets! (1893:7)

Eliot's accomplishment is regarded with pathos and reverence here. Speaking on behalf of a community of readers ("our dreams," "our secrets"), Frishman is "amazed" at her knowledge and, "most of all," at her ability to find expression for its inchoate national aspirations. She is portrayed as nothing less than an author possessed by the creative spirit of an all-knowing God who "rises in her" and gives agency to an otherwise passive organ—the eyes, which in turn penetrate the unspoken desire for national renewal.

In a twist of irony, Eliot is thus imagined as a *maternal* prophet; instead of delivering God's fury, as prophets do, she *sees* the "dreams and . . . hidden secrets" that exist in a people. And though she penetrates, she does it with her eyes. She is the female artist who looks at the collective unconscious of a people and reflects it back to them in the form of her novel. *Deronda* becomes the mirror in which the nation that has "passed" recognizes itself for the first time; Eliot, the enabler of this recognition, is likened in this passage not to the Alcharisi but to Mordecai, and like him, she is imagined as the *good mother,* constituting and organizing the national subject through her loving gaze.

In calling Eliot a prophet, it should nonetheless be noted, Frishman not only aggrandizes, but also curtails Eliot's artistic authority; if she is a prophet for the Jews, her words are not the product of artistic agency but belong, a priori, to a male God. Eliot's fate thus resembles the Alcharisi's nonetheless: both will have commanded the kind of power that exceeds its own artistic, political, and geographical limitations, and both will have been humbled at the end.

Sure enough, Eliot was bound to quickly fade away from the budding national consciousness she had helped erect. Though the character Deronda would become a sort of romantic hero, a figure of identification and a role model for early nationalists, Eliot herself would all but disappear from the national canon. When the novel is mentioned by early Zionist writers, it is always the character Deronda, not his female creator, who is credited with turning young male readers to an imagined national and masculine identity. Text and character are thus revered in several late nineteenth-century biographies; yet the name of George Eliot would hardly ever appear in Hebrew thereafter.[21]

PART II

FIN-DE-SIÈCLE
IMAGI-NATION
OF A LIBERAL
PUBLIC SPHERE
IN PALESTINE

CHAPTER 4

Herzl's *Old New Land*

Herzl and the Fin de Siècle

With the exclusion of the spin on his adoption, in *Deronda* Eliot had anticipated the very—virtually the *only*—type of West European Jewish man who would embrace Zionism at the turn of the nineteenth century: the son of a wealthy Jewish bourgeois family who could have afforded to see him liberally educated through the university system. "Simply by doing so, and without giving the matter much thought, the wealthy Jews, mainly of Germany and Austria-Hungary, created an entirely new class in Jewish life—modern intellectuals given to the liberal professions, to art and science, without either spiritual or ideological link to Judaism" (Arendt 1942/1978:145). Members of this class, a tiny minority, were both more exposed to fin-de-siècle anti-Semitism than their fellow Jews and also more knowledgeable of the structure and institutions of the modern nation-state. A turn to Zionism was therefore a logical development.

Theodor Herzl, the Austrian founder of the political Zionist movement, was representative of this class and in many ways Deronda's real-life embodiment. Son of an assimilated Viennese banker, he was educated in the law, dabbled with the theater, and wrote and edited for the liberal Austrian daily the *Neue Freie Presse* until his turn to Jewish nationalism in the mid-1890s. A real-life Deronda, yet one faced with a new wave and a new form of rabid political anti-Semitism at the fin de siècle. Since it was only the modern intellectuals who had entirely transcended the bounds of Jewish life—by virtue of their occupations, even assimilated Jewish businessman and professionals had remained essentially within the fold—"they alone were exposed without shelter and defense to the new Jew-hatred at the turn of the century" (Arendt 1978:144). Being back amid their own people, however, quickly proved "as difficult as assimilation with self-respect." Western Jewish society, as Arendt had critically observed, was organized around the synagogue and the charity, where one had to be either at the giving or at the receiving end. Too poor to be philanthropists, too rich to ask for alms, and too secularized to turn religious, "there was no place for them in the house of their fathers" either socially or politically. "To remain Jews at all they had to build a new house" (145):

> Zionism, hence, was destined, primarily in Western and Central Europe, to offer a solution to these men who were more assimilated than any other class of Jewry and certainly more imbued with European education and cultural values than their opponents. Precisely because they were assimilated enough to understand the structure of the modern national state they realized the political actuality of anti-Semitism even if they failed to analyze it, and they wanted the same body politic for the Jewish people. (Arendt 1978:146)

From 1895, following his newspaper coverage of the Dreyfus trial until his untimely death nine years later, Herzl worked maniacally, first as the self-appointed and later as the elected leader of the Zionist movement. From a respectable yet minor journalist, he had turned into the head of state, holding meetings across the globe with foreign ministers, the pope, and the Turkish sultan.[1] In 1896 Herzl published *Der Judenstaat* (*The Jewish State*), in which he outlined his political program; *Altneuland,* his only novel, was published in 1902 and in many ways reads as a sequel to *Deronda.* Where *Deronda* concludes, with the rejection of Europe as a breeding ground for character, *Altneuland* begins. If Eliot's novel ends with Deronda's abstract quest to build a "national center" for his people in the East, *Altneuland*'s protagonist actually goes there.

Though the Zionist idea had cultural roots in Eastern Europe for some time, Herzl became, almost single-handedly, its political ambassador in the West. To East European Zionists, even to those who disagreed with his program, he became not a symbol but a physical embodiment of the new Zionist movement: a tall, commanding, self-assured figure, keenly aware of his power.

> The men whom he attracted to the executive body of the Zionist movement, some of them young enough to be nearly life-long "lovers of Zion," learned from him the techniques of statesmanship, without which Zion was doomed to remain only an

object of emotion and belief. Above all they learned from him the *possibility* of statesmanship and the self-assurance to avail themselves of it. He had dared what a Rothschild never dared and a Pinsker, admirable though he was, could never dream of daring. The younger men took courage. (Lowenthal 1956:xxii)

Arguably a manic-depressive and undoubtedly a man of explosive energy and presence, Herzl met with anyone of consequence who agreed to meet him—European politicians, wealthy Jews, delegates of the Ottoman Empire—in the attempt to enlist their support for the national cause;[2] yet by 1901 he had conceded failure and declared that the Jewish nation now existed for him *only* as a literary representation: "I am industriously working on *Altneuland*. My hopes for practical success have by now disintegrated. My life is no novel now. So the novel is my life."[3]

Altneuland: From Representation to Willed Reality

In *Altneuland,* Herzl turned his energy to the education of citizens and legitimization of the hoped-for political body in Palestine through its representation, in minute detail, as a progressive, modern, just, and pluralistic "New Society." Written as the bildungsroman of Friedrich Loewenberg, a young, educated German-Jewish man who finds his way, after many twists and turns, to a newly minted Jewish society in Palestine, *Altneuland* offers the story of induction into citizenship and a detailed portrait of the new state. Over several hundred pages, Herzl discusses everything from the architecture of its houses to its prison system, its co-operative newspaper and its opera house. The novel also offers, in the image of a young male Zionist character by the name of David Litvak, an ideal image of citizenship and masculinity that would outlast Herzl's own rapidly collapsing body. It was through aesthetic identification with the symbolic figures of *Altneuland* that Herzl wanted to lure a faction of West European Jews and to prepare the East European Jewish masses, whom he generally despised and feared, for political representation in the envisioned state.

A foe, but also a product, of the antiliberal backlash that was sweeping over Western Europe at the turn of the century, Herzl repeatedly and publically argued that desire and will alone could shape reality: "Dream is not so different from deed as many believe," he wrote in 1893. "All activity of men begins as dream and later becomes a dream once more."

Many have commented, in responses ranging from admiration (Hertz-berg, Lowenthal) to contempt (Arendt), on the mixture of fiction and reality that motivated and characterized the man who coined the phrase: "If you will it, it is not fiction." The historian Carl Schorske, pointing to Herzl's affinity for fascist aesthetics, shows how Herzl "consciously and explicitly affirms dream, waking fantasy, the unconscious, and art as the sources of the power to overcome and shape a refractory social real-ity" (1981:168). In this appeal to the authority of the irrational, Schorske situates Herzl in the same historical bedrock as those against whom he was fighting—the radical German nationalist and virulent anti-Semite George Von Schonerer and Karl Lueger, author of the new Christian rad-ical left. His association with such unappetizing bed partners, it seems, have kept scholars from serious analysis of Herzl's aesthetics and politics. Or perhaps it is the structural logic of the "nation," which dictates that the nation negate its own fictionality, which precluded any serious dis-cussion of Herzl's novel. His main principles—that desire and will alone stand between dream and reality; that reality can be shaped by artistic creation, by sheer psychic energy; that great ideas need no foundation— have become, following the creation of the state, a retroactive truth.

That the transition from the "fiction" or "representation" of the na-tion to "reality" was neither linear nor unidirectional has eluded many of those who write about Herzl, on both sides of the political spectrum. Take, for example, the recent case of Jacques Kornberg, editor of the English volume of *Altneuland*, who, as late as the 2000 edition, provides the reader with footnotes that "explain" the future (now past) outcome of Herzl's vision. For example, this following passage from *Altneu-land*—"We are merely a society of citizens seeking to enjoy life through work and culture. We content ourselves with making our young people physically fit. We develop their bodies as well as their minds . . . Jewish children used to be pale, weak, timid. Now look at them!" (79–80)—is accompanied by the footnote: "Israeli children are, indeed, a remark-ably sturdy specimen with a great love of the out-of-doors and athletics," as if the book itself produced this new "specimen" directly. Kornberg does not analyze or even acknowledge the problematic of the pale/fit bi-nary, nor does he account for the ideological origins and effects of such a transformation in the "Jewish body." And yet, *it is that simple*: Herzl's text, along with other fin-de-siècle Zionist works, did, *do still* produce physically fit Jewish children, physically fit young Israeli soldiers whose photos, which have periodically yet consistently adorned the front page of the *New York Times* for sixty years now, *still* amaze. They amaze precisely because they *still* are experienced through the lens of the binary fit/pale.

The Modern Utopia: Fascination and Anxiety

When read outside of its Jewish context, *Altneuland* is profoundly a work of its time: a utopian novel that alongside Bram Stoker's *Dracula* offers a historically determined, defensive, naive, strong, and binary answer to all the "-isms" of the previous fin de siècle: not just anti-Semitism, but also cosmopolitanism, imperialism, capitalism, feminism—and the list goes on. It is, in fact, a fin-de-siècle work par excellence: fantastical, Orientalist, and sentimental, one utopia among hundreds produced as the century was coming to a close, with overt and covert politics, aesthetically not unlike (though politically very different from) *The Picture of Dorian Gray*. That West European Zionist thought was, to some extent, reactive to fin-de-siècle elements is not a new idea.[4] It is enough that Max Nordau, one of the harshest critics of fin-de-siècle culture and author of the infamous *Degeneration,* was not only a Zionist but Herzl's most prominent spokesman. Herzl himself, as his biographer, the historian Carl Schorske, has argued, was a certain type of fin-de-siècle Viennese man, vacillating between fantasies of grandeur and radical self-doubt. "When he wrote 'The State of the Jews,'" Arendt writes, "Herzl was deeply convinced that he was under some sort of higher inspiration, yet at the same time he was earnestly afraid of making a fool of himself. This extreme self esteem mixed with self-doubt is not a rare phenomenon; it is usually the sign of the 'crackpot'" (1978:165).

Arendt, who was highly critical of Herzl's legacy, nonetheless shared with him the basic desire for the politicization of the Jews and the basic understanding of political action within the realm of the national. She also shared with Herzl a nostalgia for a "pure" political sphere, whose essence she would later delineate in *The Human Condition* (1958) and elsewhere—a sphere of action, visibility, and citizenship, out of which and despite his efforts, Arendt warned, Herzl's utopian politics were all too likely to lead the Jews *once more*.[5]

If history had taken a different path, we would be reading *Altneuland* today as we read Bram Stoker's *Dracula*,[6] as a historical trace. The two works, in fact, have much in common, for both Herzl and Stoker were similarly fed both by fin-de-siècle anxieties about modernity and by an utter fascination with it. Schorske's concise depiction of *Altneuland*—"an ideological collage made of fragments of modernity, glimpses of futuricity, and resurrected remnants of a half forgotten past"[7]—is thus just as excellent a summary of *Dracula*. Both feature a break with rational thinking and the law and at the same time a fascination, almost an obsession, with technology and scientific knowledge (suspended trains in *Altneuland;* typewriters and scientific theories in *Dracula*). Both embody exactly those "subterranean currents" and "deep desires," and both turn on a crisis and a conservative solution. Fears of cosmopolitanism and unbridled capitalism, restoration of patriarchal masculinity and traditional gender roles, the alliances of a "few good men" vis-à-vis a decadent and cynical European mentality, the specter of a "New Society" (in *Altneuland*) and the "New World" (in *Dracula*), virility as a site of healthy naïveté, the purity of women's bodies as symbol of purity of nation, and anxieties about female autonomy and sexuality—all these are as present in *Altneuland* as they are in *Dracula*. It is no wonder, then, that Nordau's *Degeneration* influenced both Herzl and Stoker.[8]

"Willed Reality": Will to Action at Any Price

But on another level, *Altneuland* is a reality, having shaped at least some of the reality that is our world today. And it is precisely those seemingly utopian, fictional elements in Herzl's writing—above all the constitution of a Jewish state in Palestine—that have turned out to be *our world*. One only needs to replace the word "Fifty" with "One Hundred" in the title of Hannah Arendt's 1946 piece "The Jewish State Fifty Years After: Where Have Herzl's Politics Led?" for it to read as chillingly contemporary:

> Reading Herzl's *The State of the Jews* today is a peculiar experience. One becomes aware that those things in it that Herzl's own contemporaries would have called utopian now actually determine the ideology and policies of the Zionist movement; while those of Herzl's practical proposals for the building of the Jewish homeland which must have appeared quite realistic fifty years ago have had no influence whatsoever. (Arendt 1978:164)

Above all, it is Herzl's "furious will to action at any price": "action that was to be conducted according to certain supposedly immutable and inevitable laws and inspired and supported by invisible forces" (Arendt 1978:166) that has been his lasting, dubious legacy to Israeli "policies." Reading *Altneuland* today is unsettling because, despite the fulfillment of its utopian goals, the very issues that this novel sought to represent and contain spilled out, and continue to spill out a hundred years later.

With Israel's relations with the Palestinians at their bloodiest accord, with the state's growing isolationism; with the legitimacy and borders of the Jewish state still an open question; with a conjoining of Muslim and European anti-Semitism; with the expansion of Jewish settlements in the West Bank; with the "axis of evil" and the "with us or against us" post-9/11 mentality; with globalization and the threat of new international, contaminating Draculian terrorism; with its very existence—*Altneuland* reads as a simultaneously antiquated and contemporary portrait of present day mentality.

The "will to action at any price," and the little regard for historical reality can be traced directly to the fin de siècle. Indeed, Herzl's turn to dreams, faith, and the unconscious for political legitimacy should not only be attributed to his proximity to German fascist politics and aesthetics but to Schopenhauer and Nietzsche, and also to Freud, his exact contemporary. Herzl rejected a positivistic, foundational conception of history in favor of sheer psychic energy as the motivating force in history and narrative:

> Great things need no firm foundation. An apple must be placed on the table to keep it from falling. The earth hovers in the air. Thus I can perhaps found and secure the Jewish State without any firm anchorage. The secret lies in movement. Hence I believe that somewhere a guidable aircraft will be discovered. Gravity overcome through movement.[9]

A disturbing premise for political action, but not uncommon among Herzl's contemporaneous writers: take, for example, once again, that quintessential fin-de-siècle best-seller, Bram Stoker's *Dracula*:

> "My thesis is this: I want you to believe."
> "To believe in what?"
> "To believe in things that you cannot. Let me illustrate. I heard once of an American who so defined faith: 'that which enables us to believe things we know are untrue.'" (1993:160)

It is only by adhering to this command and replacing realist causality with the antifoundational belief that the five anti-Draculian NATO members can overpower the irrational Dracula. For Stoker, the only appropriate response to irrationality is irrationality: "You are a clever man . . . , you reason well, and your wit is bold; but you are too prejudiced. You do not let your eyes see nor your ears hear, and that which is outside

your daily life is not of account to you" (1993:158). So says Professor
Van Helsing, the leader of the anti-Draculian forces. So says Stoker to his
readers, and so says Herzl to his.

Thus, Herzl's politics were radical from the beginning. He rejected all
moderate approaches to fighting anti-Semitism through methods of rational persuasion. He refused to join the Society for Defense Against Anti-
Semitism—founded by eminent German and Austrian intellectuals—and
wrote in a published reply to them: "The time has long passed when it
was possible to accomplish anything by polite and moderate means . . .
[Instead,] a half-dozen duels would very much raise the social position of
the Jews" (Schorske 1981:160). "Crack-pot" that he was, he was "already in
closer touch with the subterranean currents of history and of the deep desires of the folk than were all the sane leaders of affairs with their balanced
outlooks and utterly uncomprehending mentalities" (Arendt 1978:165).

Altneuland was a realistic and detailed depiction of a social sphere in
Palestine that corresponded to nothing at all: a fantasy without a moor-
ing, a purely imagined "imagined community." At the same time, taking
as its departure point a decadent and racist Europe and making its protagonist a decadent and demoralized European man, it is also a specific
response to fin-de-siècle culture and the ills of (Jewish and non-Jewish)
European society. For both Stoker and Dracula, Max Nordau's best-
selling *Degeneration* was a grid for interpreting and critiquing turn-of-
the century Europe. For Herzl, it was a grid particularly for interpreting
and critiquing the condition of assimilated Jews. Nordau, who himself
eventually turned to Zionism, was for a time Herzl's speechwriter. His
imprint on *Altneuland* was great. Accordingly, *Altneuland, Dracula,* and
to a degree also *Daniel Deronda* present a growing anxiety over societal
collapse, decadence, lack of idealism, and dissipating communal bonds.
And all three novels are attempts, however heavy-handed and naive, to
resurrect faith in society, community, and authority (whether within or
outside Europe). It is for this reason that all three novels veer off from the
tradition of the mid-nineteenth-century realist novel, with its pathologi-
cal and destructive human relations, and end with an idealized portrait
of society, which is now presented as the source of human happiness and
even human survival.[10]

Against Individualism: The Primacy of the Male Communal Bond

In this turn from the radical individualism of the novelistic hero to loving communal bonds as central narrative devices, *Deronda, Dracula,*

and *Altneuland* are profoundly political yet hopelessly antidemocratic. If *Dracula* offers its readers a model of international male cooperation ("we need have no secrets amongst us; working together and with absolute trust we can surely be stronger") vis-à-vis a looming evil, *Deronda* and *Altneuland* offer a model of male love and identification as the basis for the new society. Faith, unquestioning trust, a radical end to skepticism about the other, one dare even say love between character and character, reader and author, national leader and the unformed masses are what Eliot, Stoker, and Herzl demand.

Like *Deronda*, *Altneuland* is a bildungsroman that turns on the transformation from loneliness to community, from interiority to visibility: the initiation of the "problematic individual" (Lukács 1971) to the hearth of national bonds. While *Deronda*'s alienated condition unfolds over several hundred pages, the more didactic *Altneuland* begins directly with the downtrodden and lonely condition of its protagonist: twenty-three-year-old Friedrich Loewenberg, who is sitting alone at a Viennese café. Friedrich's two best friends, the narrator tells us, died several months previously: one had committed suicide, the other "went to Brazil to help in the founding of a Jewish labor settlement, and there succumbed to yellow fever" (*Altneuland* 3). Consequently, "for several months past, Friedrich had been sitting alone at their old table." Herzl specifically presents the main condition haunting Friedrich—an assimilated young Jewish intellectual—quite simply, as *loneliness*. Friedrich lives in a world in which he is unseen and unheard by others; his existence is described as entirely private.

How the phenomenon of loneliness and ennui, described most notably in David Riesman's *Lonely Crowd* (1955), as the universal, quintessential modernist mass phenomenon, became a Jewish male problem was discussed in our previous chapter on *Deronda*. As we demonstrate there, at the end of the nineteenth century this universal modernist condition crystallizes—in the writings of Zionists, anti-Semites, and practically everyone else—in the image of the young assimilated or assimilating Jewish man. Herzl ties this state of affairs to the specific economic conditions that affect Friedrich and his intellectual friends, who had become, in Marx's terms, a "surplus" in European society:

> They were really only a kind of superior proletariat, victims of the viewpoint that had dominated middle-class Jewry twenty or thirty years before: the sons must not be what the fathers had been. They were to be freed from the hardships of trade

and commerce. And so the younger generation entered the "liberal" professions en masse. The result was an unfortunate surplus of trained men who could not find work, but were at the same time spoiled for a modest way of life. They could not, like their Christian colleagues, slip into public posts; and became, so to say, a drug on the market. Nevertheless, they had the obligations of their "station in life," an arrogant sense of class that they could not back up with a shilling. Those who had some means gradually used them up, or else continued to live on the paternal purse. Others were on the lookout for eligible patris, facing the delicious prospect of servitude to wealthy father-in-laws. Still others engaged in ruthless and not always honorable competition in pursuits where genteel manners were requisite. They furnished the curious and lamentable spectacle of men who, because they did not want to become merchants, dealt as "professionals" in secret diseases and unlawful secret affairs. Some in their need became journalists trafficking in public opinion [. . .] Friedrich would not resort to any of these shifts. (*Altneuland* 4–5)

In describing and at the same time critiquing the class of assimilated Jewish intellectuals to which he belonged, Herzl mocks the very nonproductivity of Jewish intellectuals. Barred from productive labor both by education and by a hostile society, young educated Jewish men are unable to fit in economically, and thus turn into surplus. It is this value placed on productive labor over the realm of exchange that the nineteenth century, Herzl included, emphasized with great zeal. And young Jewish intellectuals, Herzl claims, become both the primary victims of this mentality and also its primary symbols.

Private Life as Deprivation

Eliot, as we saw in the previous chapters, positions all the Jewish characters in *Deronda,* the protagonist included, in some relation to the degraded realm of exchange. Herzl makes this association much more directly and crudely. Focusing on "secret diseases," "unlawful secret affairs," and "trafficking," he draws once more the link between prostitution, usury, and Jews; young Jewish men are not only the negotiators of market exchanges, but the very objects of these exchanges: "a drug on the market," which not only changes hands but, as surplus, poisons.

Within this realm of exchange is included the journalist, Herzl himself, who is "trafficking in public opinion."

Friedrich thus resorts to spending his days at a local Viennese café. Unwilling to be reintegrated into Jewish society through marriage or business or to find a place in the larger world, he retreats to leading a completely "private life," which Herzl describes as essentially deprived. Whatever Friedrich does—thinking, reading—he does alone. And whatever he does alone leads him nowhere. Herzl's portrayal of his protagonist's deprivation is a literal simulation of Arendt's definition of the "private life" in *The Human Condition.* For Arendt, as for Herzl, "private" here is not derived from its association with private property or with the protected privacy of the home, but with the negative meaning of the original Latin word *privatus:* not in public life.

> To live an entirely private life means above all to be deprived of things essential to a truly human life: to be deprived of the reality that comes from being seen and heard by others, to be deprived of an "objective" relationship with them that comes from being related and separated from them through the intermediary of a common world of things, to be deprived of the possibility of achieving something more permanent than life itself. The privation of privacy lies in the absence of others. (Arendt 1958:58)

The Homoerotic Bond as Stepping-Stone to Communal Life

Alone and hopeless, Friedrich decides to take his own life, not before disposing of the remainder of his inheritance in the hands of a poor but feisty Jewish boy—David Litvak—and his family of Russian immigrants. Thereafter he stumbles upon and answers a newspaper ad: "Wanted, An educated, desperate young man willing to make a last experiment with his life. Apply N.O. Body, this office" (20), and thus begins his initiation into the society of men. For Mr. N.O. Body, as it will turn out, is in actuality a somebody: a German nobleman and former Prussian army officer, Mr. Kingscourt. Having made his fortune in America and been betrayed by a young wife (only the first anxiety over women's treachery displayed in *Altneuland*) the misanthropic Kingscourt takes the young Friedrich aboard his luxury yacht to an island in the South Seas, "where one is really alone": "It must be a vast, unheard of solitude, where one would know nothing more of mankind—of its wretched struggles, its uncleanness, its disloyalties" (30). And so, Friedrich's initiation away from the private realm is depicted as a transformation from loneliness to intimacy, which must occur in seclusion from the world and by turning away from it through a "full, true return to Nature." "You will know nothing more of the good and evil of this world. You will be dead to it" (32), Kingscourt tells Friedrich. It is only in solitude, in a space "outside" the world that Herzl imagines the possibility of trust and intimacy between a Jew and a Gentile, where the two men may relinquish their mutually paranoid positions. Herzl's unchanging and absolute position toward non-Jewish European society, another long-lasting Herzlian legacy to Israeli ideology and politics, is taken up by Arendt in various essays on Zionism. Herzl, she wrote, "saw little else but eternally established national states arrayed compactly against the Jews" (1978:171). In *Altneuland,* however, Herzl entertains a slightly more complex picture, suggesting a possible Jew-Gentile reconciliation in a space outside Europe:

> "I am a Jew. Does that make any difference?"
> Kingscourt laughed. "I say! That's an amusing question. You are a man. I can see that. And you seem to be an educated man. Everything else is frightfully unimportant where we are going." (32)

Like Daniel Deronda, Friedrich exits his cocoon and enters the social life through an intense bonding with an older man. Though the content of these relations is distinct (with Mordecai inducting Deronda into mystical Judaism while Kingscourt prepares Friedrich for citizenship, i.e., "manhood"), their emotional register is surprisingly similar. Both relationships are described as private, even clandestine. "With as intense a consciousness as if they had been two undeclared lovers, [Deronda and Mordecai] felt themselves alone," Eliot writes. Friedrich and Kingscourt are literally alone, spending the next twenty years (but less than twenty pages) on their "island," in a state of libertine sun and fun, at the end of which they will emerge blissfully attached:

> "You are quite mad, Kingscourt," laughed Friedrich [when Kingscourt proposes a return to Europe]. "I think too much of you to infer that you are dragging me to Europe to marry me off."
> Kingscourt was convulsed with laughter. "Carrion! Marry you off! You don't think me that kind of an ass, I hope! What should I do with you then?"

"Well, it might have been a delicate way of getting rid of me. Haven't you had enough of my society?"

"Now the carrion's fishing for compliments . . . You know very well Fritzchen that I can no longer live without you." (55)

If Proust gives us a tour de force of the intersection of homosexuality and the prenational Jew, Herzl taps into the exact currents. The year is, after all, 1902: a full two decades after the Wilde trials, years in which homosexual and Jewish identities are practically interchangeable. Herzl fully exploits this readerly knowledge: "if the crew watch us together, they will get the wrong idea of our relationship," says Kingscourt to Friedrich (38). Yet our reader *already has* the "wrong idea," just as he has the wrong idea of another Jewish character who *will not* become a member of the new state: Leopold Weinberger, a Viennese merchant with a "bald head," "a decided squint," and "very damp palms" (10). Just as they understand: *Jewish children used to be pale, weak, timid. Now look at them!* "Used to be," that is, in 1902. Even though the novelistic present is 1923, 1902 is the year the novel is published and read, in the heyday of anti-Semitic imagery, and at the exact moment that these same stereotypes are in the air. Over and against the shadow of his own tall, dark, energetic figure, Herzl taps into the well of identifications and projections around the image of Jewish men as "pale," "weak," and feminine.

Indeed, Herzl makes use of the categories outlined in *Degeneration* to portray the "degenerative" condition of assimilated Jews—not only the various European types but also Friedrich himself, whose escapade in nature has healed him, yet left him still wanting in character. Nordau associates the state of inaction and reverie with "love of the strange and the bizarre" and with a "sexual perversion" that leads to "moral insanity" (Glover 1996:66); likewise Herzl connotes a state of decay and illicit pleasures in the vicinity of the closeted island, suggesting that in the Athenian fashion, this type of intimacy between man and man, Jew and Gentile, can only be a step to something else: the induction of Friedrich into the national society of Jews and heterosexual, patriarchal marriage.

Performative Stereotypes: Aryan Fantasy and Zionist Reality

In a chapter entitled "The Colonial Drag: Zionism, Gender, and Mimicry" Daniel Boyarin (1997) uses Herzl to demonstrate what has now become a commonplace: the Zionist "postcolonial" tendency for the internaliza-

tion of negative Jewish stereotypes, in particular those of Jewish men. In
Altneuland, Herzl indeed makes use of Jewish stereotypes, and he uses
them—something that Boyarin fails to account for—*performatively.* To
understand the force of Herzl's language, we must locate it within what
J. L. Austin calls "a total speech situation," to distinguish between its
"illocutionary" and "perlocutionary" speech acts. The former, as Judith
Butler writes, are speech acts that, in saying do what they say, and do it
in the moment of saying; the latter are speech acts that produce certain
effects as their consequences; by saying something, a certain effect follows.[11] Herzl, not an unskilled demagogue, uses the weak men/strong
men binary shrewdly, to create audience identification ("it takes one to
know one") by Jews and non-Jews alike, but also, more crucially, to appeal to a collectivity that in 1902 is barely in the making. *"We took our
children out of damp cellars and hovels, and brought them into sunshine."*
In 1902, with a handful of starving Jewish colonies in Palestine, with
the chances for settlement in Palestine getting slimmer by the minute,
with a highly divided Zionist movement, and with a Jewish population
as diverse and divided as the population at large, who's the "we" here,
who are "our children"? *Altneuland* is written as "the nation-space [is] in
the *process* of articulation of elements: where meanings may be partial
because they are *in medias res;* and history may be half made because it
is in the process of being made."[12] *Now look at them,* Herzl pleads with
his reader, who is looking, at this point, at nothing at all.

Nothing, that is, but Herzl's imagination, which has come under
considerable attack in the past decade. In a scathing critique of Zionist masculinity, Boyarin argues that Herzl's (and all of Zionism's) fantasy, clear and simple, was to become an Aryan man. Accordingly, in his
life and writings, Herzl had replaced the weak/timid/effeminate image
with a "mimesis of gentile patterns of honor, that is, masculinity" and
an identification with the "honorable, vengeful, violent . . . ideal Aryan
male." Indeed, as Herzl's biographer Amos Elon writes, in 1881, when
he was twenty-one, Herzl joined (one of few Jewish young men who
were allowed to join) the Aryan-style fraternity *Albia,* where the main
activities were drinking and dueling. He even performed his first duel
successfully: his face was respectfully cut up, sewn up, and restored to its
original handsome condition. Yet Herzl's first dueling scar, his *Mensur,*
was also his last. He quickly got bored with the whole thing, retreated to
his usual isolation, and replaced dueling with reading. He was active in
the fraternity for less than a year, and resigned before his twenty-third
birthday.

Then there is Herzl's plan, teased out of his diaries, to invite famous anti-Semites for public duels. Elon describes this plan at great length:

> According to the plan, Herzl would personally intervene in order to bring things to a crisis, and therefore to a solution. If needed, he would sacrifice his life. Herzl imagined a scenario full of heroic figures and startling dramatic effects. George Von Schonerer, Prince Elois Lichstenstein and Karl Lueger were the leaders of Austrian anti-Semitism. He, Herzl, would challenge them to a duel. The sides would fight to death . . . Herzl planned meticulously and did not overlook even one dramatic effect. A spectacular theatrical gesture, he hoped, would force on people serious thought. Before the duel he would write a letter explaining his motives. If Lueger or Schonerer kill Herzl "the letter will inform the world that I fell victim to his unjust movement. My death will at least instill some wisdom in people's hearts and minds." But if Herzl kills Lueger, then he would turn his trial into an indictment of anti-Semitism. (1977:132; my translation)

Needless to say, the plan did not materialize, but Herzl wrote a play, *The New Ghetto,* that ends with a duel between a Jew and a Gentile. It is this play that Boyarin reads as the prelude to Israel's violence toward the Palestinians. "Herzl's famous passion," he writes,

> shared with many German Jews, to achieve the honor of the dueling scar, the *Schmisse,* the notorious *Mensur,* is, in this sense, a mimicry of inscription of active, phallic, violent, gentile masculinity on the literal body, to replace the inscription of passive Jewish femininity on that same body. His ultimate remedy, however, was to lead the inscription of this maleness on the body of Palestine and Palestinians. (Boyarin 1997: 307)

In this way, across the bar of history, across the bar of anti-Semitism that propelled Herzl in the first place, across a bloody and complicated history of Middle East wars, across the Holocaust, a straight path leads from *The New Ghetto* to the Palestinians, as if a direct and unproblematic line leads from Herzl's plays to his *own* politics; as if an essential category of "Jewish masculinity" was formed centuries back and carried whole throughout history, only to be replaced by an internalization of "gentile masculinity" at the turn of the twentieth century—as if, indeed, the very categories of "Jewish masculinity," "gentile masculinity," and even of "masculinity" altogether are not themselves effects of the fin de siècle and not just modified by it. If, despite their different national origins and distinct plots, *Altneuland* reads so much like *Dracula,* it is because they share a set of European bourgeois anxieties and employ similar techniques of repression around the definition of masculinity vis-à-vis the decline of patriarchy and women's liberation, a newly formed homosexual identity, and imperialism and colonialism, which far exceeds the particularly "Aryan" context.

Upon further reflection we note that even in Herzl's explicitly violent fantasies—his purported plan to call famous anti-Semites to a duel—violence is used strictly as a means of entering the public sphere; Herzl's real motive was to propel a public trial that would place anti-Semitism at the heart of public debate. One could critique, as thinkers from Benjamin to Foucault have done forcefully, the legitimacy of such "functional violence."[13] Nevertheless, it is important to note that Herzl never embraced gratuitous, Aryan-style violence; at the same time that he dreamed up duels, he was terrified of the power of the masses, of violent revolutions and of all forms of violence that surpassed the legitimate monopoly of violence by the liberal democratic state. His sentimental, exaggerated, banal, *theatrical* staging of a Jew "defending his honor," and of Jew-Gentile relations in *The New Ghetto* and elsewhere are not, we claim, *simply* the desire be an Aryan. It is a performance of violence, a performative construction of identity that situates the Jew in *fraternal* relation to the Gentile, a technique of empowerment. And of course, in *The New Ghetto,* it is the Jew who is killed. Honor, to the degree that is it achieved, is rooted for Herzl in a tragic bent toward self-sacrifice, not the infliction of violence on others.

Which is not to say that Herzl's mentality and his legacy to Zionism (not his temporary fascination with Aryan-style violence and honor code) have not ultimately led to the violent conflict with the Palestinians.

The End of Decadence in Non-European Space

In *Altneuland,* Herzl's last and definitive work, there are no duels. Rather, as we have seen, in the first leg of Friedrich's journey, Herzl stages relations between "Jew" and "Gentile" (in the form of a caricature of the "Aryan ideal," a retired Prussian officer, critical of his origins) as a play-

ful anti-Semitic/gay spectacle exchange possible only outside stratified
Europe:

> "Don't you see me as a member of a Jewish society? Me, Adal-
> bert von Koenighoff, a royal Prussian officer and Christian
> German Nobleman! No Fritz, that's too good, too good!"
>   "The Junker speaks!"
>   "Now he's piqued. You're an exception in my eyes. One's
> none." (85)

Herzl indeed deploys both anti-Semitic and homophobic knowledge. Yet it is exactly this playfulness, its reciprocity and humor ("The
Junker speaks!") that represent the potential healing of Jew-Gentile relations, the potential for forgiveness and renewal that, as Arendt writes,
are the hallmarks of citizenship. And it is exactly the passage through
the homosocial closet (that is, the secluded island) that is presented in
Herzl's narrative as abating the paranoid nature of Jew-Gentile relations,
denaturalizing national and racial divisions, and enabling Friedrich to
emerge, now comfortable in his own skin and thus ready to rejoin his
people. In both *Altneuland* and *Deronda* this will be the plot's trajectory:
an intense, instructional, and erotic intimacy between men, conducted
in privacy and secrecy, will engender a new, masculinized, autonomous
national subject. And where the newfound "public" identity has been
established, woman and family emerge. The "Old-New Land" will be a
place where European decadence, whose most poignant representative
is the Jewish intellectual or *luftmensch,* will be transformed into productive, patriarchal man.

Homesick for a bit of European culture, Friedrich and Kingscourt de-
cide on a brief return home after twenty years of exile. On the way they
discover a new sailing route, which leads to the Suez Canal, leading in
turn to a brief stop at Haifa, and finally to their "discovery" of the "New
Society" in Palestine. The year is 1923 and this "New Society," replete
with schools, industry, progressive prisons (based on the Quaker model
in which prisoners work and study), cooperative newspapers unham-
pered by dictatorial editors and wealthy backers, servants (black and
mute), and aerial electric trams, is in full motion. The spoken language
is German. Indeed, our protagonists need not go back to Europe, as they
already *are* in Europe, a recast *better* Europe, made up of socialist and
capitalist elements, and productive, clean, organized, and happily patriarchal: a *nondecadent* Europe created, mostly, by East European Jews.

Over several hundred pages in *Altneuland,* through endless depictions of streets and public buildings, governmental offices, political debates, elections, newspapers, schools, labor cooperatives, prisons, and operas, Herzl creates in minute precision a portrait of a "public realm." He describes the general elections and a "democratic" assembly where—in a manner more or less opposite that of present day Israeli parliamentary discussions—opinions are peacefully and respectfully exchanged. All information about the new place is relayed through the narration of David Litvak, one of the founding citizens of the "New Society," the same boy, it will turn out, to whom Friedrich had bestowed his inheritance. Now the former son of a poor peddler is the wealthy owner of a fleet of boats, productive and prosperous: "a tall, vigorous man of thirty" (60), "a free, healthy, cultured man who gazed steadfastly upon the world and seemed to stand firmly in his shoes" (69), "a prominent citizen" (70), "cheerful, energetic, self confident and yet modest" (83), "one of our best men," "so able and upright," "a strapping fine fellow" (134); a man who speaks "calmly," who's self-deprecating but not self-loathing ("We could not bear to part with money. For one thing we are damn greedy Jews" [65]), who's happy ("he stood on the heights of the Carmel, an expression of profound joy upon his features as he gazed out over land and sea" [70]), rich ("I am a member of the well to do class. I am a ship owner" [70]), and who is sheepishly modest ("David flushed deeply. He cast down his eyes like a little boy, and stammered, *"But*—Mr. President!" [292]).

New Society in a New World: Active and Public Duty and Fraternity

A more sentimental rendering of the masculine figure is hardly imaginable until we turn, once again, to *Dracula,* where "a fine fellow," "a good specimen of malehood," "strong," "resolute," "self-reliant," and "brave" are just some of the adjectives the male characters repeatedly use to talk about each other. Indeed, as Boyarin has written, "the nation was an instrument in the search for manliness" (1997:303), but manliness in *Altneuland* is attainable *only* within the national space. For, like Arendt, Herzl depicts the existence of a public/political space as a precondition for hu(man) *excellence.* "No activity," Arendt writes, "can become excellent if the world does not provide a proper space for its exercise. Neither education nor ingenuity nor talent can replace the constituent elements of the public realm, which makes it the proper place for human excellence" (1978:49).

The "New Society" thus enables the making of an autonomous, proud, male citizen whose ties to the world are mutual, visible, and uncomplicated. Gone are characters' "interiorities" and complex psychological makeup, for the characters in *Altneuland* are simple and flat, lacking in "private" thoughts, conflicts, emotion, and depth. This "flatness" is not only the consequence of Herzl's limited artistic talent; for as we saw in previous chapters, the Zionist novel created by the immensely talented George Eliot displayed a similar effect, with Deronda's "perennially dissatisfied and restless" (Moretti 1987) personality exchanged for descriptions of his visible actions. For both Eliot and Herzl, once a character engages within the national sphere, his actions turn public and visible.

Friedrich's journey into the nation produces similar narrative effects: "What a green, hollow-chested Jewboy you were when I took you away," says Kingscourt to the now naturalized Friedrich, explicitly linking interiority with Jewishness, "now you are like an oak." For Herzl, "hollow-chested," signals not only deformed masculinity but also, relatedly, an empty, enlarged interiority, which is now replaced by the image of an oak: strong, hard, visible, unmoving, and irremovable. This is the image of all of Herzl's nationalized male characters: hard and unchanging, demonstrating an *intentional* lack of interiority, the shedding of the Jewish intellectual's interiority and subjectivity in favor of an objective, constant, visible, surface existence. No reports of thinking, reading, dreaming, which are done in "private," that is, outside the novel, have any place in the realm of citizenship and nationality. "Action," as Arendt writes, constitutes "the only activity that goes on directly between men without the intermediary of things or matter," and that "corresponds to the human condition of plurality, to the fact that men, not Man, live on the earth and inhabit the world" (1978:7). Altogether, it was Herzl's *will* to action (not his actions themselves) that evoked even Arendt's admiration. "The mere will to action," she wrote, "was something so startlingly new, so utterly revolutionary in Jewish life, that it spread with the speed of wildfire. Herzl's lasting greatness lay in his very desire to *do something* about the Jewish question" (1978:166).

Citizenship for Herzl as for Arendt thus exists only in the realm of appearances, in the presence of others, in broad daylight, yet it is also the condition of citizenship that enables visibility and communal bonds: "Our feeling for reality depends utterly upon appearance, and upon the existence of a public realm into which things can appear out of the darkness of sheltered existence;" writes Arendt (1978:51); and in a similar vein, Herzl declares: "We took our children out of damp cellars and hovels, and brought them into the sunshine." In the "New Society," Jewish children will be brought into the light, will be en*light*ened, will exist in the realm of appearances, the realm of citizenship and political community. How is this to be done? Herzl's vision offers a "simple solution": a band of "simple" male characters who are resolute, idealistic, strong, linked to each other through an abstract sense of the "common good," an unquestioned sense of duty, and the bonds of mutual love and admiration. In *Altneuland,* it is "a free, healthy, cultured" Litvak, the one who had never been contaminated by European decadent cynicism, who is the model citizen and the magnet of admiration. In *Dracula,* not surprisingly, it is Quincey the American, whose New World simplicity, blind faith ("I heard once of an American who so defined faith . . ."), instinctive submission to authority, and natural willingness draw the admiration of the small NATO pact ("What a fine fellow is Quincey! I believe in my heart of hearts that he suffered as much about Lucy's death as any of us; but he bore it like a moral Viking. If America can go on breeding men like that, she will be a power in the world indeed" [144]).

Indeed, it is none other than the American who kills Count Dracula, rids the world of "evil," and sacrifices his own life in return. For Herzl and Stoker, both fin-de-siècle minority European writers, this vision of ideal citizenship could only be possible in a new world far from Europe. Within these new national spheres, nationhood will offer men room to become not violent and revengeful but *free* and *excellent* in the classical sense, to lead the *vitae activa,* be active, independent, and seen by fellow men. For what Herzl longed for, and what drew him to *Albia* in the first place, was not the opportunity for dueling (which he dared only once) but for fraternity, for a society of men. Herzl's idea of "public life" more explicitly substitutes male relations based on adversarial dueling with those based on working, voting, and (lovingly) debating each other. Though Herzl takes pains to depict a "confrontational" or "lively" public sphere, his portrait of the "New Society" indeed resembles a large fraternity. And that, of course, is the problem of his vision.

Unforgivable, Unforgettable: Blinkered Fantasies of Bloodless Revolution

In *Foundational Fictions,* Doris Sommers demonstrates how via "the erotics of politics" in Latin American fiction, national ideals get grounded in "natural love," which in turn provides a figure for the nonviolent consolidation of heterogeneous peoples into nations. "Romantic passion,"

Sommers writes, "[gives] a rhetoric for the hegemonic projects in Gramsci's sense of conquering the antagonistic through mutual interest, or love, rather than through coercion" (1991:6). Indeed, within the premise of the "New Society," both Friedrich and Kingscourt will find love, their homosocial erotic bonds channeled into their "proper" objects (Friedrich will marry; a grandfatherly Kingscourt will "fall in love" with Litvak's toddler boy). Yet as the novel makes clear, the erotic energy, the affective glue that links its members together is strictly operative between men. As such, the gay undertones of the island episode serve not only as prelude but also as diversion and displacement from the more conventionally homosocial sphere of the "New Society," where male-male admiration and love floods the plot, particularly as it organizes around Litvak's figure.

Indeed, in *Altneuland*, as well as in *Dracula* and in *Deronda*'s Zionist part, all transformative actions—Deronda's public embrace of Judaism, Dracula's defeat, Friedrich's induction into the "New Society"—are made possible through loving, idealized human relations. And if *Dracula* offers its readers a model of international male cooperation ("we need have no secrets amongst us; working together and with absolute trust we can surely be stronger"), *Deronda* and *Altneuland* offer a model of male love and identification as basis for a new Jewish nation. There are no descriptions of violence or conflict in *Altneuland*. Fictional characters are bloodless and lifeless. The novel does not even celebrate, as other works by Zionist writers have, a vitalist impulse.[14] It is utterly and completely sterile. Yet as in Arendt's ideal of a bloodless revolution, Herzl's defensiveness (if not blindness) against the body and its violent potential is the greatest danger of and to his vision. Neither the violence of anti-Semitism and pogroms nor the potential and inevitable violence of colonialism and national consolidation is treated in the novel in any real way. In a manner characteristic of Herzl's politics of ignorance, the novel skips from 1902 to 1923, leaving the state's foundation an open question. By then, anti-Semitism had been made a thing of the past, long gone and now forgiven, a phenomenon that can be joked about, and treated in one not very long paragraph. Litvak, the citizen-ideal, addresses anti-Semitism mainly to explain the reasons for the erection of the "New Society" to the skeptical Kingscourt:

> "At the end of the nineteenth century and at the beginning of
> the twentieth, life was made intolerable for us Jews."
> "Aha! Spewed you out, did they?"

"The persecutions were social and economic. Jewish merchants were boycotted, Jewish workingmen starved out, Jewish professional men proscribed—not to mention the subtle
moral suffering to which a sensitive Jew was exposed at the
turn of the century. Jew-hatred employed its newest as well as
its oldest devices. The blood myth was revived; and at the same
time, the Jews were accused of poisoning the press, as in the
Middle Ages they had been accused of poisoning the wells. As
workingmen, the Jews were hated by their Christian fellows for
undercutting the wage standards. As business men, they were
dubbed profiteers. Whether Jews were rich or poor or middle
class, they were hated just the same. They were criticized for
enriching themselves, and they were criticized for spending
money. They were neither to produce nor to consume. They
were forced out of government posts. The laws were prejudiced against them. They were humiliated everywhere in civil
life. It became clear that, in the circumstances, they must either become the deadly enemies of a society that was so unjust
to them, or seek out a refuge for themselves. The latter course
was taken, and here we are. We have saved ourselves." (66)

This is the only reference to the "persecutions" from which the
Jews saved themselves. There is no mention of physical violence of the
1881–82 pogroms that were the cause of most Jewish immigration to
the United States and Palestine, and were at the center of discussion in
Jewish presses. Not only is anti-Jewish violence never mentioned as a
rationale for the "New Society," but the "New Society" is presented as a
way for the Jews to protect Europe against their *own* transformation into
its "deadly enemies." In a neat Oedipal narrative, the very event that had
propelled individuation and detachment from Europe and the pain of
creating a separatist Jewish nation is repressed—even by so-called political Zionists—by the very logic of nationhood.

Arendt had commented already, in a 1944 essay titled "Zionism Reconsidered," how misguided and naive was Herzl's belief that a Jewish
nation-state would "eliminate" anti-Semitism; today, of course, we know
that the opposite is true. Herzl, Arendt wrote, appraised anti-Semitism
as "an eternal phenomenon attending invariably to the course of Jewish history through all the Diaspora centuries . . . [an attitude that was]
held to be sound precisely because it was irrational, and therefore explained something unexplainable and avoided explaining what could be

explained" (1978:147). At the fin de siècle, Stoker had both embodied such an irrational, eternal threat and given it a name—Count Dracula:

> That vampire which is amongst us is of himself so strong in person as twenty men; he is of cunning more than mortal, for his cunning be the growth of age; he is brute, and more than brute; he is devil in callous; he can command all the meaner things; he can at times vanish and come unknown. How then are we to begin our strife to destroy him? (147)

Like Stoker, Herzl rejected outright a rational, measured solution to his own Dracula—the anti-Semites of his day—the Schonerers and the Luegers who are "cunning" and "can command all the meaner things." Like Stoker, he treated anti-Semitism not as a structural, historically determined phenomenon but as a "thing," a "force of nature" (Elon 1977:100) that must either kill you or be killed by you. Yet it is precisely this binary and totalizing view that allowed Herzl to imagine a world free of Draculian anti-Semitism, if Jews were to be removed from Europe.

And it is precisely because Herzl is already "thinking" as a national subject of a nation outside Europe that he can make light of hatred suffered at the hands of another. "Forgetting," Ernest Renan writes in 1881, "is a crucial factor in the creation of a nation . . . The essence of a nation is that all individuals have many things in common, and also that they have forgotten many things."[15] Indeed, within the limits of "national discourse," pain and violence incurred by members of the nation are always and at once expressed and disavowed, sublimated through a depersonalized symbolic register (which is why, in the wake of a barrage of suicide bombing in the second intifada, traces of blood and human bodies would immediately be removed and the café or restaurant would reopen as usual within days). The national dream is of absolute insularity—the dream of banishing violence elsewhere, to a place outside its borders—and Herzl enacts this dream in his utopian work.

To no small extent, this "forgetting" of violence and humiliation and their substitution with the discourse (and new violence) of the nation has become a consequence of the nation-state. A recent essay on Herzl, begins, for example, with the following sentence:

> In the spring of 1895, the Hungarian-born, Austrian-educated, and German-identified playwright and journalist Theodor Herzl experienced a psychotic break/political epiphany, in the

wake of which he announced himself as a Jewish national leader.[16]

Just like that! Because of a "psychotic break"! The circumstances that drove Herzl to Zionism, that lurk perhaps under the psychic surface of the Jewish-American critic, are omitted, and Herzl's "Jewishness" at the end of the nineteenth century becomes a matter of private caprice. In propelling the myth of self-reliance ("We have saved ourselves")—as if one isn't bound by circumstances beyond one's control—even Herzl's critics have inherited the limitations of his vision and thought.

Positive Freedom and the Power to Begin

The case we have been trying to make up to now is that violence, revenge, and, in general, bodily expressions of masculinity were not at all the model of citizenship that Herzl offered to his readers. His road to citizenship is depicted as a psychological/pragmatic Oedipal journey of individuation from Europe, at the end of which the (Jewish) man emerges as a free, happy, and autonomous citizen, unburdened by his past and joyous in his present, without any coercion or violence accompanying this process of differentiation.

Masculine power is thus defined by Herzl as "the power to begin," not the power to overcome. It focuses on "positive freedom" (the building of a new society) rather than "negative freedom" (freedom from European constraints). It is David Litvak's mildness and notion of *forgiveness* that make him a model of both citizenship and masculinity in the eyes of Kingscourt and Friedrich. The latter, having gone through what Herzl designates as "private" existence in the Old World and hedonism and intimacy in an ahistorical state of nature, will now enter into the public sphere of a new, perfected society, where he can become active, mild, and "useful":

> "Kingscourt," [Friedrich] sighed out loud, "I am asking myself whether we did not sheer a false course when we made for our blessed isle yonder? How did we spend twenty beautiful years? Hunting and fishing, eating, drinking and sleeping, playing chess . . ."
>
> "And with an old donkey, what?" growled Kingscourt, whose feelings were hurt. "Drop the 'old donkey' stuff," laughed Friedrich. "I could not and would not live without you any more.

But, for all that, it's a pity to have not been more useful. (*Alt-neuland* 84)

And so, sensuality is replaced by usefulness and solitude by society; and the romantic space "outside" civilization is abandoned for the "nation." More than anything, in the utopian world of *Altneuland,* citizenship is modeled on the ancient Greek *polis:* on a vision of a narrowly defined "public sphere" that gives rise to the *vitae activa.* Indeed, as Eve Sedgwick (1990) has shown, at the turn of the nineteenth century ancient Greece fed into the imaginings of multiple, sometimes contradictory fantasies, including a host of male identities ranging from a separatist homosexual identity to the patriarchal, chivalrous men of *Dracula.* For Herzl, the adoption of the Greek model of citizenship cuts across many different levels. It serves to legitimize and glamorize the idea of a Jewish nation and a model of masculinity and male kinship that would both come under scrutiny if not ridicule in Herzl's high bourgeois Viennese circle.

The Nation's "Public Sphere"

As Jürgen Habermas (1991:4) has shown, the model of the Hellenic public sphere as handed down to us since the Renaissance has maintained a peculiarly normative power, not so much as a social formation but as an ideological template. Herzl's utopia, however, is quite literally based on the Greek *polis:* it is narrowly imagined as the society of free and excellent men who vote in direct elections, a "New Society" where citizens who vary in ethnic and religious affiliation—but not in class and gender—can reside in perfect harmony.

In Greek thought, Arendt writes, "the human capacity for the political organization is not only different from but stands in direct opposition to that natural association whose center is the home and the family." The rise of the city-state meant that man received "besides his private life a sort of second life, his *bios politikos.* Now every citizen belonged to two orders of existence; and there is a sharp distinction in his life between what is his own and what is communal" (1958:24). It is exactly this "sharp distinction" that, in both Herzl's *and* Arendt's analysis, is missing from Jewish political organization in the Diaspora. "The Jewish classes," she writes, "like the Jewish masses, clung together socially, linked by the never-ending chain of family and business connections . . . [forming] a curious sort of body politic" (1978:145). Based as it was on the interconnectedness of marriages, businesses, and philanthropy, this "curious" body politic existed entirely outside the purview of European political and national structures and further perpetuated Jewish isolation.

Herzl too targets the social organization of the Jewish classes (business partnerships consolidated through loveless marriages) as a prelude and antithesis to the structure of the body politic of the "New Society." Unable to participate in European public life, Herzl depicts upper-class Viennese Jews as living in an isolated, apolitical sphere, defined by property yet living a closeted life, masking their Jewish identity from even their servants. He begins the novel with a dinner party, in which Friedrich's beloved ("a sweet blond creature") is auctioned to a wealthier suitor, a member of the clothing firm Gruen and Gruen, who will consolidate her father's businesses and whose sweaty palms and bald head hold the promise of a dull, sexless marriage.[17] Within this isolated Jewish world where all spheres of life are mixed together, not only is public life absent but the social and private realms are destroyed as well, depriving people "not only of their place in the world but of their private home, where they once felt sheltered against the world and where, at any rate, even those excluded from the world could find a substitute in the warmth of the hearth and the limited reality of family life" (Arendt 1958:59).

Public and Private Domains: Space and Gender in National Life

There are, of course, in Arendt and even more in Herzl, echoes of Otto Weininger's dictum that Jews, like women, "tend to adhere together" and therefore cannot know the "true conception of the state." Against this vision of a feminized realm of association, Herzl constructs a "public sphere" of male activity, excellence, and visibility with a "private realm" whose center is the home, which not only differs from "but stands in direct opposition to political organization" (Arendt 1958:24). Unlike Friedrich's shadowy loneliness and "private" existence in the Old World, this privacy is *highly visible,* replete with descriptions of home, fertile women, and glowing children. Indeed, Herzl imagines the "New Society" along a rigid Greek model, with idealized boundaries between a public space, where male dispute and difference supposedly occurs, and a private, associationist, and patriarchal sphere, based in and on a family governed by a man. Herzl presents this model throughout *Altneuland:* from his descriptions of the strict separation of the home, business, and political life of David Litvak to his rendering of "New Society" architecture:

> From the vantage point of their enforced halt, [Friedrich and
> Kingscourt] looked up several streets, in which the architec-
> ture was fascinatingly varied. The dwelling houses for the most
> part were small and charming, intended for only one family
> like those in Belgian cities. The public and commercial build-
> ings, which could be easily recognized, seemed all the more
> imposing by contrast. (67)

"From the vantage point of Friedrich's and Kingscourt's enforced halt,"
that is, from the vantage point of Herzl's Western European readers, in a
highly condensed and deliberate staging, Herzl contrasts an "imposing,"
"easily recognized" public domain with a "small and charming" private
one. From this vantage point, one can see a most narrowly defined patriarchy, an ultra-conservative gender arrangement that isn't even masking
itself as anything else.

That the public/private distinction is ideologically and practically
moored in gender division and that its practical implementation in modern industrialized societies has resulted in greater oppression of women
than, for example, in the "mixed spheres" of agricultural life is a critique
waged by feminist social theorists for a number of decades now. Arendt
in particular has been targeted by these theorists precisely because in
her nostalgia for a "pure" public and private sphere she completely ignores the implications for women (Honig 1995). Herzl not only ignores
but consciously upholds this division as a corrective to the ills of social
organization among European Jews. In the utopian, *nondecadent* "New
Society," there will be little trespassing of the bounds of politics, home,
and gendered identities. Or, as Litvak explained to Kingscourt:

> "In our new society, women have equal rights with the men."
> "All the devils!"
> "The have active and passive suffrage as a matter of course.
> They worked faithfully beside us during the reconstruction
> period. Their enthusiasm lent wings to the men's courage. It
> would have been the blackest ingratitude if we had relegated
> them to the servants' hall or to a harem."
> "You told us on our way here," interrupted Friedrich, "that
> Reschid Bey [the Arab citizen] is also a member of your soci-
> ety. Your mention of harems reminds me of a question."
> "Which I can guess. No one is obliged to join the New So-
> ciety. And those who do not join are not compelled to exercise

their rights. They do as they please. In your own day you must
have known men in Europe who were not interested in elections, who never took the trouble to vote, and who could not
by any means have been persuaded to take office. So it is with
our women and their rights. Don't imagine that our women
are not devoted to their homes. My wife, for instance, never
goes to meetings."

Sarah smiled. "But that's only because of Fritzchen" [their
newborn son] . . .

"Yes," continued David, "she nursed our little boy, and so
forgot a bit about her inalienable rights. She used to belong to
the radical opposition . . . Now she opposes me only at home,
as loyally as you can imagine, however." (99–100)

If it takes Eliot nine hundred pages of rigorous analysis to extinguish
women's ambition (in the respective storylines of Gwendolen and the
Alcharisi) and return it, and only partially (in the case of Mirah), to
its "proper" domestic place, Herzl does it in a paragraph. Women, we
are told, participated in the "reconstruction period," lending courage
to the men through their enthusiasm for the cause. This enthusiasm,
as we had shown in our previous chapter, existed primarily in Herzl's
mind and fiction, the historical reality at the fin de siècle demonstrating a contrary trend. Yet if Herzl's core belief was that "if you will it, it
is no fiction," plenty of fin-de-siècle fiction was at his disposal for constructing his sentimental vision of idealized male-female cooperation
and submission. Most poignant, again, is the gendered plot of *Dracula*,
which moves along Herzl's exact lines: Mina Harker, the ideal wife prototype, lends excellent support to the men in their battle with Dracula;
the novel, nonetheless, ends with the birth of a son.

The year 1902 was of course a transformative period for women, with
changes in property laws and the radicalization of women's roles across
Western Europe. Herzl himself had married into considerable property
and was entangled soon thereafter in a combative relationship with a
wife whose wishes, particularly in regard to his Zionist agenda, were
quite contrary to his own. The nation therefore functioned in Herzl's
imagination as a stabilizer of marriage and women, giving rise to men's
"courage" and harmonizing men and women in their fictional struggle for a common goal. After the goal had been achieved—during the
twenty years that are markedly absent from *Altneuland*—a new, happier
patriarchal model could be reinstated, propelling women to soon "for-

get" about their "inalienable rights," settle in those "small and charming dwelling homes," and merrily delve into the traditional bourgeois role of "angel in the house."

To the extent that Sarah's story is told only from the husband's perspective (yet another reincarnation of Adam Bede), we can dismiss this narrative as an off-putting patriarchal fantasy (which it was), a consequence of Herzl's deeply conservative gender politics (which it also was), and of his own experiences in an unhappy and stormy marriage to a wife whose will he would never control. Yet as in *Deronda*, the "women question" and the "Jewish question" are bound by more intricate connections than merely those derived from the individual psychology of the respective authors.

Despite the detailed descriptions of this public realm: depictions of residential neighborhoods in which a variety of architectural styles— Moorish, Mediterranean, et cetera—are expressed, versus the uniform structures of public office buildings; a welfare society apparatus, including a penal colony for reforming criminals; newspapers in which members have shares, in the real world of the Zionist movement,[18] both the legitimacy *and* the character of this new public sphere were a source of resistance and contention, and provided little harmony. Images of women in *Altneuland* functioned to stabilize and quell these contradictions and anxieties. First, by evoking maternity and generativity, Herzl naturalizes the radical historical and political changes that the national project will entail and instead subordinates it to what is seen as the stable, self-producing ahistorical structure of the gendered, procreative family. It is no coincidence, in this respect, that the first figure our guests will encounter in the Old New Land will be Litvak's wife Sarah, "a blooming young matron," nursing mother to a beautiful, healthy boy. Thus, Herzl counters the image of a loveless, sexless, businesslike marriage in the Old World with the healthy, blushing, and procreative energy of Old New Land marriages. And just as the nation had "cured" and naturalized the corrupt institution of marriage,[19] in its new idyllic version, it serves to naturalize the nation-state.

The Private Domain: Outside the Bounds of Political Equality

Yet concurrent with this idyllic image of the family as a metaphor for the naturalness of the new nation, women and the family also function as that which is outside the bounds of the nation's political domain. As in the classical model, the potential conflict inherent in heterogeneity is thwarted through relegating all differences of identity, ethnicity, religion, and degree of religiosity to a "private" sphere associated with women and the household, whose details remain outside the purview and scope of Herzl's vision. Within the nation's "public sphere" of political action, one need only be a "man": "We ask not to what race or religion a man belongs. If he is a man, that is enough for us" (*Altneuland* 66). Now that the centuries-old distinction between Man and Jew, discussed at length in our introduction, had been dissolved by the nation-state, "Man," that is, "citizen" in the "New Society," may include Jew and non-Jew, Orthodox and secular, immigrant and native Palestinian:

> They were now in a residential section of the city, upon Mount Carmel, where there were many elegant mansions surrounded by fragrant gardens. Several houses of Moorish design had close wooden lattices over some of their windows. David anticipated their question, saying that they were the homes of prominent Moslems. "There's my friend Reschid Bey," he added . . .
>
> A handsome man of thirty five was standing beside a wrought iron gate as they drove by. He wore dark European clothing and a red fez. His salute to them was the oriental gesture which signifies lifting and kissing the dust. David called to him in Arabic, and Reschid replied in German—with a slight northern accent. "Wish you much joy in your guests!" (68)

Ignore for a moment the hard-to-swallow Orientalism of this passage, which was not atypical to its period, and you'll see how it demonstrates all we have been claiming. For the visibility of Reschid's Muslim identity goes only as far as the surface of his home and its "Moorish architecture" while identity itself is presented as "private," sealed off from the world by "wooden lattices." Like Litvak, Reschid's freedom is signified by his ability to move freely between the public sphere—the realm of the New Society—and the domestic sphere, where his wife, his children, and his "private" identity reside. These are presented as immobile as the house itself, the antithesis to the *vitae activa*. Naturally, "the Muslim wife" represents the most radical image of the "private," as her Jewish female compatriots explain:

> As they drove past Reschid's house they heard singing in a magnificent female voice.

> "She's a friend of ours," said Miriam [David's sister], "Reschid's wife. She is well bred and well educated. We often see her, but only in her own house. Reschid adheres strictly to the Moslem customs, and that makes it difficult for her to come to us."
>
> "But," added Sarah [David's wife], "you must not think that that makes Fatma unhappy. Theirs is a very happy marriage. They have charming children. But the wife never leaves her home. Surely, peaceful seclusion is also a form of happiness. I can understand that very well, though I am a full-fledged member of the new society. If my husband wished it, I should live just as Fatma does and think no more about it." (97)

Thus, the modern male-dominated nuclear family meets the tribal male-dominated nuclear family in a consolidation of men's political and economic power. For if members of the "New Society" vary in every other way, they offer little variance in class and degrees of wealth. How is the willing cooperation of women to be attained? In novels, as feminist critics have shown, that is what love is for.[20] *She used to belong to the radical opposition. Now she opposes me only at home, as loyally as you can imagine:* if *Dracula* embodies the fear of female sexuality as the road to independence, Herzl constructs female sexuality and sexual contentment as the means to women's voluntary subjugation to a strictly male-dominated old-new society.

A Sublimated Wish: "Willing Submission"

Yet these, I think, are the derivative, not primary, motivations behind Herzl's construction of the home as so clearly and radically isolated from the political sphere of the "New Society." In traditional Greek political thought, as Arendt writes, while the public realm knows only equals, the household is based on strict inequality. To command, rather than to persuade, is the prepolitical way of dealing with people; the head of the household debates with his fellow citizens, but rules over women and slaves with uncontested power. By imagining a private realm that is utterly patriarchal, where relations are not determined by "talking" and equality but by absolute submission, Herzl, who was terrified to the core by the potential destructiveness of democracy, leaves open the option of such submission. Not exactly by force, but by willed obedience: "It would have been ingratitude if we had relegated them into the servants' hall or to a harem." Instead, *they relegated themselves:* "if my husband wished it, I should live just as Fatma does and think no more about it."

These passages, we claim, demonstrate not only Herzl's fantasies about women, which were real enough, but about the willing compliance of native Palestinians to join the New Society, in its sublimated form as a fantasy about women. For as the embodiment of the "private," nondemocratic sphere, women stand for all those who could potentially remain outside the nation's public sphere: most notably, the native inhabitants. Indeed, Litvak's slippage from women's participation to Arab participation ("It would have been ingratitude if we had relegated [women] into the servants' hall or to a harem" / "You told me on our way here that Reschid Bey is also a member of your society. Your mention of harems reminds me of a question . . .") makes it clear that although Bey is an equal member of the New Society, his position in the vicinity of women's "private sphere" points to the tentativeness of and the anxiety around his political rights.

Altneuland, precisely like *Dracula,* at the end both depicts and attempts to defensively contain anxieties about democratization and theories of rights imported from the French and American revolutions. Herzl had come from a country that had no political tradition of a government by and for the people. His politics, as his fascinating diaries so clearly show, were conducted from high above, via negotiations with imperial powers and wealthy capitalists. Those who were to man the Old New Land—thousands of starving Russian Jews ready to immigrate—were as abstract to him almost as Palestine's native population. In his diaries he mentions the "people's" revolutionary fervor solely to scare Western officials—some of whom were landowners in Eastern Europe—to expedite migration to Palestine. Toward his reception by the Jewish colonists on his 1898 visit to Palestine he remained largely cold, yet what had moved him to tears was the sight of the young daring horsemen on their little Arab horses. "I was reminded," Herzl writes, "of the Far West cowboys of the American plains whom I once saw in Paris."[21]

Of Herzl's vision on colonization of the land, *Altneuland* provides little insight. What is known is that by the time of its publication, he had forsaken the idea of simply buying stretches of land from the Ottoman government. Thus, it is only in Herzl's narrative slippage from women's rights to the "reconstruction period," to "men's courage" to the question of inclusion/exclusion of Muslims, that Herzl gives the reader a narrow glimpse of the imagined founding moment of the New Society. It is, in fact, the only reference in the entire book to the "reconstruction" period, those twenty years that are missing from the novel, in which the "New Society" came to be. It is also the only mention of the word "courage." "On the whole," Litvak relates, "it was a bloodless operation" (65). Honor, revenge, dueling, and violence—all those features that Boyarin and others have presented as the core of Zionist masculinity—are utterly absent from *Altneuland;* it was exactly these elements that remained outside its public sphere and for which citizenship in the New Society substituted.

Personal Politics, National Dream: The Dream of Nonviolent Discord

For Arendt, violence is the "pre-political act of liberating oneself from necessity and entering the realm of freedom." It is justified in the private sphere as the means of mastering necessity: that is, becoming free, but is never a part of the political process (1958:31). Over and against von Clausewitz's famous dictum that designated war as "the continuation of politics by other means," Arendt's post-Holocaust, post-Hiroshima writings sought to radically separate power from violence, arguing that they stand to one another in a nondialectical, asymmetrical relationship.[22] Thus she adopted the Aristotelian model by which violence is always instrumental, a view that, as our reading of *Altneuland* demonstrates, Herzl shared. The New Society has no army ("We are merely a society of citizens seeking to enjoy life through work and culture. We content ourselves with making our young people physically fit. We develop their bodies as well as their minds"[23]), and supposedly, as we have seen, is pluralistic and democratic. Political debate and a process of elections are depicted in *Altneuland* but, naturally, no detrimental conflict ensues. Enemies or opponents of the New Society have simply been left outside the borders of its city-state.

It is of course a fictional dream about the easy containment of debate and hostility. If Herzl had not trusted the democratic process for his own people, an attempt to approach the native Palestinians was certainly outside his purview. Indeed, even the figure of Reschid Bey—the prototypical Muslim member of the New Society—was in fact modeled on a Turkish official with whom Herzl had dealt politically and befriended: Westernized, friendly, and cooperative ("He studied in Berlin . . . His father was among the first to understand the beneficent character of the Jewish immigration . . ." [68]). Thus Herzl would never make serious attempts to broach the inhabitants of Palestine, but rather appealed to the Imperial forces in the area (first Turkey, later Britain)—a blunder that Arendt (1978:164–77) considered Zionism's gravest mistake.

Was Herzl truly blind to the possibility of violent Arab resistance, or did he choose to remain strategically ignorant? A tough question to answer about a man for whom reality and fiction were so closely intertwined. What *Altneuland* does demonstrate, however, is that the locus of Herzl's energy and emotional investment, and that of his followers, did not rest with the Palestinian or Arab issue. As in the case of *Daniel Deronda,* the "East" is presented as the solution to a bildungsroman that had reached an uncrossable impasse in Europe. If Herzl's politics were conducted from above, his turn to the nation was above all felt and articulated by him as a solution to his *personal* problems and those of his fellow young, assimilated Jewish men. For these Western European Zionists, no less, though in different ways from Socialist Zionists, "Palestine functioned as an ideal place, out of the bleak world, where one might realize one's ideals and find a personal solution for political and social conflicts" (Arendt 1978:144). It was and remains a personalized politics, narrowly focused on the salvation of the self and little concerned with others.

Certainly, Herzl had avoided the question of Others by propagating fantasies of willing submission to the authority and sovereignty of the "New Society" (which are not only about the willing submission of women and Arabs but also about Arab society and *its* own coercive mechanisms, as void of all force and violence, and as held together by tradition alone). This had also enabled him to envision the sovereign authority of the nation as maintained—how ironic today—sans violence. Or perhaps, that is, with only the threat of violence. Because an implied threat is nevertheless in place in *Altneuland:* "It would have been ingratitude if *we* had relegated them into the servants' hall or to a harem." *We* decided to give them equal rights, *we* can take them away at our pleasure and relegate *them* elsewhere.

Though Arendt's vision of a violence-free "public sphere" makes a mockery of Herzl's rigid and naive pseudo-democratic portrayal of the "New Society," the critique that has been launched at Arendt at least since 1968 is highly applicable to Herzl's imaginings as well. Arendt, Habermas claims,

> dissociated power from the teleological model, to project the
> consensus-building force of communication as a coercive-free

force. At the same time, Arendt narrowed the political to the practical on the basis of an outmoded Aristotelian notion of praxis, thus reducing politics to a pristine, violence free realm. For this Arendt pays the price of screening all strategic elements out of politics as violence, severing politics from its ties to economic and social environment in which it is embedded in the administrative system, and being incapable of coming to grips with appearances of structural violence. (1983:174)

To the extent that Arendt was and remains one of Zionism's most insightful critics, she shared Herzl's nostalgia for a democratic public realm that would be shielded from both structural and spontaneous violence. Such a realm had been imaginatively constituted by *Altneuland* and in and by Israeli democracy, with its direct elections and political debates. Yet at the same time, Herzl's narrow political vision, particularly the elimination of violence and coercion from his account and the relegation of violence to a nonpublic space or a state of exception that warrants no debate, continues to haunt Israeli politics today.

PART III

THE TRAGEDY
OF ZIONISM

CHAPTER 5

Nationhood and the Birth of
Jewish Tragedy at the Fin de Siècle:
A Quick Overview

In the chapters that follow, I turn to the construction of Zionist nationality, national feelings, and a national subject in turn-of-the-century *Hebrew* literature, written mostly, though not exclusively, in Russia and the Ukraine. It is in this body of works, which latter-day scholars will retrospectively deem the beginning of the modern Hebrew canon, that a national subject and sensibility are most significantly forged; and it is the consciousness and paradigms constituted by these works that will affect post-statehood culture most profoundly.

The single overarching hypothesis examined in the subsequent readings is that alongside and in the service of its nationalist turn, fin-de-siècle Hebrew literature came to be dominated and infused by *tragedy*, both as an aesthetic form and a political-emotional category. Tragedy, of course, is an imprecise and highly debated term. Its definition has spanned from Aristotle's stress on the "fear and pity" it arouses in audiences, to Dorothea Krook's now dated paradigm of a story that centers on a flawed hero who comes to grief on account of his flaw and reveals through his suffering the power of gods and destiny (1969:17)—to the broader definitions laid out in Arthur Miller's "Tragedy and the Common Man" (1949) or Raymond Williams's *Modern Tragedy* (1966). For all of these theorists, nonetheless, tragedy remains a form of art based on human suffering that offers its audience some degree of pleasure (whose nature is debated), an aesthetic response to the instance of suffering rather than the suffering itself.

There is, of course, no shortage in suffering among the Russian Jewish masses at the turn of the nineteenth century: pogroms, poverty, migrations, disintegration of families, and intergenerational wars, to name a few of its sources; yet it is the *response* to these events, which is not only a product of the events themselves but of broader historical and intellectual currents, including the very turn to nationhood, that constitutes Hebrew tragedy. The aesthetics of tragedy not only serve the political aim of Jewish nationhood but in fact create national feelings and consciousness and delineate, I argue, a blueprint for masculine citizenship in the specter of the tragic hero.

Let me be precise here. Modern Hebrew literature *does not* embrace the grandiose glamour of Greek, Shakespearean, or even Wagnerian tragedy. Its subjects *are not* fallen kings and rulers (as Yosef Hayyim Brenner had put it: "We are not aristocrats!"[1]); its sensibility is essentially modern and modernist, focusing on the normative individual and his daily life. Nonetheless, *elements* of tragedy and a tragic outlook both color its portrayal of the nation and of the modern individual in his encounter with daily life, and affect the reader's response to the content and form of these works. Elements such as fate, fall, blindness, sacrifice, sin, and extreme, grandiose suffering figure in one form or another in many early Zionist works; suffering, in the works of Micah Josef Berdyczewski and Brenner, for example (which will be discussed in subsequent chapters), is intense, almost transcendental. For these and other early Zionists, the worst state is mediocrity, muddling along in present Diasporic conditions or surrendering to lightweight opiates (a good marriage with a handsome dowry and the like). It is this tragic hue and sensibility, I argue, that distinguishes the nationalist-oriented Hebrew bildungsroman from its previous mid-nineteenth-century incarnation.

As an artistic form, tragedy went through a long hiatus, stretching roughly from the Renaissance to the late nineteenth century. It is Schopenhauer's philosophy and, most profoundly, Friedrich Nietzsche's *Die Geburt der Tragödie, Oder: Griechentum und Pessimismus* (*The Birth of Tragedy, Or: Hellenism and Pessimism*) that in the 1880s signaled tragedy's renewed prestige and rebirth in European culture. "Tragedy returns as an everyday experience," Terry Eagleton writes, "at exactly the point when a democratic age has grown wary of it as ritual, mystery, heroism, fatalism, and absolute truth" (2003:96); it returns therefore as a feature of modernism, in its postrationalistic search for modes of vitality, beauty, and feeling. For Nietzsche, whose impact on early Zionists was monumental, classical Greek tragedy embodies the supreme libidinal energies of pre-Christian culture; by witnessing the depth of human suffering as it is played out on stage, he argued, Athenian spectators could surpass their atomistic, petty lives and feel an elevated, collective, Dionysian existence passionately affirmed. It is in this sense that Hebrew writers, most notably Berdyczewski, elicit the tragic in their works as well; and it is also in this sense, as I argue in the last chapter of this book, that tragedy has functioned and continues to function in the production of Israeli national feelings.

Tragedy figured in a number of ways in early Zionist literature: First, it allowed for the acceptance and elevation of suffering, when the *repression* of suffering—humoring or muddling along in it—was even for rationalist Zionist writers like Ahad Ha'am and Leo Pinsker a terrible sin. Second, it colored the *confrontation* with or response to Jewish suffering (the Kishinev Pogrom of 1904, for example, in Hayyim Nahman Bialik's "In the City of Killing") by positing a tragic hero who is affected by hurt but not entirely a victim. And third, it provided a paradigm through which the daily disappointments of young, assimilation-aspiring Jews could be understood within a larger, more politicized framework.

For both as an ideology and a structure of feeling, Zionism emerges as thousands of young Jews abandon traditional Jewish life and embark on numerous paths of migrations: to European cities, to the United States, and in the rare case, to Palestine. Hebrew fiction, particularly in the short bildungsroman genre that dominated it from the mid-nineteenth century to the early twentieth century, makes their struggles for self-fulfillment and wholeness its main subject. The autobiographical similitude of these narratives has been stressed by scholars like Dan Miron (in his numerous works) and Alan Mintz (1989), who have argued that turn-of-the-century Hebrew prose creates a vision of modern, secular interiority and individuality unprecedented in Jewish life. Yet my reading suggests that these works should be read as more than autobiography, that they should be understood through the prism of what Williams has called "liberal tragedies": plots in which the liberal right to individual self-fulfillment clashes not only with the existing social order (in this case with traditional Jewish life and its rigid customs) but also with the destructive forces inherent to the hero himself. Indeed, the premise of the fin-de-siècle Hebrew bildungsroman is the liberal dream of an escape from a false network of connections and customs associated with traditional Jewish social life; yet invariably, as these stories conclude, there is nowhere for the protagonist to get away *to*. A typical plot ultimately leads to the hero's fall, which is also where liberal tragedy meets classical tragedy in Hebrew literature, and to the denouncement of individual desire for the implicit embrace of common aspiration. Through its depiction of the acute failure, self-division, and suffering inherent to the liberation project of the individual Jewish man, a new collectivist, mythical-historical consciousness is born.

Modern Hebrew works thus revive notions of fate and sacrifice as well as blindness or flaw, coupling a theoretical critique of the flaws of Jewish life (Pinsker's critique of Jewish Diasporic life, for example) with fictional liberal tragedies—tales that are invariably grounded in blindness to one's origins and that lead the protagonist to near destruction. If psychoanalysis, whose invention was precisely contemporaneous with the advent of Zionism, secularizes fate by theorizing the individual's compulsive return to his family of origin and thus inscribes tragedy within its modern developmental theory, modern Hebrew discourse makes a similar move within a national context. What hovers above its modern, liberal trajectory is an aura of sin and punishment: the desertion of the homeland and the disregard for national roots come to haunt its protagonists, whether they are conscious of these forces or not.

"Sadness in Palestine?!" Franz Kafka had sarcastically written to Max Brod after reading some pages (in Hebrew) from a novel of Brenner's.[2] Indeed, though Zionism in Eastern Europe (as opposed to Herzl) offered itself as an answer and antidote to Diasporic Jewish misery, it did not, I argue, produce an alternative vision of the painless life. Rather, much of its identity and the source for national feelings centered on visions of sacrifice, pain, and suffering, typically of the individual young man. Yet the "sadness" or pain depicted in modern Hebrew literature was different from both the inglorious mundane suffering of ordinary Jews in Yiddish literature and also from Kafka's comedic brand of sadness. It was more closely linked to tragedy.

Hebrew literature inherits the tragic mode through the engagement of some of its authors with the works of Nietzsche and through a conscious and unconscious dialogue with fin-de-siècle German and Russian works. Yet tragedy's allure for early Zionists and their later followers is derived from more than a desire to expand the national canon and incorporate new artistic forms into its realm of cultural production. Tragedy touches the nation's deepest reaches, providing an artistic and political outlet precisely in those areas where the nationalist vision is most vulnerable to conflict and indeterminacy.

One such area is Zionism's vacillation between its Jewish identity, which is tied to its religious history, and the demands of a secular nation-state. As a form that arises with the advent of the democratic age (in fifth-century Athens), tragedy is perhaps the most potently appropriate genre to represent this predicament; it vacillates, that is, between theology and democracy, propelling a vision of the individual as both autonomous and bound by destiny, the prototype of democratic citizenship. Even in modern tragedy, Georg Lukács writes, "God must leave the stage, but must yet remain a spectator" (1974:154). With its mixture of theological and secular elements and its mixed message of freedom and duty, autonomy and destiny, death and life, tragedy, as Una Ellis-Fermor argues, forges an equilibrium between religious and nonreligious values, while endorsing neither (1945:17); it was thus, I argue, highly compatible with the particular brand of theological politics of Jewish nationhood. Moreover, if Zionism, like other liberally oriented nationalisms, moves between the explicit aims of liberating the individual Jewish citizen and simultaneously subjugating him to the nation-state, tragedy offers a way out of this predicament: a model of tragic responsibility, in which the individual is bound to the group by forces beyond his control or his choosing.

The absorption of the tragic into its culture also allowed Zionist discourse to universalize the particular Jewish national experience, to Hellenize it, and to a degree even to Christianize it, thus answering the modern nation-state's demand for universalizable particularity. If the rebirth of tragedy at the late nineteenth century reaffirmed, as Williams maintains, a Greco-Christian tradition—a link between Greeks and Elizabethans, Hellenes and Christians—Zionism (discreetly and indirectly, as such a link is all but explicitly forbidden and blasphemous) inserted Judaism into this narrative. Tragedy universalizes Jewish suffering, elevating a tragic hero who to some degree expresses a secular, universal fate, a hero whose actions are understood not from within the realm of faith but from within the realm of ethics.

Tragedy, finally, was fit for Zionist national discourse because it allowed it, as it did for Nietzsche's philosophy, to be at once modern and antimodern. Indeed, a critique of modernity is echoed in the works of many early Zionist thinkers: myth against rational inquiry, action against interiority, "life" against strict morality, the recovery of primal energies not in the service of Reason (as is the case in the *Haskalah*, the "Jewish Enlightenment" period) but for the purpose of what Terry Eagleton in his reading of Nietzsche calls "the ecstatic yea-saying to life's sheer obdurate imperishability" (2003:53). And yet, in their acute *self-consciousness*, early Zionist thinkers were also thoroughly modern, acknowledging the nation's need for salutary myths (in Ahad Ha'am's "Moses," for example) and for techniques that would make action in the present possible, including a selective historical amnesia. Tragedy is exactly the form in which such duality between modern and antimodern worldviews can coexist.

A poignant feature of its modernity, which became acutely relevant to national culture in the post-statehood years, is its ambivalence toward willed sacrifice, namely, the individual consciously giving his life to service the group. Tragedy both enacts and alleviates this ambivalence, turning sacrifice into victimhood, or at any rate, to an act not consciously chosen by the individual sufferer. Consider, for example, Moshe Shamir's *Hu halakh ba-sadot* (*He Walked the Fields*, 1947), a popular post-statehood novel-turned-screenplay that ends with the hero's questionably suicidal, questionably heroic sacrifice. Read by audiences as tragedy, the representation of this death had a symbolic-cathartic effect on the budding national community, triggering not only a renewal and affirmation of general life (the effect that Nietzsche imagines classical tragedy to have had on Athenian audiences) but of general guilt that, as Williams has argued, can move people "more deeply than the consummation of any order of life" (1966:191). Thus, especially when tragedy (both in its literary and psychological permutations) moves to *Eretz Yisrael*, it becomes closely linked with ambivalent images of male sacrifice, which are read within the domain of the tragic. Without any relationship to the actual circumstances of the hero's death, the blind force that propels what is seen as a tragic action comes to stand metaphorically for the blind force of the nation at large, revealing to its members a grander potential and essence.

Tragedy, as Timothy Reiss (1980:284) asserts, plays out the chaos at the core of the social discursive order, and it is in this sense that the tragic mode is both ideological and counterideological. In the nation's formative years in particular, though to a degree today as well, tragedy allowed for the "inexpressible" that eluded explicit national ideology to be experienced in the realm of culture. It was especially in images of male sacrifice, as I maintain in the last chapter of this book, that this "inexpressible" received expression, producing in readers and audiences a feeling of national belonging and essence that transcended the annihilation of its representative member: the individual hero.

At least since the 1970s, and alongside the persistence of the tragic outlook in Israeli culture and society, Israeli writers, artists, and scholars have produced counternarratives to tragedy. The representation of Woman's position vis-à-vis male-centered tragedy is, I think, of key importance here, and by way of interrogating and challenging its structure, I end this book with a reading in the works of two contemporary female Israeli writers.

CHAPTER 6

Kishinev and the Making
of a Jewish Tragedy

On the eve of April 6, 1903, a wave of attacks against the Jews of Kishinev, capital of Bessarabia, began. For two, and in some areas for three, days, homes and businesses were looted and destroyed; men, women, and children were beaten, mutilated, and murdered; women were gang-raped. The perpetrators were mostly young men: neighbors, students, and business partners of the victims. The violence left forty-nine people dead and 592 wounded, and over seven hundred homes and businesses looted and destroyed (Goren 1991:9).

These three days in Kishinev mark for many historians a pivotal formative moment in modern Zionism.

By 1903, Russian Jews had already lived through other pogroms; in the late 1910s and early 1920s, more than a thousand pogroms in the Ukraine alone would claim thirty to seventy thousand lives (Kadish 1992:87); still, Kishinev, with "only" forty-nine dead, became at least until the Holocaust a code word for the brutalization and vulnerability of Jews worldwide, the most traumatic event in modern Jewish memory. For a nominally local occurrence, it elicited numerous articles, letters, and photos in major newspapers across the globe, including the *Times* of both New York and London; it drew significant political responses in Russia, England, and the United States, and made it into the larger cultural sphere—into plays, songs, poems, and essays—some of which are recited even today (Roskies 1989:145–68).

What served most dramatically to insert Kishinev into the vocabulary of generations of Jews was not a photograph,[1] newspaper article, or eyewitness testimony but *a Hebrew poem*—"Be-ir ha-hariga" ("In the City of Killing")—by the romantic Hebrew poet Hayyim Nahman Bialik. In Israel, where I grew up, this poem is an integral part of the school curriculum and recited on many occasions. I do not remember when I first read or studied it, but the words "Kishinev" and "pogrom" seem to have been part of my vocabulary for a long, long time. This is not an obvious matter. Like many who have been raised in nations prone to recycling poems for public use, my experience has been that, along with the names of overly didactic elementary school teachers, such poems tend to eventually dissipate from memory. "In the City of Killing" did not.

From Kishinev to a "City of Killing"

"In the City of Killing" was published in 1904. The thirty-one-year-old Bialik was by then known as a literary maverick in the world of modern Hebrew letters. He had already published an earlier poetic response to Kishinev—"On the Slaughter"—a moving, anguished elegy that was enthusiastically received. It begins with these lines:

> *Sky, have mercy on me!*
> *If there be in you a God and to that God a path*
> *and I have not found it—*
> *you pray for me!*
> *I—my heart's dead and there's no prayer left in my mouth*
> *and no strength and no hope any longer—*
> *how long, and until when, just how much longer?*
> *Hangman! Here's my neck—come kill!*
> *Crop me like a dog, you have the axe-arm,*
> *and all the earth is to me a block—*
> *and we—we are few in number! . . .* (Hadari 2000:11)[2]

In "On the Slaughter," the poetic speaker is equated with pogrom victims, the tone is knowing and resigned, and the poem in its entirety registers a pervasive sense of helplessness and a portrait of a mass of undifferentiated peoples destined for repeated attacks. The possibility of vengeance is briefly raised—"and cursed be he who cries: vengeance! / Such a vengeance, the vengeance for a small child's blood / Satan himself never dreamed"—only to be rejected as grossly inadequate and futile.

Bialik was not content with this first poem. Having stayed put in Odessa as the pogrom unfolded, he decided to go to Kishinev and examine things at close range. He was charged—or rather got himself charged—with heading an inquiry panel commissioned by the Jewish Historical Committee, and spent May and June of 1903 interviewing sur-

vivors and collecting testimonies. By 1904, Bialik emerged from many
months of labor with a resolute decision not to publish a single testimony;[3]
instead he composed the epic poem that for many was to transform the
representation of and response to Jewish suffering. It begins thus:

> *Rise and go to the town of the killings and you'll come to the yards*
> *and with your eyes and your own hand feel the fence*
> *and on the trees and on the stones and plaster of the walls*
> *the congealed blood and hardened brains of the dead.*
> *And you'll come from there to the ruins and stop before rents*
> *and pass by the pierced walls and shattered ovens,*
> *where the axe's head bit deep, to burst and deepen holes,*
> *baring the black stone and shears of brick all burned*
> *and they'll look like the open mouths of black and mortal wounds*
> *that have no remedy, that have no cure,*
> *and your feet will sink in feathers and stumble over heaps*
> *of the fragments of fragments and smithereens of smithereens*
> *and defeat of books and scrolls,*
> *the annihilation of divine labor and fruit of working like a dog;*
> *and you will not stand by the carnage but pass by there on your path—*
> *and the rye blooms before you and pours perfume in your nose,*
> *and half the buds will be feathers, and their smell the smell of blood;*
> *and in your spite and against your heart you'll bring their strange*
>   *incense*
> *like the tender spring to your bosom—and it will not be loathsome to it;*
> *and with a multitude of golden arrows the sun will pierce your liver*
> *and seven rays from every grain of glass will dance in your torture.*
> *For the Lord called the Spring and the slaughterer together:*
> *the sun rose, rye bloomed, and the slaughterer slaughtered.*
> *And you'll flee and come to a yard, and this yard will have a heap in it—*
> *and on this heap they'll have beheaded two—a Jew and his dog.*
> *One axe did for both of them and in one heap they were thrown*
> *And in the mixed blood of both—pigs will snuffle and roll;*
> *tomorrow a rain will come down, and sweep it to one of the wasteland*
>   *streams*
> *and blood will not longer scream from the gutters and garbage pails*
> *for it will be lost in the deep water and feed the thorns—*
> *and all will be as nothing, all go back to as if it never were.* (Hadari
>   2000:1)

In every respect, this second poem represents a dramatic deviation from the first. If in "On the Slaughter" the poetic speaker is a man, presumably the poet himself, here the speaker is God, addressing himself to a human messenger with a command to bear witness to and register the violence, horror, and shame of the pogrom. If in the first poem, the poetic speaker is *a victim* ("Hangman! Here's my neck—come kill!"), and the underlying assumption is that of an unbroken chain of identification between poet, poetic speaker, pogrom victim, and reader—all of whom are understood through the sign of collective helplessness ("and all the earth is to *me* a block— / and *we—we* are few in number"), in the second poem the speaker (God), witness, and reader are differentiated from the victims through several layers of spectatorship.

There is no "we" in "In the City of Killing." Quite the opposite. Though he is commanded to live among survivors, to see "with [his] own eyes" the horror and the shame, God's addressee, the entity molded *through* God's commands, is instructed to remain apart and aloof ("and you will not low with their crying"), to become an angry, repulsed, *solitary* figure faced with the humiliation of the Jews. If, as I have argued in the previous chapter, early Zionist theory reconfigures Jewish history as *tragedy*, if it deems the Jewish nation as one repeatedly punished for abandoning its political existence, Bialik, I argue, molds Kishinev's witness as *a tragic-hero-in-the-making*. By "tragic" I mean not merely sad or hurt but fated, doomed, grand, tragic in the classical sense: an Oedipus, a Hamlet. Unlike Oedipus and Hamlet, the witness does not act out the consequences of his destiny; yet he is the only figure in the poem who is charged with what Karl Jaspers has called "comprehending the tragic atmosphere" (1953:75) and the only figure commanded to respond *tragically* to the abomination of Kishinev: to experience anger and guilt and recoil from sentimentality, to be transformed by the tragic condition of the stateless Jews and be primed for *future* self-sacrifice on their behalf. Set apart from his maker (God) and his people (the collective victims of the pogrom) the witness is both an avenger and a sacrificial figure, primed *to become* tragic through the encounter with the suffering and humiliation of his people and his God. "In struggle," Jaspers writes, the tragic hero "becomes aware of that power for which he stands, that power which is not yet everything" (76). "In the City of Killing" details the *process,* the emotional rite of passage that this struggle constitutes, which is also the process through which the Jewish witness is universalized and inscribed into the classical, that is, Western, tradition. The poem depicts the excruciating, painful, violent journey through which Jewish suffering—the witness's suffering, that is—is transformed into tragic suffering, and as such its subject is not the pogrom but something else, something new: the making of a tragic figure, a presence not quite foreign but not quite kin, an exasperated, fascinated, hardened male witness, poised for tragic action. Through *his* struggle, as I will show, the witness becomes a subject, a blueprint of a citizen in a future nation-state, a symbol as well as a scapegoat for the imagined national community-in-becoming, and a sign of potential national renewal and invigoration. It is the emergence of this tragic figure out of the ashes of Kishinev that renders the illegible suffering of Kishinev meaningful and seals it as *destiny.*

The Making of Suffering into Tragedy

For most theorists of tragedy, real life suffering does not constitute tragedy. Tragedy, for Aristotle as for Nietzsche and as for the radical Franco Moretti, is located in the *representation* of suffering, and it is only through such artistic representation that the value of suffering can be released. "War, revolution, poverty, hunger; men reduced to objects and killed from lists; persecution and torture; the many kinds of contemporary martyrdom; however close and insistent the facts, we are not to be moved in a context of tragedy," Williams writes; "Tragedy, we know, is about something else" (1966:62).

Bialik knew this, and it is perhaps for this reason that he decided to forsake actual survivor testimonies, straightforward individualized narrations that tell of drunken teenage neighbors, ransacked furniture, and rational acts of self-preservation for a highly stylized rendering of the horrors, trading city for nature, shops for stables, inner courtyards for "boulders," those same drunken teenage neighbors for "centaurs" and "wild boars," individual women for "virgins" and "daughters of [the] race." It is perhaps for this reason that he deploys visual, sensational, highly eroticized synecdochic images—"wheels with spokes splayed wide"; "corpses drunk with blood"; "pulverized bones"; "spike smeared with human blood and brains"; a "disemboweled chest filled with feathers"; a "beheaded" couple: "a Jew and his dog"; "a case of nostrils and nine inch nails"; "a baby found by the side of his stabbed mother / still dozing with her cold nipple in his sucking mouth"; a ghost "crying without tongue"—to conjure up a mental image of the pogrom. Blood, rape, cellars, secret horrors: the poem's strong eroticization of the violence, a central feature of *Hamlet,* for example, is typical of tragedy, which as Terry Eagleton notes, "often betrays a certain kind of sensationalist subtext, an aura of violence or exoticism, of sweetly heightened sensations and covert erotic pleasures" (2003:10). Bialik does not only, as Miron (2005) has claimed, acknowledge an erotic fascination with the violence, he deliberately creates a mood of dark, unspeakable, sexual horror that engulfs the witness and by extension the reader.

Spanning nearly three hundred lines, the witness is thus commanded by God to "rise and go to the town of killings," to abolish the physical distance between himself and the horror, to go to and from cellars, attics, stables, synagogues, graveyards, and outhouses and to never recoil. He must learn in graphic detail the methods, weapons, and modes of violence; he is instructed to watch rape and "slaughtered human beings hung up from beams like fish." He is allowed no way out: "Shut up! And silently bear witness," "do not go out from among them," "be locked here in the dark and bury your eyes in the ground," "open the gate reluctantly . . . and a black fear will swallow you up, an abyss of secret horrors." Following the witness's footsteps, the reader is invited to a macabre tour of Kishinev and of the range of feelings that such encounter with horror evokes.

Fear and Pity

For Aristotle, tragedy performs the politically valuable service known as catharsis: the draining off of an excess of enfeebling emotions such as pity and fear. By feeding us controlled doses of such emotions, Aristotle argues, tragedy cleanses us from experiencing too much terror and tenderheartedness. We are shaken but not stirred to run away. Tragedy, more contemporary critics tell us, creates a "didactic of otherness and intimacy" in which pity, the impulse to approach, and fear, the impulse to retreat, are brought into perfect equilibrium: "this 'me and not me' is what the pity and fear precept is groping for" (Eagleton 2003:160–61). Hume stresses tragedy's pleasurable effect on the spectator: the dance of distance and proximity from others' horror and the amalgamation of pain and pleasure that it ignites (1985:424). Joseph Addison claims that tragic pleasure is derived from exactly these spectatorial relations, from the ability to compare our own secure situation to the havoc on stage (Eagleton 2003:169–71).

But *Kishinev*? Kishinev was not just a representation, it happened to *our people*. And Bialik went there, and stayed there, for two long months, and saw and heard everything. Nonetheless, or perhaps for this very reason, Bialik creates a spectatorial distance between the violence of Kishinev and the experience of a reader, whose take on Kishinev is filtered *through the witness's spectatorial position.* More than a direct representation of the pogrom, "In the City of Killing" is a narration of the psychological and ethical journey through which the witness comes to face it. Though the poem's graphic language and its profoundly negative portrayal of pogrom victims calls us to retreat, the narrative of the witness's psychological journey in the realm of trauma calls us to approach and identify. In shifting between the shocking details of the scene of violence and the near serenity at the scene of witnessing ("the rye blooms before you and pours perfume in your nose"), between a mood of sadness and pity ("and you will hear there the cry of their ruin and be swept up in their tears") to one of horror and fear ("and a black fear will swallow you up, an abyss of secret horrors" / "and the hair of your flesh will stand on end and fear will call on you with trembling"), between fatalism ("the sun rose, rye bloomed, and the slaughterer slaughtered") and sadism toward the victims, the poem explores the range of feelings the spectator of Kishinev both fends off and invites. The poem articulates, as Miron (2005) has convincingly argued, the kind of psychical defense that is triggered by one's sense of impotence and festers into sadism; it does so without shame, allowing the reader to take in controlled doses of the Kishinev horror at the same time:

And the rye blooms before you and pours perfume in your nose, / and half the buds will be feathers, and their smell the smell of blood; / and in your spite and against your heart you'll bring their strange incense / like the tender spring to your bosom—and it will not be loathsome to it; / and with a multitude of golden arrows the sun will pierce your liver / and seven rays from every grain of glass will dance in your torture: It is exactly the encounter with the deadness, detachment, and even pleasure of violence, the encounter with the traumatic otherness within the self that Bialik's witness models for readers of the poem. It is exactly the picture of violence in the other *but also in the self* that is set up to mirror, echo, dramatize, mediate, and also shape going forward their response to the Kishinev carnage. A dubious ethical position, it nonetheless rings true. Eagleton explains its potency thus:

> In the deepest sense, to exclaim "This isn't me!" of the tragic victim is not to disown the agony but to acknowledge it. It can mean that confronted with this unbearable pain, all iden-

tity, including one's own, has now dwindled away, leaving nobody even to make the act of identification. What we share, in
Lacanian parlance, is no longer a question of the imaginary—
rivalry, mimesis, antagonism, sympathetic identification—or of
the symbolic—difference, identity, alterity—but of the *Real* . . .
Only relationships based on a mutual recognition of the *Real*—
of the terrifying inhuman installed at the core of the other and
oneself, for which one name is the death drive—will be able to
prosper. What has to be shared, to by-pass a mere mirroring of
egos, is what is foreign to us both. And this is what is expelled
from the world of consciousness and civility. (2003:164)

Bialik manufactures for his readers such a portrait of "the Real," and
it is for this reason, I think, that the Kishinev poem has lingered in my
mind for so long.

A Tragic Response

For Hegel, one of the first modern theoreticians of tragedy, the direct
confrontation with horror is *the* key element of tragedy; it is only by
"looking the negative in the face and tarrying with it," by confronting
and holding on to death, that the tragic hero's spirit can finally triumph
(1977:19). And "In the City of Killing" is a tragedy precisely because it
articulates the demand, perhaps for the first time, for a *tragic comprehension* of Jewish suffering and history. Again and again God commands the witness to "not budge" from the deadly scene but take it all in.
Take in "things that poke holes in the brain and are enough to kill / your
spirit and your soul to an eternal death"; take it in and "bury it in your
heart before it breaks." Take it all in *and remain silent*: "refrain and stifle
in your throat the scream," "do not shed a tear," "gnash your teeth and
dissolve":

> and I'll be cruel—and you will not low with their crying
> and if your roar bursts out—I will stifle it between your teeth;
> they can profane their catastrophes alone—you will not profane it.
> The calamity will stand for generations—a calamity unmourned,
> and you will build on it a fort of brass and a wall of steel
> of deadly fury, hatred deep as hell and secret loathing
> and it will take hold in your heart and grow there like a serpent

and you will suckle off one another and will not find any peace;
and you will keep it hungry and thirsty—and then destroy its fort
and like a nest of cruel vipers send it forth
and on the people of your anger and compassion in a day of thunder set
    it loose. (Hadari 2000:7)

They can profane their catastrophes alone—you will not profane it.
Most dramatically, the demand for the witness's tragic comprehension,
for his fury, hatred, and steeled anger is articulated against the poem's
radically exaggerated images of uncomprehending, passive, and pathetic
pogrom victims. If witness is charged with suffering *tragically,* with a
mixture of agony and grandiosity, *their* mental state is "merely" that of
suffering or grief, what C. S. Lewis has called the "uncouth mixture of
agony and littleness" (1961:78). The pogrom survivors are cast as dull
and petty sufferers, human ghosts and beggars bereft of any grandeur,
and Bialik pounces on them with astonishing cruelty—"beaten slaves,"
"broken vessels," "there's no point to your deaths as there was no point
to your lives"—an attack so extreme that it propelled the Yiddish master
Sholem Jacob Abramowitz to dub "In the City of Killing" a "poetic pogrom" (Miron 2005).

Tragedy and the Zionist Idea

Indeed the poem launches a shocking assault, but one deeply rooted in
the staple Zionist explanatory narratives of the period. One need only
turn to a major Zionist foundational text, Pinsker's *Autoemancipation*
(1882/1944), to detect the overtones of tragedy and a mythic structure
in the quasi-scientific polemic—the tale of a people repeatedly punished
for the original sin of deserting their homeland:

> Among the living nations of the earth the Jews occupy the po-
> sition of a nation long since dead. With the loss of their father-
> land, the Jews lost their independence and fell into a state of
> decay which is incompatible with the existence of a whole and
> vital organism. The state was crushed by the Roman conquer-
> ors and vanished from the world's view. But after the Jewish
> people had yielded up its existence as an actual state, as a po-
> litical entity, it could nevertheless not submit to total destruc-
> tion—it did not cease to exist as a spiritual nation. Thus the

world saw in this people the frightening form of one of the
dead walking among the living. This ghostlike apparition of
a people without unity or organization, without land or other
bond of union, no longer alive and yet moving about among
the living—this eerie form scarcely paralleled in history, unlike anything that preceded it or followed it, could not fail to
make a strange and peculiar impression upon the imagination
of the nations. And if the fear of ghosts is something inborn,
and has a certain justification in the psychic life of humanity,
is it any wonder that it asserted itself powerfully at the sight of
this dead and yet living nation?

Fear of the Jewish ghost has been handed down and
strengthened for generations and centuries. (1944:77)

Pinsker suggests at least implicitly that *Judeophobia*—a deep-seated,
timeless, and universal psychic phenomenon for which legal rights or
emancipation are no match—is a direct punishment for yielding the
state. So long as the Jews remain a nation without a political identity,
a ghostlike nation, they will invoke the fear of ghosts, in distinct places
and for supposedly distinct reasons; that is their original sin, for which
they are collectively punished. So long as they do not resume political
existence, they will remain ghosts. Yet the prolonged death-in-life condition had, according to Pinsker, sapped out of even this ailing people
the will to cure themselves: the drive for political existence,

In a sick man, the absence of desire for food and drink is a
very serious symptom. It is not always possible to cure him of
this ominous loss of appetite. And even if his appetite can be
restored, it is still a question whether he will be able to digest
food, even though he desires it. The Jews are in the unhappy
condition of such a patient. (1944:76)

Bialik too depicts the Jews of Kishinev as living-dead: their lives are
"cursed," their "hearts" "a desert and drought"; and like Pinsker, Bialik
creates an ambiguity around the cause for this condition: are they attacked because they are nearly dead, or are they nearly dead because
they are attacked? Whatever the causality, they now carry within them
a larger curse, a fate of impending doom: "the note of death is on their
brows." Living survivors live a ghostlike life ("So the wick will smoke
when the wax is done, so the old horse pull when his strength is gone"),

and those who died cannot properly die. Like Hamlet's ghost, they walk among the living and haunt and terrorize the reluctant witness:

> *And you will go down the hill of the city and find a vegetable garden*
> *and a great stable in the garden, the stable of killing.*
> *And like a camp of giant owls and terrible bats,*
> *fears sprawl over the corpses drunk with blood and tired.*
> *There on the floor of the stable, thrown to earth,*
> *wheels with spokes splayed wide, like fingers sent forth for blood*
> *their spikes still smeared with human blood and brains.*
> *And toward the end of the day, when the sun tilts to the West*
> *wrapped with clouds of blood and waistcoated with flames*
> *you'll open the gate reluctantly and come to the stable yard*
> *and a black fear will swallow you up, an abyss of secret horrors:*
> *fear, fear all around . . . it wanders in the stables, soaks the walls, and*
>   *ferments in the silence.*
> *And from under the mounds of wheels, among the cracks and holes*
> *you can still feel a fluttering of pulverized bones*
> *moving the wheels balanced across their backs,*
> *squirming in their death throes and trampled in their own blood;*
> *and one last secret groan—the voice weak with pain*
> *still hangs on the branch above your head as though congealed*
> *and a low, an endless sorrow, simmers there in fear.*
> *It is the spirit oppressed from suffering and great torment*
> *that locked itself here as in gaol,*
> *here in the endless pain and will not yet be parted from it*
> *and a single black Presence, weary with sorrow and exhausted,*
> *broods here in every corner and cannot find comfort,*
> *wants to weep, and cannot, wants to roar and keeps quiet,*
> *and silently festers in mourning and secretly stifles,*
> *spreads its wings over the spirit of martyrs with its head under one wing*
> *keeping its tears in the shadow and crying without tongue.* (Hadari
>   2000:4)

Bialik's poem thus corroborates and dramatically expands the repertoire of symbols, images, and metaphors that Pinsker uses to mythologize the highly diverse and idiosyncratic condition of Jews. And he attempts to insert Kishinev into the Western imagination precisely by couching it in the deeply ingrained symbolism of Hamlet's tale. "To the graveyard, beggars!" the poetic speaker addresses survivors of Kishinev:

Dig for the bones of your fathers
and of your sainted brothers and fill with them your bundles
and hoist them on your shoulders and take them to the road, fated
to merchandise them at all the trade fairs;
and you will seek a stand at the crossroads where all can see,
and lay them out in the sunshine on the backs of your filthy rags
and with a parched voice sing a beggar's song over their bodies
and call for the mercy of the nations and pray for the kindness of the
*   goyim,*
and where you've stretched your hand you'll stretch it further,
and where you've begged you will not stop begging. (Hadari 2000:9)

Increasingly, as the poem progresses, the particular suffering of
Kishinev victims is presented as the collective destiny of the Jews: "Uprooted grass this race—and do the uprooted have hope?" asks the poetic
speaker; "so cries a nation that is lost, lost" (6). Echoing Pinsker's much
used image of the Diasporic Jew as eternal beggar ("he is not a guest,
much less a welcome guest. He is more like a beggar; and what beggar
is welcome?"[4]), pogrom survivors are depicted in language both generic
and shockingly carnivalesque. If *Autoemancipation* is a theory of Jewish
nationalism, "In the City of Killing" is exhibit A. Bialik turns the three
days of Kishinev into the timeless *tragedy* of a nation collectively and
repeatedly punished for having forsaken and lost the will for political
existence.

The Social Meaning of Rape

Perhaps the most shocking (and factually false) critique of Kishinev survivors is lodged in the much studied rape scene of "In the City of Killing," where Jewish men are depicted as hiding and "peeping out of holes"
while their wives and sisters are gang-raped:

Go down . . . and come to the dark cellars
where the pure daughters of your race were defiled among the pots and
*   pans*
woman by woman under seven after seven uncircumcised,
daughter in front of mother and mother in front of daughter,
before killing, during killing, and after killing;
and with your hands feel the filthy pillowcase and blushing pillow,
den of wild boars and raping paddock of centaurs

with the axe's blood dripping and steaming from their hand.
and see, oh see: in the shade of the same corner
under this bench and behind that barrel
lay husbands, fiancés, brothers, peeping out of holes
at the flutter of holy bodies under the flesh of asses
choking in their corruption and gagging on their own throats' blood
as like slices of meat a loathsome gentile spread their flesh—
they lay in their shame and saw—and didn't move and didn't budge,
and they didn't pluck out their eyes or go out of their minds—
and perhaps each to his soul then prayed in his heart:
master of the universe, make a miracle—and let me not be harmed.
And those who survived their contamination and woke from their
*   blood—*
their lives abhorred, the light of the world dunned and all their lives
*   made loath*
forever, the profanation of soul and body inside out—
And their husbands emerged from their holes and ran to the house of
*   God*
and blessed the miracles of the Holy One Blessed be He their refuge and
*   respite;*
and the priests among them went out and asked their rabbis: "Rabbi!
*   My wife,*
what is she? Allowed or not allowed?"
and everything returned to its course, and everything fell into line.
(2–3)

In contrast to the depiction of the rest of the violence at Kishinev, told as we have seen via brief synecdochic images, the story of the rape is recounted in narrative form and great detail over dozens of lines. Like Hamlet's staging of a play within a play, the witness becomes a spectator of a spectacle of eroticized violence, now presented for the poem's readers. Why was the rape scene so central to Bialik's rendering of the pogrom? Scholars have given various answers to this question—ranging from Bialik's overidentification with the raped women, to his metaphoric references to the Book of Ezekiel.[5] In a recent essay, Michael Gluzman demonstrates how the story of the rape of Jewish women and particularly the phrase "the flesh of asses" (*bsar hamorim*) is taken from Ezekiel's description of the lovers of two Jewish women, Aholah and Aholibah, "whose flesh is as the flesh of asses, and whose issue is like the issue of horses" (Ezekiel 23:20). The prophet Ezekiel, Gluzman claims, "creates a rhetoric of national rage that condemns the nation through a gendered metaphor which identifies idol worship with sexual infidelity" (2005:26; my translation); Bialik borrows the metaphor of the cuckolded nation and implements it in his critique of Jewish male passivity at Kishinev.

We might, however, also pay attention to Bialik's portrayal of the rapists as a "den of wild boars and raping paddock of centaurs," taking as his source not the Hebrew Bible but classical mythology. For in Greek mythology and its later renditions centaurs embody the essence of rape (Zeitlin 1986:132); most prominently, these semidivine hybrid crosses between man and beast are associated with a myth that takes place at the wedding of Pirithous, king of the Lapithae. In the wake of the centaurs' attempt to carry off the bride and the rest of the Lapith women, a defense is mounted by Pirithous and Theseus, another hero and founder of cities; the centaurs are driven off and destroyed, patriarchal order is resumed, and the myth becomes a recurrent theme in the monumental art of the great temples that were constructed after the triumph of Greece in the Persian wars. Mostly, the myth of the centaurs and the Lapith women has been read as an important metaphoric representation of the Greeks' defense of their own women against the Persian invaders (Zeitlin 1986:132–33).

Classic myth and images of Greek gods held tremendous value for early Zionist culture in its negotiation with questions of male virility, the boundary between Judaism and Hellenism, and the definition of national identity. Here too the myth of the raping centaurs has clear allegorical value. Against the model set by Lapiths/Greek men's prowess in the defense of their city and their women, Jewish men are posited as cowardly, selfish, and worse. Bialik does not, as Micah Berdyczewski implicitly does, condone rape as a sign of male potency and virility, yet his juxtaposition between the barbarity of the "centaurs" and the cowardly "civilized" response of Jewish men (prayer, consultation with the rabbis) suggests that the latter are the worst offenders. Because they presented no resistance to violence ("they fled the flight of mice and hid like ticks,/ and died like dogs where they were found") and because they did not appear to be truly affected by it ("they didn't pluck out their eyes or go out of their minds") the men of Kishinev are depicted as precisely *antitragic*. Unwilling to directly face ("peeping out of holes") nor comprehend their own tragic state, for them the "calamity" of Kishinev is "mourned" no sooner than it has happened: *And everything returned to its course, and everything fell into line.* Survivors are blamed not only for their inaction during the pogrom, but for not *comprehending* the enormity of the pogrom's meaning in its aftermath, for not becoming a Hamlet, an Oedipus—"they didn't pluck out their eyes"—for simply carrying on as before, for not even noticing that something smells rotten in the state of Kishinev, for *being comforted*:

> *And if you rose early tomorrow and went to the crossroads*
> *you'd see many bits of men all groans and sighs,*
> *swarming the windows of the rich and hanging about their doors*
> *crying aloud their wounds as a hawker does his goods;*
> *who has a cracked skull, and who a hand-cut bruise*
> *and every one puts forth a grimy paw and bares a broken arm,*
> *with eyes, the eyes of beaten slaves . . .*
> *And masters who are merciful take pity on them*
> *and hand them from within a stick and a knapsack for the cracked*
>   *skull,*
> *say "Blessed be He that rid us of them"—and the beggars are comforted.*
> (Hadari 2000:8–9)

Indeed, "In the City of Killing" "performs" the essential elements of Pinsker's Zionist theory. It literally evokes the images of lifeless Jews begging among the healthy nations. And in casting the rapists as a pack of centaurs, associated in Greek culture with untamed nature itself (Kirk 1970:52–62)—in reality they were mostly drunken teenagers, neighbors, and associates of the raped women—it deems the violence against the Jews as a timeless force of nature, not a local, historically specific occurrence.

Moreover and most importantly, the reference to the myth of the centaurs, the abduction and defense of the Lapith women, and the implicit link to the Greek-Persian wars fixes the Kishinev rapes squarely as a question of national defense. Boundaries of the nation are allegorized via the penetration of women's (virginal) bodies by "uncircumcised" barbarians; female bodies are associated with the city-state itself, penetrated and left undefended. The nation that is not yet a nation becomes a nation precisely because it needs to be defended. And where the Jewish men of Kishinev have miserably failed, the witness is called to observe and internalize in preparation for future action. *His* affiliation with the raped women, as opposed to the private nature of the affiliation of "husbands, brothers, and fiancés," is asserted in national/collective terms—"pure daughters of your race"—after which he is ordered to engrave the offense in his soul and maintain there it forever:

And you too, you too, son of man, shut the gate behind
and be locked here in the dark and bury your eyes in the ground
and stand here till you lose track of time and are one with the sorrow
and fill your heart with it for all the days of your life
and the day your soul is bankrupt and lost all its holdings
it will be to you a remainder and a poison cup
and it will lurk in you like a curse and fright you like an evil spirit
and it will grip you and press you like the pressing of a bad dream;
and you will bear it in your bosom to the four corners of the earth
and you will seek and you won't find for it a sound of lips. (4–5)

The poem does two things then. It constructs, out of the highly idiosyncratic individual stories of survivors of Kishinev, and particularly
through the rape scene, an image of "a nation": a helpless, passive, non-
descript, ahistorical, effeminized collective, sick and destined for repeated brutalization by forces as timeless and unpredictable as nature
itself, yet nonetheless *a nation;* concurrently, it erects a new masculine
subject—the witness—differentiated from the nation yet poised as a
(future) actor on its behalf.

In contrast to Kishinev's people, who are painted with broad archetypal strokes, regarded en masse, and implicitly identified as village
Jews, poor beggars, an undignified chorus of sentimental wailers, and
traditional country folk (Kishinev was in fact a small industrial city), the
witness's suffering is articulated through a universal and highly modern
sensibility; he is addressed simply as "son of man," and we read of the
bankruptcy of his soul, the loss of his bearing, the failure of language,
his solitude, all of which are associated for the early Lukács (1974) with
both tragedy *and* the modern condition. Less of a human figure than a
modern tragic *presence,* the witness is the binary opposite of the highly
recognizable, mundane portrait of village Jews. In contrast to their col-
lectiveness, he stands alone; in contrast to their incessant "wailing, weep-
ing and wild cry," he utters not a sound.

This silence, what Walter Benjamin in *The Origin of German Tragic
Drama* calls "the inarticulacy of the tragic hero," is central to the tragic
essence of Bialik's witness. "The tragic hero," Benjamin writes,

> has only one language that is completely proper to him: si-
> lence . . . in his silence the hero burns the bridges connecting
> him to God and the world, elevates himself above the realm of

personality, which is speech, defines itself against others and
individualizes himself, and so enters the icy loneliness of the
self. The self knows nothing other than itself; its loneliness is
absolute. How else can it activate this loneliness, this rigid and
defiant self-sufficiency, except in silence. (1977:108)

For modernity, as it is understood by Benjamin, common consciousness is false and only a violent passage through hell will return it to true
cognition, "purged and demystified," demanding, as it does of King Lear,
a painful self-transformation (Eagleton 2003:34). It is in part for this
reason, Benjamin contends, that tragedy was rediscovered by modernity, and it is at least in part for this reason that it becomes important
for modern Zionists as well. The silence of Bialik's witness in the face of
Kishinev *is* the sign of his modernity. Not only are his actions narrated
exclusively by God, not only do we understand him through God's commands and never through his own words, but the prohibition against
language and crying *is* God's most forceful command to him: *Gnash
your teeth and dissolve.* For the contemporary tragedy theorist Roy Morell, the mere confrontation with "the worst" that tragedy depicts is in
itself a source of value, the value of a shock that brings with it true cognition (1965:26). Indeed, through his silent encounter with suffering the
witness is propelled by God to sink to the edge of psychosis, to a place
beyond language, beyond personality, beyond the social, a place of utter meaninglessness, the place where Oedipus and King Lear have been,
where human ties and his very identity will "dissolve," where his soul will
become "bankrupt and [lose] all of its holdings." Like Oedipus's flight
into the desert—"Forth from thy borders thrust me with all speed; set
me within some vastly desert where No mortal voice shall greet me any
more"—the tragic witness is instructed to "rise and flee to the desert"
and there, outside the realm of the social, let loose his scream. That is
how the poem ends:

*And now what have you left here, son of man, rise and flee to the desert
and take with you there the cup of sorrows, and tear your soul in ten
    pieces
and your heart give for food to a helpless fury
and your great tear spill there on the heads of boulders
and your great bitter scream send forth—
to be lost in the storm.* (9)

Minority/Majority; Universal/Particular

To understand the extent to which Bialik's epic poem inaugurated a tragic outlook and a new, tragic, universal figure into Jewish culture, let us briefly compare it to another literary response to the Kishinev Pogrom: a short Yiddish story titled "Tsvey Antisemitn" ("Two Anti-Semites") also published in 1904 by the Yiddish master Sholom Aleichem (Sholem Rabinowitz). The story's protagonist is Max Berlliant, a traveling salesman with distinct Jewish features and a highly recognizable identity, a quietly assimilating Jewish man:

> Max's eyes are dark and shining, his hair the same. It's real Semitic hair. He speaks Russian like a cripple, and, God help us, with a Yiddish singsong. And on top of everything he's got a nose! A nose to end all noses . . . True, our hero did avenge himself on his beard. Beardless now, and decked out like a bride, he curls his whiskers, files his nails, wears a tie as glorious as what the Lord God himself might have worn had he ever worn a tie. Max has accustomed himself to the food in railway restaurants, but he continually vents his bitterness on the pigs of this world. If even half the curses he heaps on the species were to come true, I would be happy. But what's the use of being fussy? Might as well be hung for a sheep as for a lamb, so Max took his life in his hands and began to eat Lobster. (Howe and Wisse 1979:115–16)

Like Bialik's poem, Sholom Aleichem's story takes as its subject not the pogrom but the Jewish response to it. Soon after the Kishinev Pogrom, Max the salesman is forced to travel to Kishinev on business, a trip that he dreads and wishes to avoid:

> It must surely have happened to you while sitting on a train that you passed the place where some great catastrophe has occurred. You know in your heart that you are safe because lightning doesn't strike twice in the same spot. Yet you can't help remembering that not so long ago trains were derailed at this very point, and carloads of people spilled over the embankment. You can't help knowing that here people were thrown out head first, over there bones were crushed, blood flowed, brains were splattered.

Max knew he was bound to meet people in these parts eager to talk about the pogroms. He would have to listen to the wails and groans of those who had lost their near and dear, and he would also be forced to endure the righteous exhortations and malicious remarks of the Gentiles. So the closer they came to Bessarabia, the more he tried to find some way of escape, some way to hide from his own soul. (Howe and Wisse 1979:116–17)

"Two Anti-Semites" thus explores, as "In the City of Killing" does, the ambivalent relationship of an individual Jewish man to the victimization of other Jews. Yet the affinity between the two works stops here. If the story depicts the familiar mechanisms of shame and passing, the poem is decidedly unconcerned with Gentiles, passing or publicly shaming the reader. If the story, in its 'pain-laden, familiar Yiddish comic irony, explores and concurrently mocks a highly recognizable figure: the poorly assimilated Jewish merchant, at once differentiated from and overidentified with his Jewish brethren, the poem presents an entirely new masculine subject: the *tragic* Jewish male figure, silent and devoid of name, language, identity, and personality, a universal "son of man." This imagined figure does not *happen* to be at Kishinev for work; he is commanded *by God* to go there and directly and deliberately bear witness to Jewish suffering, to the worst, most violent suffering.

Max Berlliant, on the other hand, decides to avoid Kishinev altogether. He purchases an anti-Semitic paper, *The Bessarabian*, at a train-station kiosk and hides beneath its pages as the train rolls through the accursed city; soon after, he discovers that the Jewish passenger lodged across from him is doing the exact same thing with the exact same paper. "It's a proven fact that the readers of anti-Semitic newspapers are mostly Jews," the narrator tells us, as the two characters inevitably and hilariously "out" each other as well as the reader. The story, with its central image of the train rolling by, is about the desire for escaping pain and history. As Deleuze and Guattari put it, in minor literature "everything leads to laughter" as it stakes out "the path of escape" (1986:2). Indeed, by deploying the tropes of disguise and twinship, "Two Anti-Semites" is the opposite of tragedy: it is *comedy*, and comedy cannot contain news of death. "In the City of Killing" by contrast is all about the containment and internalization of death; it is through his tragic confrontation with death that the witness is inserted into the history of Jewish suffering and made to stay there.

This last point is key to my argument. For if Sholom Aleichem's protagonist cannot face Kishinev, it is only because he cannot, despite his
best lobster-eating efforts, adequately differentiate himself from its Jewish victims. Kishinev for him is at once too far and too near, and "Two
Anti-Semites" is about the impossibility of fully embracing or fully
shedding an unwanted minority identity.[6] Bialik's witness, by contrast,
is clearly distinguished from the victims of Kishinev; and it is precisely
because of this distinction that he, and by extension, Bialik's readers, can
face the horrors of Kishinev and not be swallowed by them. Max can be
read only under the sign of irony; the witness is anything but ironic. His
imagined presence is grandiose and all-encompassing, marking a budding majority consciousness at the center of its own making.

Political Theology

A major substantial difference between what I have shown to be "minority" and "majority" aesthetic renderings of the Kishinev Pogrom is
the paramount presence of *God* in the Zionist poem. Theological frame-
works are often utilized in the formation narratives of national movements;[7] yet for Zionism, which attempted to form a nation-state out of a
world religion, the relationship between theology and national politics
was particularly tight and fraught with a deep contradiction. "On the
one hand," Hannan Hever writes, "Zionism presented itself as wanting
to found a nation like all nations, and therefore as universal. For that
purpose it erased its primordialism, whose dominant expression was its
religion. On the other hand, it needed religion for its Jewish identity"
(2005:67; translation mine). The solution, Hever claims, was a kind of
perpetual ambivalence around religion, by which religion is simultaneously evoked and erased in secular "national" culture. "In the City of
Killing" seems to enact this ambivalence directly. The poem, as scholars
have long noted, is steeped in theology; it features God as poetic speaker,
relies heavily on the biblical prophetic mode, contains biblical allusions,
and references the Book of Ezekiel directly.[8] Much of early Zionist discourse is closely embedded in the use of such theological allusions and
rhetorical modes, and Bialik in particular was thoroughly versed in the
Bible and other traditional sources. Yet, as we have seen, the poem also
contains a harsh critique of traditional religious life, unleashing a rhetoric of rage at the praying men of Kishinev, asserting the impotence of
God and religious fellowship and utilizing the prophetic mode exactly

for the purpose of buttressing the secular/universal criteria by which the witness is both constructed and judged.

Much of earlier scholarship on "In the City of Killing" downplayed the theological significance of the poem, either reading its theological dimensions as mere aesthetic tools for the poem's political function, or subordinating them to nonreligious categories such as "the sublime."[9] In recent years, scholars have tended to reevaluate these readings, arguing that from the beginning mainstream Zionism was an interpretation of religious myth rather than a strict substitution of a secular national sphere for religion.[10] In a highly convincing recent reading, Hever demonstrates that the supposed secular/universal/national ideals embedded in "In the City of Killing" are in themselves rooted in theological discourse and that the poem, like other early Zionist works, cannot fully contain a clear demarcation between religion and secularism (2005:66–68). Utilizing Jacques Derrida's term "différance," Hever calls the distinction between religion and secularism in Zionist discourse "flexible," arguing that the two stand in a supplementary rather than an oppositional relationship to one another (67).

Much of the poem's ability to maintain this supplementary relationship between secular/national values and a religious framework is hinged, I think, on our understanding of "In the City of Killing" as tragedy. For the God of the Kishinev poem, it is immediately revealed, *is not* the biblical God. Weak, erratic, half-crazed, it is a purposeless God who sends the witness in all directions with contradictory instructions and without aim; a God who speaks directly to witness and victims; a God that walks on earth and feels shame and pain, who *wants* to weep but withholds:

> *And I too in the heart of night will go to the graves,*
> *Stand and look at the bodies and be secretly ashamed*
> *And yet, by my life, says God, if I shed one tear.*
> *And great is the pain and great is the shame.* (Hadari 2000:5)

It is a God who suffers from all the weaknesses, inconsistencies, and follies of humans, a half-human God in dire need of man's help, a *Greek*-like God who asserts his own impotence ("for you have found me in my shame and saw me in the day of my distress"), looks to humans for answers ("And great is the pain and great is the shame. / And which is greater? You tell me, son of man!"), and longs to be rebelled against by survivors of Kishinev:

And why do they plead with me?—Speak to them and they'll thunder!
They'll raise a fist against me and protest their insult
The insult to all the generations from the first unto the last,
And they will shatter heaven or my stool with their fists. (7)

Reaching beyond biblical sources and a biblically inspired divine speaker, Bialik turns to the classical tradition for its vision of pagan gods and to Greek tragedy, where more than anywhere else the divine and the vernacular, the theological and the political intertwine in flexible, supplementary ways.

The incorporation of the qualities associated with the ancient gods into a portrait of the God of the Jews is a radical and bold move. For it is precisely the transcendent and omniscient nature of the Jewish God *as contrasted with the gods of Greek mythology* that has underscored Judaism "nontragic" essence for theorists of tragedy from Hegel to George Steiner. For Hegel, the long tragedy of the Jewish people can arouse neither pity nor terror, only horror, because it is divorced from Greek heritage and is incapable, on account of its utterly transcendent God, of incarnating the divine in the human sphere (de Beistegui and Sparks 2000:13). The basic claim is this: in the power relations between the Jewish God and man, say that between God and Abraham, there could never be a tragic element. God is transcendent and all-empowering; man is an inconsequential servant. Within the framework of such radically asymmetrical power relations there could be no struggle, only blind obedience. Kierkegaard, for this reason, pits the story of Abraham/Isaac against Agamemnon/Iphigenia to prove the latter's tragic essence (2006:76). There are no tragic figures in the Bible, Steiner (1980) likewise claims, not even Job, who as an aristocratic and noble figure hit with inexplicable suffering comes closest.

Yet in the Kishinev poem Bialik reverses this equation entirely. A humanly imperfect, powerless God, commanding neither wrath nor intimidation, endows his witness, his self-created tragic figure, with the capacity for intimidation and wrath. God's power is presented by Bialik as equivalent and utterly dependent on the power or powerlessness of his people—"your God is as poor as you, poor he is in your living and so much more so in your deaths"—while the witness is split off from and raised above all sufferers. A far cry from Abraham's ominous, all-powerful, all-knowing transcendent God, God looks to man for answers: with God's authority half gone, the witness, imagined as we have seen as tragic-hero-in-the-making, assumes divine status. It is exactly the turn to the ethics, aesthetics, and theological world of Greek tragedy that allows the poem to maintain a flexible shifting relationship between its religious identity and secular/political/national aims. And it is exactly the premise of tragedy that allows for a reading of the witness as *citizen,* a figure who at once is a free agent and an object of total control and obedience.

Tragic Responsibility

In their elaborate work on the politics of Greek tragic drama, Jean-Pierre Vernant and Pierre Vidal-Naquet demonstrate how tragedy's simultaneous and normative engagement with divine *and* individual agency enabled Athenian society to transition into democracy and early notions of citizenship (1988:78–79). Concurrent with the emergence of tragedy in sixth-century Athens, democracy, they claim, demanded that individuals act and be viewed as morally responsible agents; but the ancient understanding of individuals as bearers of collective sin and playthings of the gods died hard. "Oh, suffering dreadful to behold . . . what madness has struck you . . . what daimon has crowned your destiny that was the work of an evil daimon?" the chorus lamented as a blinded Oedipus entered the stage; Oedipus, Vernant and Vidal-Naquet claim, may have chosen to mutilate his own eyes but this self-sacrifice, like all the events that led to it, were understood by the Greeks as dictated from above. In tragedy, tensions between the civic and the divine world views were played out, amalgamated, and resolved. And it was there, in the "twilight zone between politics and myth, civic and religious alliance, ethical autonomy and a still cogent sense of the numinous," that "a tragic sense of responsibility" first emerged: a vision of an autonomous individual who nevertheless is unfree and bound to a collective and its mythic past (1988:4).

This model of tragic responsibility provided a formula well suited for the aim of Zionist nation building. The tragic framework allowed for the seamless amalgamation of politics and religion and masked real differences between Zionists regarding questions of religion and state. It also allowed early Zionist culture to place at its center an image of a tragic hero who looms larger and brighter than "the people" and yet is bound to them and their God with invisible shackles, who at once is a morally responsible agent and a subject of total control. For Bialik too, and for subsequent Hebrew writers whose works we will approach in the coming chapters, tragedy evolved around an image of a tragic male figure, autonomous yet eternally bound in fated, inexplicable ways to God and to his "nation."

Thus, though he is construed in an antithetical, ambivalent, and even hostile relationship to the mass of Jewish victims, and though he is to be understood as superior to them, the tragic witness of "In the City of Killing" is also a kinsman, eternally and unequivocally bound to his people and poised to sacrifice himself on their behalf. "Your people," "your nation," "pure daughters of your race": the witness's affiliation with the nation is asserted again and again. Commanded to drink from their "poison cup" and bear it within him "for all the days of [his] life," he is anointed with *responsibility*, the responsibility of a citizen: "Do not go out from among them!" Replacing Sholom Aleichem's discourse of shame and passing with the discourse of citizenship and *tragic responsibility*, Bialik creates a tragic figure that must not only bear witness but sacrifice itself in the name of the nation and its God.

Guilt and Sacrifice

The tragic narrative of "In the City of Killing" that I have thus far delineated goes something like this: having sinned and deserted their land and political existence, the Jewish people are doomed to a ghostly life and repeated violations; at last, as these violations have reached a level of unprecedented horror, a male tragic figure appears who in silence is made to comprehend the depth of the calamity, assume tragic responsibility for the nation, and prepare for heroic sacrifice. Guilt, as Jaspers writes in *Tragedy Is Not Enough*, is a key component in the making of such a tragic hero:

> Tragedy shows man as he is transformed at the edge of doom. Like Cassandra, the tragic hero comprehends the tragic atmosphere. Through his questions he relates himself to history. In struggle he becomes aware of that power for which he stands, that power which is not yet everything. He experiences his guilt and puts questions to it. He asks for the nature of truth and in full consciousness acts out the meaning of victory and defeat. (1953:75–76)

If "Two Anti-Semites," as we have seen, is about the protagonist's desire to escape his guilt, "In the City of Killing" establishes the witness's guilt directly and traces a path for atonement. God *demands* of the witness to experience the authentic guilt that the people of Kishinev lack:

> *And see, oh see: while they fester in pain*
> *all succumb to weeping, raise a dirge with their wails*
> *and already they're drumming on their breasts and telling of their guilt*
> *saying: "We're guilty, we're traitors"—and their hearts don't believe*
>   *their mouths.*
> *Can a shattered vessel sin and shards of clay be accused?* (6–7)

Survivors of Kishinev—embodying the ailing nation at large—not only lack comprehension: they are not worthy of guilty self-sacrifice and atonement. "Can a shattered vessel sin and shards of clay be accused?": even as they stand before God on the Day of Judgment, they perform empty gestures of guilt; having been broken already, they cannot experience authentic guilt nor be held accountable for the outrageousness of the violence or the dire state of the nation. They are the "lost" nation, the sickly people whom Pinsker had diagnosed with the loss of the will to live. Only the tragic witness alone is bestowed with pain, shame, and guilt and is therefore worthy of sacrifice:

> *and you will know that it's time to low like an ox tied to the altar—*
> *and I will toughen your heart and no sigh will come.*
> *Here are the calves slaughtered, here they lie all—*
> *and if there are prices to pay for their deaths—tell me, how will they be*
>   *paid?* (5)

Like an ox tied to the altar: the image of the ox sacrificed for the calves, strength bound and sacrificed for weakness, is both tragic and arresting. The witness must *himself* become the sacrificial figure, the scapegoat for the community's sins, the *first* to seek atonement. Yes, he is distinct from the nation of sufferers, but he is also their noblest representative and must account for them: "And I will take you . . . to your brothers who survived the massacre / and you will hear there the cry of their pain and be swept up in their tears." The tragic witness is the one and the only one who can answer his "brothers'" needs, amend their misdeeds, and take vengeance for God's humiliation all at once. "If there are prices to pay for their deaths—tell me, how will they be paid?" God asks of the witness; it is a rhetorical question, of course, for both collector and debtor are embodied in the tragic figure himself. It is a structure of male sacrifice that will dominate Zionist and Israeli culture for a long time to come.

Judaism/Hellenism

We have seen then that much of the appeal, much of the uneasy magnetism of Bialik's poem was drawn exactly from the unholy mixture of biblical and Greek references through which it is constructed—the language of prophecy, the flawed and half-human Jewish God dressed in pagan garb, the sensational bloody narrative, the tragic male figure— from the unconscious crossing and recrossing of the bar that separates Jewish and Hellenic culture. No small matter, if we consider a history as well as a long-standing tradition that positions Judaism and Hellenism in adversarial relations.

The turn to tragedy, however, did not appear in the world of Hebrew letters in a void; much of early Zionist culture, in line with fin-de-siècle European culture at large, flirts with imagery of the ancient Greek world. "Long before the Hellenizing Jews in Palestine tried to substitute Greek culture for Judaism, the Jews in Egypt had come into close contact with the Greek way of life and thought," writes even the conservative Ahad Ha'am in his influential essay on "Imitation and Assimilation" (1894/1970:72). And the popular Hebrew poet Saul Tschernichowsky, known as "the most Hellenic" of modern Hebrew writers, locates one of the first and most dramatic displays of idealized Jewish masculinity in the figure of the god Apollo. "Le-nokhakh pesel Apollo" ("Before a Statue of Apollo"), a celebration of vitality, life, action, beauty, and youth, was published in Hebrew in 1899 and begins thus:

> *I come to you, forgotten God of all ages,*
> *god of ancient times and other days,*
> *ruling the tempests of vigorous men,*
> *the breakers of their strength in youth's plenty!*
> *God of a generation of mighty ones and giants,*
> *conquering with their strength the bounds of Olympus,*
> *an abode for their heroes, and adorning with garlands*
> *of laurel-leaf the pride of their foreheads—*
> *masters of their idols and like unto them,*
> *adding to the councils of the world's rulers;*
> *a generation of god on earth, drunk*

with the plenty of life, and estranged
from a sick people and tribe of sufferers.
Fresh youth-god, magnificent, full beautiful,
subduer of the sun and life's hidden truths (translation by Sholom J.
Kahn; published in Silberschlag [1968:97–98])

Tschernichowsky is believed to have composed "Before the Statue of
Apollo" following a visit to Greece; yet it is also possible to locate the
precursor to Tschernichowsky's cultural investment in the Greek male
figure in the contemporaneous works of Friedrich Nietzsche, who had
a notable enabling effect on early Zionist thinkers.[11] Nietzsche, whose
writings were widely circulated among Zionists, mobilizes a sensual language that declares as its aim the liberation of masculinist Dionysian
energy from centuries of effeminized Christian sensibility. Zionism in
turn develops a parallel discourse of liberation, through which the Jewish
masculine body, paralyzed by centuries of repressive Jewish law (including the prohibition on making symbols) is released, unbound, and re-
made through an amalgamation of Greek and biblical imagery. Zionism,
after all, emerged in the last decades of the nineteenth century, when
Hellenic culture loomed large in the European imagination. Melville,
Wilde, Stoker, Nietzsche, Freud: for many late nineteenth-century writers, and the Hebrew writers are no exception, Hellenic culture served as
the philosophical backdrop but also, as Sedgwick (1990:131) has shown,
as a platform and a license for the adoration of the vital, unbound male
figure: "Here he comes; and, by Jove—lugging along his chest—Apollo
with his portmanteau!" so exclaims an admiring spectator of Melville's
Billy Budd. Tschernichowsky's ecstatic love song to the male God—"Fresh
youth-god, magnificent, full beautiful"—evokes exactly those same sentiments: an admiration of male body and strength untainted by centuries of Jewish/Christian experience and suffering.

Trouble is, of course, that as the nineteenth century turns into the
twentieth, there is plenty of suffering in store for Russian Jews like Tschernichowsky, Berdyczewski, and Bialik: poverty, expulsions, anti-Semitic
laws, and then Kishinev. If just five years earlier, "Before the Statue of
Apollo" could inaugurate a discourse of masculinity and a male figure
that stands apart from the "sick people and tribe of sufferers" and re-
presses the effects of suffering from its own self-representation, Kishinev
had rendered this discourse and this figure radically inadequate and naive. And so in its stead, Bialik develops the *discourse of tragedy,* organi-

cally bringing fin-de-siècle Hellenic imagery into the Jewish fold and creating a sensibility and an aesthetic of suffering that is still, I think, with us today.

Tragic Masculinity

For nearly a decade now, as we indicated in our analysis of Herzl, scholars have understood early Zionist masculinist culture through the lens of colonial mimicry. Boyarin, who was the first to suggest this paradigm, argues that Zionism was and still is modeling itself on a "mimesis of gentile patterns of honor," on an internalization of the "honorable, vengeful, violent . . . ideal Aryan male" (1997:277). This framework, as I hope my reading has demonstrated, is far too limited in scope. For as we have seen, "In the City of Killing"—perhaps the most significant cultural artifact produced by early Zionist culture—presents a model of Jewish manhood that is neither active, violent, nor directly vengeful; it suggests a figure primed for action yet also strangely arrested, passive yet intensely committed. Silent and inarticulate, led blindly by God, tied to the destiny of its nation and primed for sacrifice: more than the image of the autonomous male subject violently defending his nation's honor, the witness becomes the representation of tragic fate and self-sacrifice as the poem ends not with a call for vengeance but with the witness's futile lonely scream in the desert.

The ambivalent and deeply pessimistic image of the tragic male figure holds, I think, tremendous political significance and the kind of grip on the public imagination that an explicitly violent "Aryan" masculine image could never hold (which is why a story like Berdyczewski's "Red Heifer" could never rival the popular appeal of Bialik's Kishinev poem). This figure is important, indeed crucial, to the production and re-production of feelings of national invigoration and renewal in early Zionist and later Israeli culture. True, in its supposed message of defeatism and determinism ("the sun rose, rye bloomed, and the slaughterer slaughtered") tragedy appears as the form most opposed to social renewal and change; yet it is precisely tragedy's deep pessimism that, as Williams asserts, is most indicative of its revolutionary potential (2006:127). The desert that seals the tragic fate of Bialik's witness-turned-tragic-figure is not only a place of supreme loneliness and desolation, a place outside civilization, a place where all meaning is lost; it is also the road to the promised land after the Exodus from Egypt, the place where Oedipus flees to, but also where he is found and finds his true identity: the place where everything can begin once more. "Whether with joy or in fear, it doesn't matter," Deleuze writes: dreaming of a "desert island" is "dreaming of pulling away, of being already separate, far from any continent, of being lost and alone—or it is dreaming of starting from scratch, recreating, beginning anew . . . The idea of a second origin gives the deserted island its whole meaning, the survival of a sacred place in a world that is slow to re-begin" (2004: 10, 14). It is in the witness's confrontation with "the worst," with the loss of reality as he knows it, that a tentative new world whose essence is still unknown is cautiously suggested by the poem.

Thus, despite its graphic imagery and the horrific historical circumstances out of which it was born, "In the City of Killing" seems to have had a regenerative effect on both readers and the poet himself, who while still at Kishinev composed and published a lighthearted poem titled "With the Sun." The poem consolidated the contentious and divided world of European Jewry around a tragic myth of Jewish history and suffering; it offered a model of witnessing and response that was both steeped in the glamorous aura of tragedy and that spoke to readers' modern sensibilities; it allowed for readers to meet the witness and each other on the common ground of trauma, impasse, and the ultimate dissolution of meaning, from which, the poem implicitly suggests, a new beginning is possible. "The cornerstone of a new order has to be, like Oedipus at Colonus, the reviled and unclean . . . It is this inhospitable terrain, this kingdom whose citizens share only the fact that they are lost to themselves, which we hold most deeply in common," Eagleton (2003:164–65) writes of the community-building effect of tragedy. Indeed, the witness's solitary tragic stance in the face of Kishinev was written precisely to be heard and emulated by thousands, and by all accounts it was. "Through this poem," reported the influential literary critic Yosef Klausner, "came a thorough and major change in the Jewish people's mood: the slouching Israel had become erect, as if iron had been cast into the veins of the elderly nation."[12] No need for further unpacking of phallic imagery here, I think. "In the City of Killing" had offered readers, to borrow Williams's efficacious phrase, a new "structure of feeling."

CHAPTER 7

"Nietzsche: I Want to Become One"

Knowledge kills action, action requires the veil of illusion—it is this lesson that Hamlet teaches.

—FRIEDRICH NIETZSCHE, *THE BIRTH OF TRAGEDY*

"Nietzsche: I want to become one."

—MICAH JOSEF BERDYCZEWSKI, UNDATED
LETTER WRITTEN SOMETIME IN THE 1890S

The following is, more or less, a staple biography of young male Zionists of Berdyczewski's generation and class: A turn-of-the-century Hebrew writer, he is born in 1865 in Miedzyborz, Poland, a small town and cradle of Jewish Hasidism, and becomes a brilliant young Talmudic scholar. At seventeen he begins to stray: a taste for "profane" books resulting in outing, shaming, and expulsion from the Yeshiva, as well as from a marriage and the comforts of a wealthy father-in-law's home. From there follow a series of increasingly larger cities: First, Volozhin, where Berdyczewski studies at a more progressive Yeshiva, a hotbed of Zionist activity. Then, Odessa, where he becomes acquainted with Ahad Ha'am and other Zionist "free-thinkers." Third stop: Breslau, where he studies philosophy at a local university, reading Heine, Tolstoy, Dostoyevsky, Balzac, Zola, Rousseau, Kant, and Schopenhauer. Fourth stop: Berlin, where the twenty-eight-year-old Berdyczewski falls hard for the works of Friedrich Nietzsche. Continuing to his fifth stop, the University of Bern in Switzerland, he completes a dissertation "On the Relationship Between Ethics and Aesthetics" and is awarded a doctorate in philosophy in 1896. The dissertation is a detailed extrapolation of Nietzsche's *Birth of Tragedy*, though Nietzsche, who was snubbed by Berdyczewski's mentor, is rarely mentioned in this work by name. Initially dabbling in German prose, Berdyczewski soon becomes a Hebrew writer and a Zionist, moving between Berlin, Odessa, and Weimar, where among other adventures he visits the housebound Nietzsche and his sister Elisabeth (Golomb 2004:74–76).

Minus the doctorate, it was the *standard* profile of young Eastern European Hebrew writers and Zionists (Miron 1987a; Brinker 2002:131–34). The last third of the nineteenth century was a period of extreme mobility and unrest for European Jews, more than half of whom were living throughout the Russian Empire. Tens and later hundreds of thousands of them—mostly young men—were abandoning the learning institutions of Orthodox Judaism, undergoing a process of secularization and dreaming of a European education. A European education was hard to come by, particularly when one did not read, as these men did not, any non-Jewish European language and one no longer believed, as these men did not, in the possibility of impending assimilation. The pogroms of 1881–82 and the tepid government response in their wake were widely considered proof that achieving equal rights in Russia in the foreseeable future was unrealistic. The rapid process of secularization, on the other hand, created for Eastern European Jews acute dilemmas of personal and collective identity. Throughout the Russian Empire, as the literary historian Menachem Brinker writes, "New trends of thought were discussed to improve the situation of Jews as individuals and as a group." In contrast to the earlier "Jewish Enlightenment" period, "these solutions no longer included the Europeanization of Jews":

> Different movements were operating for the organized immigration to the United States, for cultural autonomy for Jews in the nations in which they resided, for enlistment in the Russian socialist movement, and finally for gradual immigration to *Eretz Yisrael* and the erection of a new Jewish center.
>
> The fermenting Jewish youth wrangled between these options. Yet even those youngsters who were still living a partial Jewish life had lost faith in the ability of the rabbinical authorities to lead them. According to the model set by the educated Russian youth—though for utterly different reasons—the young began to look to writers and literary intellectuals for spiritual guidance. (2002:132; translation mine)

Nietzsche, Schopenhauer, Dostoyevsky—these were the new scriptures for the young East European Jews who were actually able to read them in Russian or German. The rest—the vast majority, that is—would absorb them indirectly, through translations, citations, or their conscious/

unconscious internalization in Hebrew literature and essays. Why Hebrew? Because Hebrew and Yiddish were for many of these young men the *only* languages in which they were literate. "In the absence of a gymnasium or Russian or German university education," Brinker writes, "the only language available to these young men in their autodidactic onslaught on European belles lettres, history and science was the Hebrew language, which they knew from their religious training." Hebrew thus became the mediating language between European culture and these increasingly secularizing young men (Brinker 2002:131), who became readers and writers of a host of new Hebrew books and journals. The number of readers who purchased and read these works—including a Hebrew language daily—multiplied thirtyfold from the beginning of the nineteenth century. And the Hebrew writers of the day—Smolenskin, Lilienblum, Frishman, Ahad Ha'am, Berdyczewski, and Brenner—became the spiritual and intellectual beacons of the day (Brinker 2002:132–33).

This renaissance in Hebrew literature was not directly synonymous with the Zionist movement; nonetheless, it is in works of late nineteenth-century Hebrew writers that what can be called a national consciousness first emerges. In varying degrees of self-consciousness, Hebrew works of this period ended up representing, creating, and consolidating for early Zionism what Lauren Berlant has called "national fantasies": images, signs, ideas, and theories that organize the consciousness of individuals and instill in them political feelings linking them to the "nation" and to one another (Berlant 1991:57). What had been for some writers and readers an attempt to enter European culture via the mediation of Hebrew resulted in the modernization and expansion of the Hebrew language and the beginning of a Jewish national culture.

No European writer penetrated this Hebrew cultural scene as deeply and broadly as Nietzsche. No other European writer played a more prominent role in its emergent "national fantasies," appearing (even as a fictional character) in slogans, essays, translations, polemics, and prose works. In what follows I trace not the entire spectrum of Nietzsche's influence on Zionist culture—a subject long treated in countless articles and books[1]—but a single aspect of Nietzsche's oeuvre that was deeply internalized by early Zionist consciousness and has remained, I think, a powerful category ever since: *the idea of the tragic.*

Nietzsche and the Zionists?!

It is, of course, a strange alliance, on both sides. Even without considering Nietzsche's prominence in Nazi ideology, Nietzsche's stance on Jews and Judaism has been a subject of debate for quite a while now.[2] Yet in the entire oeuvre of fin-de-siècle Hebrew works that directly or indirectly evoke Nietzsche's ideas, there is no mention or assessment, or for that matter puzzlement over Nietzsche's evocation of the "Jews" in *Genealogy of Morals* and elsewhere. With the exception of a handful of articles written in the 1930s and 1940s—mostly devoted to "proving" Nazi misuse of Nietzsche's works—there is no such mention or assessment or puzzlement in the scholarly works evaluating Nietzsche's impact on Zionism. There is, in short, no puzzlement over early Zionists' lack of puzzlement. Some early Zionists (Ahad Ha'am, Hayyim Nahman Bialik) frowned at the image of the Blond Beast, yet nonetheless absorbed Nietzsche's images and ideas into their own writings. Nietzsche, it seems, excited early Zionist writers and critics so much that they could not intuit his works' elastic potential for fascist manipulation. They could not intuit it because Nietzsche's works spoke intimately to their half-articulated (and sometimes quasi-fascistic) desires: their critique (to put it mildly) of institutionalized religion, their longing for the aesthetic life, their thirst for power and transformation, their discourse on masculinity that was heavily imbued with Nietzschean language.

The extent to which early Zionists, most notably Berdyczewski, were *real* Nietzscheans and the depth and length of Nietzsche's impact on them has been debated by scholars for over a century. To some, the marriage of Nietzsche and nationalism made by early Zionists could not be stranger—"it's hard to imagine an idea more disgusting for Nietzsche," Brinker writes[3]—except, of course, that Nietzsche's potential uses for nationalist agendas have by now been aptly proven. But modern Hebrew writers did not exactly dip into the well of Nietzsche's works for images of racial superiority—that would have required a highly complex misreading in the case of the Jews—it was rather that their concerns were quite compatible with Nietzsche's. Most prominently it was "the death of God," the recognition that for the educated classes of the late nineteenth century, Western religion was no longer the source of all being and moral value. Nietzsche deemed the death of God "the greatest event in history," and through the project that began with *The Birth of Tragedy* sought to give Europeans an analysis of the cultural underpinnings of their world, one that could potentially culminate with a "newly redeemed innocence of becoming" (Allison 2001:viii). Though ancient Greek culture had long been established as the basis of Western Christian civilization, Nietzsche sought to "uncover" and make use of *its* aesthetic and historical genealogy, particularly through an analysis of the cultural dynamics and worldview that enabled classical Greek tragic drama. The age of tragedy was long gone—its decline had already begun, according to Nietzsche, after the Greek victory in the Persian wars; yet the tragic model could potentially be revived once more at the specific historical junction of the late nineteenth century. Nietzsche had seen in the works of Wagner such a possibility for the "rebirth of tragedy," though he later bitterly renounced them (Allison 2001:16).

Modern Hebrew writers—each and every one of them having gone through some process of secularization and doubt—experienced the "death of God" hardly as a pan-European phenomenon but as a lived crisis. The historical genealogy that they were considering, out of which they emerged and against which they rebelled, was not, of course, Nietzsche's peculiar version of Judeo-Christian history but the rabbinical tradition. Yet the historical narrative told by these writers reads quite like Nietzsche's version of Western history at large: the story of how a "civilized" religion, eclipsing the ancient Greek-Hebrew world, had eradicated the fundamental force of "life" in individuals and groups. In the preface to the 1886 edition of *The Birth of Tragedy*, titled "An Attempt at Self-Criticism," Nietzsche famously launches his critique of Christianity thus:

> Behind the [Christian] mode of thought and valuation, which must be hostile to art if it is at all genuine, I never fail to sense *hostility to life*—a furious, vengeful antipathy to life itself . . . Christianity was from the beginning, essentially and fundamentally, life's nausea and disgust with life, merely concealed behind, masked by, dressed up as, faith in "another" or "better" life . . . For, confronted with morality, life *must* be continually in the wrong because life is essentially amoral—and eventually, crushed by the weight of contempt and the eternal No, life *must* then be felt to be unworthy of desire and altogether worthless. (1886/1995:23)

Against this Christian worldview Nietzsche juxtaposes classical Greek culture, which in its celebration of the artist-god Dionysus affirmed life in an entirely antimoral way. Dionysus, as contrasted both with Apollo (the embodiment of form, beauty, order, and individuation) and Socrates (rationalism and intellectualism), represented the instinctual elements in human expression: the sometimes violent drives of intense emotion, sensuality, intoxication, frenzy, madness, and collective outbursts of ecstatic celebration. In the ancient world Dionysus was celebrated in "festivals of extravagant sexual licentiousness" where cruelty and sensuality were intertwined (Nietzsche 1995:23). In later periods, the Greeks managed to infuse Dionysian culture with a dose of Apollonian restraint and transform it into tragic art, which Nietzsche considers the noblest achievement of Greek culture and a testimony to its "extraordinary health." Though tragedy is embedded in the "duality" of Apollo and Dionysus, Nietzsche often refers to it as "the Dionysian art": its power derived exactly from its sanctioning of violence and immorality as integral to human life (60). In *The Birth of Tragedy*, Nietzsche traces both the birth and the death of tragedy, drawing obvious parallels between the decline of the tragic age and that of European culture at the late nineteenth century. "A tremendous hope speaks of this essay *The Birth of Tragedy*,"[4] he writes in 1888, lashing out against the pessimism of neo-romantic writers like Schopenhauer and, as David Allison notes, never ceasing "to explore the resources needed for a new age of human achievement" (2001:27).

Late nineteenth-century Hebrew writers developed a discourse and a genealogy parallel to Nietzsche's, but one that traced its roots to ancient biblical culture: at the foundation of what had come to be regarded as repressive, book-centered, antilife rabbinical Jewish tradition was a living, vibrant culture that could potentially be reclaimed for the spiritual and physical healing of late nineteenth-century Jews and Judaism. Nietzsche gave modern Hebrew writers an intellectual framework, a usable historical/genealogical analysis, and *a language*, not only *his* words and sentences (which they cited profusely, with or without referencing the source) but a literary boldness: the use of corporeal metaphors, the evocation of sensual imagery, a freewheeling attitude toward evidence, a license to lash out. "The Jewish nation is a mummified body without moisture and feeling senses," writes the turn-of-the-century critic David Frishman.[5] "We must unlock the vital powers of the nation and let loose its fettered instincts . . . Jews must free themselves from an 'inner ghetto—the ghetto of unfree spirituality,' to come loose from the compulsion of a tradition divested of sensuality . . . New Jewish view of life should be suffused with something profound and soulful, with a new power, a new beauty," cries Martin Buber.[6] "Oh, The Book," Frishman again: "How miserable has it made us? It took our heart and gave us the mind, took the feeling and gave us logic; it took away the power todream and bid us to count and calculate; the power of the imagination, the desire to live, it took away our freedom from us and in their stead it gave us the Word" (quoted in Parush 1992:33; my translation).

And above all, Berdyczewski:

> I recall from the teaching of our sages: Whoever walks by the way and interrupts his study to remark: "How fine is that field—forfeits his life!"
>
> Yet I assert that then alone will Judah and Israel be saved, when another teaching is given to us, namely: Whoever walks by the way and sees a fine tree and a fine field and a fine sky and leaves them to think on other thoughts—that man is like one who forfeits his life! Give us back our fine trees and fine fields! Give us back the Universe![7]

Even the writings of the positivist Zionist thinker Ahad Ha'am, who repeatedly challenged Berdyczewski's Nietzscheanism and its relevance for Zionist culture, bear the imprint of Nietzschean language: evocations of sickness and health, corporeal metaphors, images of subjugation and power. A "powerful national self," he writes, is one whose metabolism is strong enough to incorporate appropriate foreign elements into its core identity, while discarding those elements that are indigestible: "The plastic power of a man, a people, a culture . . . is determined by the capacity to develop out of oneself in one's way, to transform and incorporate into oneself what is past and foreign . . . it adopts out of foreign material everything that can be useful to it and can be incorporated as an integral part of itself; everything else is discarded." Nietzsche, of course, posits a similar metaphor of psychic health at the beginning of Essay 2 of *The Genealogy of Morals:* "To remain undisturbed by the noise and struggle of our underworld of utility organs working with and against each other; a little quietness, a little *tabula rasa*"; for Nietzsche, as for Ahad Ha'am, forgetting or discarding are not *vita inertia* but an active, positive force of repression that, using a nutrition metaphor, prevents one from eating too much while digesting. Ahad Ha'am blames Berdyczewski for exactly this: for importing Nietzsche whole and undigested into Hebrew culture and for corrupting the impressionable, searching Jewish youth.[8] Yet in allowing himself to incorporate, loosely and half-consciously, portions of Nietzsche's writings into his own elegant essays, and to "forget" that he had done so, Ahad Ha'am himself adopts Nietzsche's values and ideas.

We can see then how deeply Nietzsche reaches into Zionist culture, if he informs even the writings of the most avid self-proclaimed anti-

Nietzschean positivist. Not only had Nietzsche affected Zionist thought profoundly, but his impact was profound precisely because Zionist thinkers and Nietzsche alike were fed by similar historical/intellectual currents. In the wake of the final collapse of the Enlightenment ideal of a "common humanity"—a collapse whose repercussions were felt most acutely and painfully by European Jews—would come, as Terry Eagleton writes,

> Schopenhauer, for whom the malignant will stirs in our most casual gestures; Marx, for whom death-dealing conflicts are masked by Apollonian consensus of bourgeois democracy; Nietzsche, who detects a repressed history of blood and horror in the fashioning of civilization itself; Freud, who likewise sees culture as the fruit of barbarism and for whom we are all potential monsters, as the criminal features of Oedipus can be traced in the blissful countenance of an infant. (2003:96)

And might we add Zionism, whose seemingly optimistic message of national renewal is supposedly at odds with Schopenhauer and Nietzsche but whose project is historically concurrent with and deeply affected by them. Works of late nineteenth-century Hebrew writers—considered today as the origin of the modern Zionist canon—were steeped in Schopenhauerian/Nietzschean/Freudian antirationalist language and the discourse of instincts, drives, and emotions. A political response to the doomed hopes of Jewish assimilation and the ideals of the "Jewish Enlightenment," early Zionist discourse, like Nietzsche's writings, was mired in the critique of reason.

And it is against this backdrop that we should assess the emergence of the aesthetics of tragedy in Zionist culture.

A Bloody Red Heifer

Berdyczewski was by far the most "serious" Nietzschean among the modern Hebrew writers, engaging with his writings in many essays and polemics. In what follows, however, I propose to look at Nietzsche's impact on Berdyczewski's *fiction*, a topic that has received relatively little scholarly attention.

Berdyczewski's "Red Heifer" (1906) is a short story about a group of drunken common (i.e., nonritualistic) butchers who abduct, subdue, kill, dismember, and devour an extraordinary red heifer owned by a fellow townsman: "a red Dutch heifer, of such beauty and health and roundness of body as were never seen in *Dashia* [the town where the story takes place] before." It is perhaps the first (and only) depiction of an orgiastic Dionysian state in the Hebrew language.

> At midnight the prized heifer is stolen from its owner's compound and violently dragged to a nearby house where:
>
> Seven people greet it in the cellar, wearing fur jackets, armed like peasants, their faces already on fire. They have already drunk a few glasses, and the small candles burning in the darkness make the cellar appear like the underworld. They begin to turn and pat the cow.
>
> All of a sudden, a powerful butcher rises and tries to push the cow to the ground, but her legs are strong as steel. His friends come to help him and they fiercely wrestle with the beast. She falls to the ground; her eyes are filled with fury. She tries to strike a man, but drives her head into a brick wall; the entire cellar trembles. A big, strong butcher crawls beneath her body and ties her back legs with a thick rope. Another does the same with her front legs. The rest pile themselves on top of the cow, and finally push her to the ground. She tumbles and lets out a strong cry, attempting to force the ropes apart. Her attackers hold her down with a vengeance, which they did not even know had been inside them. Outside the rain begins to pour on the cellar roof. The wind is soaring, and the exasperated butchers shed large drops of sweat. They signal to each other, remove their clothes, roll the sleeves of their undergarments above the elbow, and feel prepared, as if the time of a great battle has arrived. What has come over them? *A force that was pent up inside them needs release.*
>
> One of the butchers, a former ritual slaughterer [who for various violations was now forbidden to practice his trade], stands apart quietly, sharpening his old knife, and testing the edge of the blade with a fingernail. Once again, the butchers hold the cow, some grabbing her front and some her back legs. Two of them, the bravest, pull her head backward. And here the butcher-slaughterer raises his blade and passes it across the smooth neck. The animal lets out an earth-shaking, horrible scream, and a stream of blood erupts. A thick current of blood, visible through the dim light, begins pouring. And

the blood floods and washes the ceiling and the walls and the floor and people's trousers, hands and faces. With her remaining strength, the heifer struggles, then trembles; the ground around her becomes a river of blood. The murderers then carry her to the side, where an hour later she takes her last breath and dies. Man has triumphed over beast!

One of the butchers stabs the heifer's belly. Others begin to rip her skin off. They do this with restrained force and a passionate resolve that they have never felt before.

Flayed, the animal is dismembered, her head and legs detached from her body. One of the butchers cannot restrain himself, and above some burning coals of a pit flattens the cow's liver, which is then eaten unsalted and with gluttonous pleasure, everyone passionately licking their fingers. A large bottle of wine stands in the middle of the room, and they drink and eat with great enthusiasm. Like the priests of the temple in ancient times, these people are now partitioning the sacrificial animal before the altar. This has not taken place, however, in *Beth El* or in *Dan,* but in the Jewish town of *Dashia;* not before the ten tribes were exiled, not in the northern Israelite kingdom, but in the year five thousand six hundred and forty five of the creation. (1995:88)[9]

An odd and disturbing short story, "Red Heifer" has no climactic plot development, no named characters, no dialogue, no moral lesson. The story is told by an unnamed, cautious first-person narrator—"I, the narrator, was not there and did not witness things with my own eyes, but I have heard them from credible persons"—who prefaces the action with multiple yet evasive details about the butchers' craft, the townspeople, and the perfection of the beloved red heifer. Though the narrator offers various excuses and meager defenses, he provides no sound explanation for the butcher's actions. Except, that is, for the gluttonous, violent, intoxicated pleasure, which is reportedly embedded in the act itself. The reader is never told whether the butchers planned or repented their actions, and their punishment is relayed in one vague sentence. The story's focus is on the violent action itself, and that is its startlingly revolutionary statement.

Down to the author's very choice of a mutilated cow—an animal believed to have often been mutilated at Dionysian orgies—"Red Heifer" is modeled precisely after Nietzsche's portrayal of Dionysian festivals, those "awesome, joyful, and occasionally fear-inspiring expenditures of energy and eroticism that transgress the general rules, norms and codes of individual and social existence" (Allison 2001:19). In _The Birth of Tragedy_, Nietzsche elaborates at great length on what he read as the violent, ecstatic rituals of Dionysus's worshipers. "In nearly every case," he writes,

> these festivals centered on extravagant sexual licentiousness, whose waves overwhelmed all family life and its venerable traditions; the most savage natural instincts were unleashed, including even that horrible mixture of sensuality and cruelty which has always seemed to me to be the real "witches brew." (_The Birth of Tragedy_ Sec. 2, 39)

Berdyczewski, however, traces the roots of the violent, ecstatic cruelty of the butchers to biblical rather than pagan culture, as the story's title, and its very action, refer to a sacrificial ritual described in Numbers 19:

> And the Lord spake unto Moses and unto Aaron, saying,
>
> This _is_ the ordinance of the law which the LORD hath commanded, saying, Speak unto the children of Israel, that they bring thee a red heifer without a spot, wherein _is_ no blemish, _and_ upon which never came yoke.
>
> And ye shall give her unto Eleazar the priest, that he may bring her forth without the camp, and _one_ shall slay her before his face:
>
> And Eleazar the priest shall take of her blood with his finger, and sprinkle of her blood directly before the tabernacle of the congregation seven times:
>
> And _one_ shall burn the heifer in his sight; her skin, and her flesh, and her blood, with her dung, shall he burn:
>
> . . .
>
> And a man _that is_ clean shall gather up the ashes of the heifer, and lay _them_ up without the camp in a clean place, and it shall be kept for the congregation of the children of Israel for a water of separation: it _is_ a purification for sin.

"Red Heifer" thus represents a narrative parallel to the one told in _The Birth of Tragedy_, but one that taps into the sacrificial elements of the biblical instead of the Greek past. The narrator, nonetheless, emphatically stresses its setting in the present ("this has not taken place, however, in *Beth El* or in *Dan,* but in the Jewish town of *Dashia;* not before the ten tribes were exiled, not in the northern Israelite kingdom, but in the year five thousand six hundred and forty five of the creation"). The days of bloody ritual slaughters and sacrifices, the story suggests, are long gone, yet their traces are relived in the sudden and inexplicable burst of violence of a group of Jewish butchers, one of whom, the narrator tells us, has lost his license as a ritualistic slaughterer and all of whom indulge often in petty crimes and thefts. The ritual slaughter, understood under the sign of atonement for the sins of Israel against their God, is turned in Berdyczewski's story into a tale of rebellion against institutional religion and a crime with no causality or meaning. It is in fact a travesty—an unholy and unclean imitation of the sacred ritual, and as such a willful disobedience. And it is the offering of a disobedient *text* (the story), as nobody was sacrificing real heifers in either Halakhic or Dionysian modality, to flout the ritual text in Numbers 19. The mere linguistic description of the wild slaughter is culturally a transgressive rebellion equal to the deed.[10]

The narrator emphasizes the offense against Jewish law—the laws of *kashrut* (dietary law), ritual slaughtering, and theft—as well as against the norms and conventions of the Jewish town ("from the day of its foundation, *Dashia* did not experience such an onerous day"). Yet he also complains about the burden of rabbinical Jewish law ("Just think of the meat that's lost through the ritual slaughtering, whether it is pronounced un-kosher on the spot, or at a later stage by the ritual slaughterer, or whether it is un-kosher because of a lung adhesion, or because of one of the other eighteen rules of uncleanliness . . . People want to live . . ."), which, he suggests, maintains communal order at the expense of the repression of "life." Since the destruction of the Temple in Jerusalem, it should be noted, the *study* of the ritual that was no longer performed was the direct and obligatory sacrificial substitute for the ritual itself. Yet in contrast to Talmudic study, the sacrificial ritual of the ancient Temple in Jerusalem, like Greek tragedies, had a performative function, simultaneously curbing *and* providing a communal outlet for violence. And it is this regulatory function of ritually controlled violence, which had become mummified and bound into language in the obligatory practice of Talmudic study, that Berdyczewski, like Nietzsche, both celebrates and mourns.

Similarly to Nietzsche, Berdyczewski also acknowledges that the Dionysian aspect of human experience is Janus-faced. He displays, on the one hand, the deadly effects of uncurbed, unregulated, orgiastic violence, yet he also affirms the Dionysian as the essence of life itself, an essence that in Nietzsche's account had seeped into the makeup of the Greek psyche, and enabled Greek tragic art, as well as Greek military prowess in their heroic defeat of Persian invaders (*The Birth of Tragedy* 76). Berdyczewski's narrator draws a similar link between the immorality of the butchers and their heroic courage:

> Cruelty is the legacy of the butchers. Thus, as a rule, butchers are no weaklings, and when a scuffle erupts in town, they are the first to strike. The entire spiritual nation fears these solid-bodied, hot-tempered butchers; if one upsets them, they know no mercy.
>
> There is also a good side to all of this. For many days, the Jewish nation was feeble, fearful of the sound of a falling leaf. During pogroms, a hundred Jews would flee one drunken peasant, and succumb without protest to the breaking of windows and tearing of pillows and covers. Instead, the butchers learned to protest, to arm themselves with sticks and axes and to offer protection when needed. Such an event took place in *Dashia* a generation ago, before Jews learned to congregate and protect themselves. Is there any wonder that they are considered the first heroes of Israel? (1995:94)

Today, Nietzsche argues, no ritualistic or aesthetic mechanism for the release and containment of violence exists. Greek tragedy, which functioned in the aesthetic realm similarly to those original sacrificial rituals, had all but been eclipsed by two thousand years of Christianity. He therefore calls for the resurrection of tragedy—the reincarnation of Dionysian festivals in the aesthetic realm—in modernity and presents the *tragic idea* as a usable moral/epistemological category for the modern reader. To this call, early Zionist literature had responded in its unique expression. Berdyczewski in particular offered his story to readers with a similar purpose: to ignite a tragic sensibility, the shock of "life."

"Life" Versus the "Book"

"Life" contra "book"—the clash between religious law and life—is a theme that had occupied Hebrew literature since the advent of the "Jewish Enlightenment" in the late eighteenth century, when the process of secularization, migration away from shtetls, and the encounter with modernity began to affect Jews on a mass level. The meaning of this theme, how-ever, had changed dramatically in the late nineteenth century when for Hebrew writers, saturated as we have seen they were in Schopenhauer, Nietzsche, and Freud, "life" came to mean the libidinal unconscious en-ergies lurking at the depth of both individual and collective subjects. As Dan Miron succinctly summarizes:

> The concept of "life" is identified in mid-nineteenth century [Hebrew literature] as a dialectical socio-historical category that develops through the battle between generations. With the advent of realism, "life" is identified with the Jewish socio-economic market: realist portrayal of different types and of market relations; "man" is a product of society. Yet in the 1890s, with the understanding of the emotional world as springing out of an instinctual-libidinal ground and flooding the rest of the personality, including its rational and moral sides, "life" becomes a psycho-biological category. This new perspective affects all genres, including social tracts, in which the discus-sion shifts from socio-economic reform to the "return" of the "nation" to its sources of national-emotional-libidinal exis-tence, ancient sources that went dry after two thousand years of exile. (1987a:13; translation mine)

Both Miron and Hamutal Bar-Yosef (1997) have demonstrated the ex-tent to which early Zionist discourse was saturated with the language of instinct, irrationality, dreams, and the unconscious. Ahad Ha'am views genuine national feelings as essentially springing from the unconscious of a people as he denounces the pedantic rationalism of *Wissenschaft des Judentums,* the "science of Judaism" inaugurated by nineteenth-century German-Jewish historiographers. ("History knows only the hero who still lives in men's hearts and exerts influence on human life. What does it matter to history whether the source of this influence was once a walk-ing and talking biped, or was never anything but a creature of the imagi-nation"; "Moses," 1904; quoted in Simon [1944:103].) Theodor Herzl, founder of the political Zionist Movement, prefaces his program for a Jewish nation with the sentence: "All activity of men begins as dream and later becomes a dream once more" (quoted in Schorske [1981:165]). In her recent attempt to read Zionist culture through its foundational texts, Jacqueline Rose (2005) organizes this turn to the unconscious un-der the chapter heading "Zionism as Psychoanalysis." Indeed, as I have noted in my earlier discussion of Gourgouris's *Dream Nation* (1996), all formation narratives of national identities can be read as dreams; yet Zionism in particular shares a direct affinity with psychoanalysis. Conceived at the same time and in the same place (Vienna, 1890s), both psychoanalysis and Zionism are neo-romantic responses to mid-century rationalism, both are libratory discourses, and both privilege the libido and the unconscious as the psychic places in which a person's or a nation's prehistory has left its traces.

As the definition of "life" becomes synonymous with instinct and unconscious drives and forces, Berdyczewski and other fin-de-siècle Zionist writers construct a genealogy of Jewish history that gradually comes to imagine not the rabbinical tradition in itself as having sucked "life" out of the Jews but rather the condition of exile; centuries of absence of political existence, of powerlessness, decentralization, and dispersion had divorced the Jews from "life" and made them overly reliant on "the book," their only common glue. Anti-Semitism, the raison d'être for modern Zionism, also comes to be understood as an unconscious psychological phenomenon. This, as we have already seen, is the basic explanatory narrative for Leo Pinsker, whose *Autoemancipation* (1882) diagnoses both Gentiles and Jews with an incurable psychic illness. Pinsker's is, as we argue in the previous chapter, a pessimistic, tragic philosophy, portraying a seemingly tragic cycle for the Jews from which there is no recourse except, tentatively, by way of national independence.

And yet, behind the early Zionists' veil of pessimism and their harsh critique of Jewish life hovers the possibility of renewal and invigoration; within the psyche of the nation that had lost its will to live lie, according to Pinsker, dormant desires. Beyond the instinct for self-preservation represented by the reactive, near-death nature of Diasporic life lies a will to power, a desire that desires itself:

> The consciousness of the people is awake. The great ideas of the eighteenth and nineteenth centuries have not passed by our people without leaving a trace. We feel not only as Jews; we feel as men. As men, we, too, wish to live like other men and be a nation like all nations. And if we seriously desire that, we must first of all throw off the old yoke of oppression and rise manfully to our full height. (1944:82)

"Red Heifer" answers, in a sense, this call for action, demonstrating the working of active, spontaneous male desire. Two thousand years after the abandonment of an autonomous political existence whose center was the Temple in Jerusalem and whose ritualistic ceremonies afforded the nation with appropriate libidinal discharge, "life" reappears in the form of random acts of violence. For all their random horror, the butchers' actions, as we have seen, are presented by Berdyczewski as a manifestation of life itself, a demonstration of Jewish "will to power," a desire to subdue, a desire for the sole sake of desiring, springing up in all its amoral and ecstatic force. Here Berdyczewski aligns himself much more closely with Nietzsche than with Schopenhauer, the former moving away from the latter's vision of life as unworthy of living except through the disinterested will-less drive and locating the will to life exactly in the destructive and violent instincts. Within the deeper instinctual drives represented by Dionysus lay power (*Kraft*) and force (*Macht*): the desiring energy in individuals and groups that goes beyond the instinct for self-preservation.[11] And the representation of such desire in the butchers—a distilled, synecdochic example of the entire nation's will to power and its desirous/aggressive potential—is, I think, what Berdyczewski aims at in the seemingly simple story of the red heifer's subjugation: *A force that was locked up inside them needed release.* Against the anemic vision of "the spiritual nation" ("poor Jews do not buy much meat") the story presents the desire for and the internalization of flesh as a sign of vitality and potential renewal.

Disindividuation and Identity

Yet more is at stake here for Berdyczewski than representing Jewish will to power. For it is important to note that "Red Heifer" depicts not only a state of heightened desire but also one of merging: the condition of violent intoxication when all actors and all actions and desires *merge into one.* Throughout the entire ordeal, we are told, the butchers are perfectly synchronized, communicating without a word: "They signaled to each other, removed their clothes, rolled the sleeves of their underdress above the elbow, and felt prepared, as if the time of a great battle had come . . . One of the butchers stabbed the heifer's belly. Others began to rip her skin off. *They did this with restrained force and resolute emotion, one that they had never felt before.*" In the butchers' synchronized, unmediated actions, all individuality and subjecthood disappear. The butchers are neither named nor attributed any dialogue; mostly they are portrayed through verb actions: "rising," "pushing," "pinning," "tying." There is, the story's very language suggests, no individual "interiorities" behind the butchers' actions: they *are* their actions. Berdyczewski creates for Hebrew literature a model of a subject who isn't an individual subject, of a will that isn't hampered by a thinking subject, an image of pure force, of "life" as it manifests itself in uncontrollable, instinctual life. In his reading of *Birth of Tragedy*, Gilles Deleuze calls this state the "abnegation of ego," the Dionysian state of pure desire (1983:17).

As boundaries of law and decorum are lifted and intoxication, violence, and merging heighten, the butchers recognize themselves for the first time: feeling a power "that they had never felt before." Such recognition subsequently engulfs the entire townspeople, who upon discovering the butchers' violence the next day began staring "into each other's eyes . . . as if a solar and a lunar eclipse had occurred simultaneously." In the mutual gaze, in which there is both terror and amazement, they too seem to recognize their own violent origins for the first time. The release of collective, transgressive desire in the story is thus presented as disrupting all individual identities, be it of a person, a town, or a nation. For even as the heifer's slaughter is traced back to ancient Jewish ritual, the onslaught on Jewish dietary law and the covenant shatters the facade of Dashia's regulated communal life. In its stead Berdyczewski offers a metaphysical model of merging and collectivity born out of the crushing of the preexisting order and the spontaneous release of deeply buried desires.

The Individual, the Collective, and the Making of a Citizen

My argument that Berdyczewski celebrates the state of disindividuation in "Red Heifer" requires perhaps some clarification, since Berdyczewski, in stark contrast to Ahad Ha'am, has traditionally been read as the "champion" of the individual subject in its battles with the collectivist spirit. "Give a chance to live to a single individual," Berdyczewski writes in "The Question of Culture" (1900), "and the mass will follow after its own accord" (quoted in Hertzberg [1997:299]). In her essay on "The Myth of the New Jew," historian Anita Shapira goes as far as crediting Berdyczewski with igniting the myth of the lone Zionist pioneer: "Against the burden of history and the blocking rational conclusions that are the product of generations of experience," she writes, Berdyczewski argued for "the spontaneous creativity of the individual who dares to rebel against the institutions of the past and who views himself at the center of Creation and its purpose" (2002:115; translation mine).

The making of the "individual" and the assertion of individuality indeed had been one of the explicit aims of fin-de-siècle Hebrew works. As Miron has shown in great detail in his monographs on Bialik, Berdyczewski, and their contemporaries, the "Hebrew Renaissance" period had created the conditions under which radical individuality could be negotiated and represented as such. The corpus of Bialik's lyric poetry, where the various moods of the romantic poet are interrogated, the short stories of Berdyczewski and Brenner, where individual sensations are depicted in great detail: if, as we have seen, the late nineteenth century and the turn to nationalism had triggered for West Europeans like Eliot and Herzl a backlash against radical individualism, for East European Hebrew writers they seemingly had an opposite effect.

Indeed, though Bialik and Berdyczewski were contemporaries of Eliot, they have at least a partial affinity with West European works produced a century earlier—British and German romanticism and the post–French Revolution novel in which, as Nancy Armstrong (2005) has argued, the image of the sovereign individual was created. Flaubert's *Sentimental Education* comes to mind, or even the early Eliot of *The Mill on the Floss*. It was not so much the novel, which in Hebrew was still in its infancy, that held common ground with these works, but short stories in which an individual protagonist sets out to become free from his station in life, from his family, and from religious and moral constraints, and find an authentic identity. This quest for individual liberation is at the heart of the works as well as the lives of many early writers, and Berdyczewski's biography is in this sense a case in point, as are his radically liberated butchers. Yet "to become fully individuated," Armstrong writes, "the British subject [depicted in the late eighteenth-century novel] had to posses some piece of presocial humanity in the form of desires that exceeded the limits of his or her social position, desires originating at the very core of himself that made it impossible for him to fit in" (2005:61). The exploration of such desire constituted the chief thematic preoccupation of fin-de-siècle Hebrew works. The turn away from both traditional Jewish life and assimilation into European culture had produced a psychological and literary sensibility whose locus was the individual, his sensations and his quest for an unmediated encounter with the world.

And yet, to the extent that the move to Jewish nationalism constitutes a new individual and a license for radical individuality, it also demands that a new collectivity be formed and social bonds, even if transformed, be maintained and strengthened. As Etienne Balibar so amply demonstrates in his genealogy of the post-1789 modern subject, the radical

individuality afforded by national liberation projects often is quickly negotiated into new structures of collectivity. And it is in this sense that the
physical liberation of Berdyczewski's individual butchers brings about
just such a new, radicalized collectivity. In going against the traditions
and institutions of traditional Judaism they represent a new collective
spirit, one that deviates from Jewish particularity and merges with a
more universal experience of rupture. Indeed, "Red Heifer" offers precisely such a vision in the image of the nameless and featureless butchers: the dissolution of individual subjects in favor of a vision of an original, collective being, a phenomenological world-force that transcends
individual experience. There is a dialectical paradox here, for in their
respective works, Ahad Ha'am and Berdyczewski each depict the opposite of what they declare. In the writings of Ahad Ha'am, who argued
bitterly with Berdyczewski over the question of the individual versus the
Jewish collective, the nation is modeled exactly on the individual human
body, complete with interconnected organs, a heart, a digestive system,
interior organs, interiority, feelings; and in Berdyczewski's writings, images of individual characters—the butchers are just one example—are
vague and abstract. If Ahad Ha'am's vision of the Jewish nation ("The
Law of the Heart" [1894], "Flesh and Spirit" [1904]) is an "Apollonian"
quest for order, form, and clear division between individual bodies and
the body politic ("When the individual loves the community as himself
and identifies himself completely with its well-being, he has something
to live for; he feels his personal hardships less keenly, because he knows
the purpose for which he lives and suffers"[12]), Berdyczewski strives to
present a phenomenological world beyond individuation as a basis for
the nation.

Pitting the narrator's ambivalent, tentative tone against the butchers'
cruel, active, experiential mode of being, "The Red Heifer's" deeper contrast thus appears to be not only between instinctual desire and religious law—even as the butchers' actions are against the covenant and the
moral law, they are also as we have seen a reincarnation and continuation
of ancient religious life—but also between a modern/dialectical/rational
versus an instinctual/active mode of existence. *Dionysus Versus Socrates:*
this, as Deleuze (1983:13) has convincingly argued, is the deeper opposition in *The Birth of Tragedy,* as well: dialecticism, skepticism, rationality,
individuation, knowledge grounded in logic and formal analysis against
the experiential epistemology of tragic aesthetics. Berdyczewski's narrative is similarly dichotomous. The story pits the narrator's dialectical
convulsions and moral ambivalence, his vacillations from condemna-

tion to admiration, his reticence in general ("I myself, the narrator, was not there and did not witness things with my own eyes . . . Butchers aren't saints, and I don't want to make excuses for them, but if not for this event, I would not consider them evil . . . People want to live, yet they are plagued by base, uncontrollable, unrefined instincts . . . I do not judge, only narrate") against the butchers' blind will to power, embodied in their actions alone.

Berdyczewski's image of the Jewish nation is thus an eternal, metaphysical phenomenon, a force beyond individuals, order, politics, conventional Jewish history and identity. He rejects not only the alienation and emptiness of the modern assimilated Jew, but also the equally hollow pretenses of traditional Jewish life. Only when stripped from its narrowly defined Jewish identity, "Red Heifer" implies, can Dashia and the Jewish nation at large achieve a more authentic collective identity. Berdyczewski, as Bernice Glatzer-Rosenthal writes, searched for "the deepest part of the individual and of society" in order to find an authentic self or humanity (Golomb 1996:101). In his scholarship he thus turned in particular to the myths and ecstatic rituals of Hasidic Judaism. Within this universe of Dionysian-like disindividuation, boundaries between Judaism and the "world," the particular and the universal, were seemingly lifted. Similarly, in "Red Heifer," as the shock of spontaneous desire and violence shatters Dashia's facade of Jewish law and morals, its people come to feel their deeply collective identity as an eternal, unconscious phenomenon.

This was for Berdyczewski the essence of national feelings and identity.

Like the classical tragedians who recovered the old Dionysian myths (Allison 2001:53) he sought to revive the Dionysian/ancient Hebrew ritual as a literary spectacle for his modern readers. He embarked on the course of an independent researcher, collecting Hasidic myths and writing a revisionist history of Judaism that recovered moments of active revolution. In his fiction he strove for a similar effect; *a thick bow of blood, visible through the dim light, began pouring. And the blood flooded and washed the ceiling and the walls and the floor and people's pants, hands and faces:* it was, I think, the conscious aim of Berdyczewski's literary project, not only to depict the opposition between the "book" and "life," rationality and instinct, individual and collective, but to actually arouse, to wet, to stir up, to awaken what he perceived as the dried-up Jewish political body and individual bodies of Jews, to revitalize the well of energies, bodily fluids, and the emotions, including fear, horror, and disgust that had supposedly dried up,[13] and thus to develop a basis for a tragic aesthetic for modern Hebrew literature.

"Between Two Camps": Zionism and the Limits of Liberal Tragedy

It is possible to trace the engagement with the limits of rationalism and individuation and the negotiation between individuality and collectivity in Hebrew literature to the autobiographical or mock-autobiographical bildungsroman that, in direct contrast to its fortunes in West European culture, rises to popularity at the fin de siècle. As Alan Mintz has shown, the autobiographical bildungsroman was historically foreign to the Hebrew tradition; yet as modernity belatedly affects the East European Jewish masses during the *Haskala* (the "Jewish Enlightenment" of the late eighteenth to mid-nineteenth century), the Yiddish[14] and Hebrew bildungsroman gains momentum. The publication of Moses Leib Lilienblum's Hebrew novel *Khataòt Neurim* (*Sins of Youth*) in 1876 spurs a host of subsequent works, and with the advent of the Hebrew Renaissance around the turn of the century, the genre comes to dominate modern Hebrew prose (Mintz, 1989:3–24).

Like the European bildungsroman, these Hebrew works contend with the liberal desire to transcend one's origins and place and find individual happiness. In Berdyczewski's early short story "Makhanayim" ("Between Two Camps"), published in 1899,[15] a young Jewish man, Mikhael, escapes his provincial home for a dream of university studies in Germany. Orphaned by his mother's death at a young age and raised by a remarried father whom he loathes, Mikhael declares his radical individualism and disowns his origin and any memory of it ("He has no people and no birthplace anymore. A free man living alone. He does not belong to the bonds of family and tradition and memories. He has no memories at all. He does not wish to know them"[16]). Through autodidactic teaching—previous attempts to enlist the help of a Russian tutor having ended in humiliation—he seeks to remake himself as a rational, autonomous, secular subject. Living in poverty and hunger, surrounded only by his books and devoid of human ties, Mikhael makes a meager living at a printer's shop, battles to master the Russian and German languages and to tackle difficult philosophical concepts, sleeping long hours and strolling around the city. In time, he is befriended by the Polish wife of the drunken shoemaker from whom he has rented a room and is drawn inexplicably to her silent, contemplative adopted daughter Hedwig—the product, it will turn out, of a forbidden liaison between a Jewish student and a German washerwoman. He encounters the girl at home and around the city and spins pastoral fantasies of a dreamy union ("He will leave civilized life and return to nature, will wear simple clothes like a farmer; and she will walk barefoot, covered by only a heavy coat and thin garments. She will sing at dusk as the cattle return from the fields; his voice will echo hers."[17]). Yet he also encounters an older German prostitute, with whom he develops a sexual liaison. Soon the prostitute is revealed as his beloved's biological mother, and Mikhael, tormented already by irrational forces—his unbound sexuality, involuntary memories of his mother's death and his father's hasty remarriage, flashes of the hostility of his hometown—collapses from this final and fatal blow to his dream of a pure, reasoned, self-sufficient life.

On the surface, "Between Two Camps" is a typical nineteenth-century formation narrative of abandonment of Jewish tradition and home for a cosmopolitan, urban European life. Spurred by the mass migrations from shtetl to large city and written almost exclusively by authors who underwent such a journey, Hebrew and Yiddish literature treated this theme throughout the nineteenth century, from Lilienblum's aforementioned autobiography, saturated as it was in the modernizing and Europeanizing ideals of the "Jewish Enlightenment," to *sifrut ha-tlushim* (literature of the alienated) of the early twentieth century, which depicted the eventual collapse of these ideals. Stories in the latter category—and "Between Two Camps" is a classic example—inevitably ended with the protagonist's disillusionment, loneliness, and loss.

Mintz, and before him Dan Miron (1987a), have stressed the particular individual, autobiographical elements of "Between Two Camps" and other contemporaneous bildungsromane, demonstrating how they deviate from earlier, more didactic models of Hebrew literature. A uniquely modern feature of these narratives, they have argued, is the investment in and representation of erotic life, and most commonly of an erotic crisis, which seems to drive their plots and provide a new center of gravity. As for psychoanalysis, the unique and deeper sense of self for these writers is rooted in sexuality. Thus the investment in the erotic is read as further proof of the autobiographical nature of these texts, which attempt, as Miron has particularly argued, to stake out the core libidinal components of the unique self for the first time in the Hebrew literary tradition.

Indeed, turn-of-the-century Hebrew bildungsromane bring into existence the "living," "sensual" modern Hebrew individual, a subject whose center is himself and whose creation is enabled precisely by the rejection of minority identity and the turn to the nation. As Etienne Balibar had shown, a similar evolution in the modern European subject becomes manifest in the wake of the French Revolution, as the quest for freedom becomes inscribed in the very inner texture and contradictions of the represented individual. Yet what must also be stressed is that "Between Two Camps" ends in the utter and unmediated *failure* of the protagonist's quest for individuation, the betrayal of his individual desires, a failure that must be understood in political terms. Thus, the nationalist sensibility that creates the conditions for the creation of the individual simultaneously undermines his quest in the service of the new collectivist fabric of the nation. In her reading of the European novel's genealogy Nancy Armstrong delineates a similar trajectory:

> During the early nineteenth century, the novel offered up the national landscape as one in which individuals could become fully themselves. The novel extends this apparent invitation to expressive individualism, however, only to show that unrestrained individuality had to be contained, cut down to size, degraded, domesticated, or else subjected to some violent act of repression. Through this process of self-expansion, loss and self-contradiction, I am suggesting, fiction drained away desire from the bad subject in order to reinvest it in the imaginary nation. (2005:63)

In a similar vain, I argue, turn-of-the-century Hebrew bildungsromane both "invite" individuality and violently undercut it. It is not individual erotic desire (which, as Miron rightly suggests, constitutes the locus of the Hebrew bildungsroman) that is negated by these plots but the failure to achieve (sexual and other) fulfillment within the rationalist liberal framework as well as within the domain of erotic-romantic heterosexual love. Such a failure, the subject of many Hebrew bildungsromane, ultimately and implicitly designates the "nation" as a proper object of erotic investment. And within this resolution, I argue, as within the economy of desires outlined by *Daniel Deronda*, it is Woman who gets invested with excessive, unrestrained individualism.

Let us turn here to an example: the short novella *Bakhoref* (*In Winter*)[18] by the Hebrew prose writer and literary critic Yosef Hayyim Brenner. Published in 1903, the story is a first-person mock-autobiographical narrative that begins with the narrator's exclamation: "I don't have a future or a present." The narrator, Yirmiya Fireman, then proceeds with the details of his autobiography, culminating with the tale of his unrequited love for Rahil, a beautiful, socially ambitious, and seemingly unapproachable young woman from his hometown, whose only desire is to emigrate from Russia to Belgium. The narrator traces his life from a miserable early childhood marred by poverty, hunger, and rags, as well as by a suffocating, unattractive mother and an ignorant, arrogant, and self-deluded father. From there, the usual/familiar list of tribulations follows: the strict and narrow Jewish education, the evolution of male friendships, the gradual loss of faith, the immersion in early twentieth-century ideological wars (Zionism versus Marxism), the desertion of the hometown, the encounter with Dostoyevsky, Nietzsche, and Schopenhauer, the wanderings across Russia from city to city, the failed returns home, and finally, the aborted "affair" with Rahil, whom the narrator is unable to approach and loses to another, a failure that unfolds over half the novella and brings about Yirmiya's emotional collapse. As in "Between Two Camps," the final scene of *In Winter* ends with the protagonist's ruin as he lies face down on the snow-covered ground of a European train station, going nowhere, freezing and alone.

In both "Between Two Camps" and *In Winter,* protagonists' attempt at the quest for self-fulfillment, which is at the basis of liberal ideology, is truncated suddenly and violently. In both plots, this liberal ideology so completely collapses that they may be read as instances of what Raymond Williams has coined "liberal tragedy": narratives like Ibsen's *Brand* or Tolstoy's *Anna Karenina* that trace the radical desire for and eventual failure of individual self-fulfillment and happiness (Williams 1966/2006:123).

This collapse, as we have noted, is brought about in both bildungsromane through the protagonist's failure to regenerate himself through romantic/erotic bonds. And in both cases, the impeding element is traced back to incestuous desire, which in "Between Two Camps" in particular is represented directly. Indeed, as Mikhael surrenders to incestuous relations with a prostitute who turns out also to be his future mother-in-law, he is confronted not only with his own immorality and loss of innocence but with his likeness to the adulterous father he disowned and abandoned. "What happens again and again [in liberal tragedy]," Williams writes, "is that the hero defines himself against an opposing world, full of lies and compromises and dead positions, only to find, as he struggles against it, that as a man he belongs to this world, and has the destructive inheritance in himself" (1966/2006:123).

Not only the futility of liberal values is demonstrated in these plots but also, significantly, the impact of Freudian psychology on the consciousness of modern Hebrew writers. For in both works, the explanation given to the necessary failure of erotic happiness is Oedipal. Miron, who has written extensively on Brenner's works, puts great emphasis on this point. In a sharp break with mid-nineteenth-century Enlightenment Hebrew prose, he argues, *In Winter* focuses almost exclusively on the eruption of sexual desire in the form of the narrator's attraction to Rahil and its attendant shame and failure. All preceding autobiographical details—the intricate study of the narrator's family and early childhood—are provided strictly as explanatory framework for this failure, which Miron attributes to Yirmiya's deep hatred of and identification with his contemptible father:

> [Yirmiya] Fireman cannot allow himself the attempt to fulfill his desires, because he physically identifies with his father and, through this identification, deems himself a loathsome sexual object. He is not worthy of touching a beautiful woman's body; no sexual liaison between them should be allowed . . . Fireman is a young man who despises his masculinity, that is, himself, with all his heart . . . How could such a man avoid Oedipal self castration? (1987a:238, 240; my translation)

Virtually nowhere in early Zionist literature is there a loving, active, lasting relationship. Never does it exist between children and parents. The parent-child relationship is guilty as such, and every move toward new relationships ends in failure and guilt as well. For both Mikhael and Yirmiya discovering the parental face behind the adult mask marks a rude awakening and an instantaneous end to the quest for individual self-fulfillment. Both are marked with terror in the face of parental inheritance, and both are therefore incapable of acting on their desire. Nor are they able to return to the parental home. Trapped in a place from whence "there is no going forward or backward" (Ibsen, *When We Awaken*, 1900, quoted in Williams 1966/2006:68), turn-of-the-century Hebrew bildungsromane end in what Williams calls "tragic stalemate": "the self alone, detached from the reality of the world and relationships, withered and wasted, to be redeemed only by return" (1966/2006:124).

Yet it is not merely Oedipal relations and parental inheritance that appear to haunt protagonists but a complicated web of ancestral inheritance and a *generalized* sense of guilt that reaches beyond the nuclear family. There is, of course, a paradox here. As literary characters in Hebrew fiction come to be understood as individuals and their conflicts read as internal, and as "life" comes to mean libidinal energy and instinct, *interiority* comes to mean something larger than the individual. "Man has a single internal life, and its roots are located beyond his individual existence," Berdyczewski writes in his doctoral dissertation.[19] Thus, Mikhael's fate in "Between Two Camps" is finally determined by a complicated past, much of which reaches beyond the Oedipal triangle: his widowed father's hasty marriage, the illicit affair between the Jew and the Gentile whose product is the dreamy Hedwig, the legacy of an entire people's past sins. Worst of all, the story seems to imply, is Mikhael's own sin: the denial of his deeper, truer ethnic or national origins. That one cannot move past one's ancestral origin is the unequivocal message of the endings to both Berdyczewski's and Brenner's stories, as Yirmiya dreams that he is a fly whose legs are being torn off one by one while Mikhael is depicted as unable to move, touching "his legs and arms to check if they had not broken and fallen off of him." As Miron has convincingly argued, what these endings imply is not only the fantasy of dismemberment of the legs but a representation of self-castration and self-sacrifice that is at the basis of the Oedipal tragedy.

Both Berdyczewski and Brenner, avid readers of Schopenhauer, powerfully evoke this sense of original sin and generalized guilt; "The true sense of tragedy," Schopenhauer writes in *The World as Will and Representation,* "is the deeper insight that it is not his own individual sins that the hero atones for, but original sin" (quoted in Eagleton, 2003:52). They evoke it *seriously,* not only, as Miron suggests, in its psychological-Freudian dimension or in the form of the self-inflicted guilt of a Godless liberal subject, but as a mytho-historical phenomenological force that comes to haunt their heroes. The sin, which underlies their works but is never directly articulated, is the desire for self-fulfillment when national existence has been forsaken, the investment of erotic energy in Woman instead of People; it is the sin of forgetting one's national origins and identity, of abandoning the tribe.

In this evocation of sin and ancestral origins, Berdyczewski and Brenner align themselves as closely with classical tragedy as with modern liberal tragedy. Their protagonists, it should be emphasized, are not classical tragic heroes, yet their *qualities* are closely associated with ancient tragedy: blindness, fate, an intensity of commitment even to a spurious goal (and political Zionism in Brenner's work was often portrayed as a spurious goal[20]), extreme suffering, self-sacrifice. "Between Two Camps" in particular, as Miron (1987a) has demonstrated, presents an unmasked rendering of the Oedipal myth, complete with incest and self-mutilation. Like Oedipus, Mikhael leaves home, blind to the larger implications of his identity, only to shockingly encounter it through the trappings of accidental, tragic incest; and as in *Oedipus Rex,* it is only through the protagonist's symbolic blindness at the end of the story that true identity is rendered possible.

Literary incest, as Terry Eagleton has written, is "a matter of keeping things in the family" (2003:162), a trajectory that binds each generation to the previous one and hinders the renewal of the individual through normative procreation patterns. In "Between Two Camps," as we have seen, the possibility of such renewal is seriously questioned; and even as it does not depict incest directly, Brenner's novella raises similar doubts. From *In Winter's* very first scene, the nuclear family comes under assault as the narrator outlines his erotically charged relationship with his mother, his disgust with his father, his own "family romance" with his best male friend. Here, as in Brenner's later writings, lateral marriages and the neat substitution of one generation for the next appear never to materialize. The entirety of Brenner's corpus, in fact, is riddled with family "substitutions": absent fathers are replaced by a tenant, orphaned children adopt a passer-by, tight all-male relationships supplant the family (*Mesaviv la-nekuda* ["Around the point"]). No one can separate, people are implicated by each other's lot, and each pays for the actions of his forebears.

Yet incest, which implies an unbreakable bond with the past, also functions in the stories as a metaphor for self-division. Incest brings one *too* close to the source of one's identity, breaking the boundaries between self and other and resulting in alienation and blindness (the inability to see without the proper distance). An "enigma of otherness and affinity" (Eagleton 2003:162), it establishes one as both stranger and kin to one's family, nation, and tribe. This, in short, is the conflict embodied in both "Between Two Camps" and *In Winter,* which utilize the depth structure of ancient tragedy in order to evoke, play out, and resolve the internal rift of thousands of readers: the conflict between a felt alienation from the Jewish world (and especially the immediate family) and a pull toward a collectivist calling.

What I am suggesting here is that while early Zionist writers were committed to expressing individuality, they simultaneously curbed its excesses by depicting its dangers and failures and implying that it be channeled to collectivist objects. Their air of imagined citizenship functioned, as Armstrong argues in relation to the European novel, as "a kind of supplement as well as a limit on subjectivity" (2005:58) in which individualism had to find a social form of expression beyond erotic love (and assimilation into European society). Aesthetically committed to representing individual desire while also renouncing individualism, these works end in perfect ambivalence or stalemate that, I argue, can only be resolved within the realm of the tragic, which affords a way out of the liberal dilemma of individuality and individuation. In its emphasis on both will and destiny and its grounding in the Dionysian, tragedy presents an aesthetic and political possibility out of the liberal paradigm embodied in the bildungsroman, and implies a realm beyond it.

That despite their professed Zionism at the time, Berdyczewski and Brenner do not (as Eliot and Herzl do) align nationalism with idealized erotic bliss, that they choose instead to represent these protagonists' fall, and furthermore, that they fail to explicitly resolve the conflict with "national" rebirth and instead load the reader with the overwhelming pain and suffering of their protagonists should thus not be read as evidence of their pessimistic nihilism alone, but of what Nietzsche calls in *The Birth of Tragedy* a "pessimism of strength." "Strife, for Schopenhauer," Nietzsche writes, "is a proof of the internal self-dissociation of the Will to Live, which is seen as a self-consuming, menacing, and gloomy drive, a thoroughly frightful, and by no means blessed phenomenon" (1995:56). For Nietzsche it is something else entirely: the *process* through which a new, healthier world is born, the process of "becoming" that, as Allison stresses, was precisely what Nietzsche was after in *The Birth of Tragedy*. Pain, suffering, and conflict are central to the process of becoming and carry for Nietzsche, as for these early Zionist writers, the future possibility of renewal and transformation.

It is no wonder, therefore, that *In Winter* especially offers a taxonomy of psychical and physical pain unparalleled in Hebrew literature: "My past is buried in the sand, filthy; the facts that I know more than remember, not only do not fit into the skin and flesh of one corpse, but are black and heavy" (1978:104); "my past is dark and loathsome and miserable" (155); "I am miserable. Everything hurts me and everything is hard for me"; "I'm a worm and not a man, crawling, pathetic, pitiful, depressed" (161); "I walk like a shadow" (142).[21] Brenner's narrative assaults the reader with evocations of pain and suffering, from "shadows," "dark visions," and "hidden tears" that haunt the narrator to the literal moans and groans that litter the narrative. It is the pain experienced in the wake of incest or unrequited desire that signifies a possible change: the collapse of boundaries and false divisions within the individual, the complete and simultaneous burst of all depressive/anxious boundaries and the flood of the ego with repressed material.

In *Birth of Tragedy,* Nietzsche associates such transformation most directly with *bodily* pain: "In the doctrine of the Dionysian mysteries, *pain* is pronounced holy: the pangs of a woman giving birth hallow all pain; all becoming and growing—all that feeling of life and strength, where even pain still has the effect of a stimulus, gave me a key to the concept of *tragic* feeling."[22] Brenner, a serious reader of Nietzsche, had in particular adopted this psychology of pain. In his works we have something new entirely in Hebrew literature: detailed descriptions of physical pain. "Surges of small needles" that run along the narrator's spine, a heart that feels "like raw flesh" (155); a narrator who is "hungry like a dog" (168), suffering from recurring headaches—"I am sitting alone. Night. Oh, why am I not screaming from the intensity of my pain?" (170); "I am miserable. Everything hurts me and everything is hard for me"; "A full fifteen hours I slept in my clothes and shoes. Disgusting. My head is exploding . . . all my body parts hurt" (167); "I groan, tortured like a murderer, from the depth of my boredom, from the horror of my torments" (169). For long stretches of the narrative, *In Winter* reads as "more of a cry than a discourse" (*The Birth of Tragedy* 57).

If we remember that at the beginning of the twentieth century, few were actually experiencing pain *in Hebrew*—that is, Hebrew was still not a vernacular, spoken language—we can perhaps understand the depth of Brenner's ambition. Pain, as Elaine Scarry (1985) has written, eludes representation in any language, let alone in a language in which it was not spoken about. Brenner's attempt to depict physical pain, *in Hebrew,* broke from a Jewish literary tradition, Yiddish or perhaps that of Kafka, that repeatedly masked and sublimated pain through humor and metaphor. It collapsed boundaries between text and reader, making *In Winter* an uncomfortable read, and by forcing pain into avenues of communicability with readers and writers of Hebrew transformed the Hebrew language in the process.

It is through this representation of the suffering and sensations of the male subject, I further argue, that Hebrew literature of the fin de siècle creates an image of a *universal* national subject. That this suffering had many significant external causes—both in Europe and in early twentieth-century Palestine—is beyond doubt. That male suffering, however, should be portrayed in literature and that it should enthusiastically be received as a theme by readers is indicative of something else. The turn to nationalism had afforded the space for the display of male suffering in literary works. From Bialik's romantic autobiographical poetry— which as Miron has demonstrated moves along an axis of regression, depression, and elation—to Brenner's sickly protagonists, Hebrew literature not only positions the male subject at the center of its discourse but interrogates his every mood, sensation, and pain.

What is further implied in these works, I think, and links them to "Red Heifer" is that once the conflicts and inner divisions of the liberal subject have been eclipsed by pain and suffering, a new recognition can potentially set in and a process of disindividuation and merging with the world at large and the Jewish nation in particular can begin. As Berdyczewski writes in his 1897 doctoral dissertation, *On the Link Between Ethics and Aesthetics:* "*Man has a single internal life, and its roots are located beyond his individual existence. These roots bring him, gradually and slowly, to a recognition of the unconscious, of consciousness, of the act, regardless of whether they will end in action and creation, or in the consumption of life*" (1999:85). This recognition is not articulated directly in Berdyczewski's fiction works, nor is a new identity found or even discussed; yet what they suggest, I think, is that the pain and suffering embedded in the individuation process enable a future and a gradual, reluctant, ambivalent movement toward common desire and aspiration, a tentative merging within a new collective vision.

The Transition to Palestine

This link between individual suffering and pain and the purging and renewal of collective consciousness will repeat cyclically, as I show in the next chapter, throughout the twentieth-century Hebrew canon. Suffering and pain, reconstituted in later works more precisely as "sacrifice" for the collective will continue to inflict Brenner's protagonists as he immigrates to Palestine and becomes a cultural icon for the budding Jewish national community. The sufferer in both art and life is individual, yet his suffering bears meaning for the national community at large. "Only by particular examples of annihilation [of individuals] are we made clear as to the eternal phenomenon of Dionysian art, which gives expression to the will in its omnipotence, as it were, behind the *principium individuationis,* the eternal life behind all phenomena, and despite all annihilation," Nietzsche writes in *The Birth of Tragedy* (59). And as Brenner had stated, "there is hope that personal sacrifice of individuals will succeed in changing the course of Jewish history" (Shapira 2002:122). In his fiction, as in thought patterns that will become rooted in pre- and post-statehood culture at large, notions of pain and sacrifice recast as tragic sacrifice will be deemed necessary for the nation's felt identity.

In Palestine/*Eretz Yisrael,* the reality of strife and conflict lent itself naturally to the tragic discourse that took root in fin-de-siècle European Hebrew literature. Tragedy as an aesthetic category and structure of feeling resolved conflicts within the individual subject but also, I claim, around his relationship to the emergent national community, and also to native Palestinians. More than in actual ideology, national "feelings" and national "guilt" would be cultivated around the suffering or sacrificial *male* figure and his encounter with the reality of strife around him. Woman, meanwhile, as figure of excessive individuality (Brenner's Rahil, for example) would be brought into the national fold not (as for Herzl) through her recasting as partner in idealized marriage and romantic love but rather as *witness* to male suffering and tragic sacrifice.

Berdyczewski's and Brenner's stories, like most (though not all) fin-de-siècle Hebrew works not only reject marriage and romantic love but also display a *revulsion* at heteronormative patriarchy. In contrast to the argument that aligns Zionism with the invention of the masculinized, heterosexual Jewish man, these early Zionist works often depict deep conflict around masculinity and manliness.[23] The plot that centers around the collapse of love and mutual desire thus also gives rise to a thinly disguised fantasy to escape inscription within the patriarchal, heterosexual, future-oriented, procreative order. Male suffering and affect in general eclipse such patriarchal order and suggests, as we have seen, broader visions of collectivity and belonging.

It is in the works and person of Yosef Hayyim Brenner that what I outline above is most dramatically and "tragically" demonstrated. That Brenner both understood and represented *himself* through suffering, pain, and, ultimately, tragic self-sacrifice is conveyed throughout his works and particularly in his torturous letters to his fiancée and later wife, Haya Broyda, to whom he was married for only several months. The letters, a litany of illness, headache, and nagging depression ("Am thinking of those terrible moments, when everything is a terrible weight on me"[24]), convey both the centrality and grandiosity of male suffering in Hebrew literature. They reflect a desire for Brenner's female companion to witness his suffering and also to bear the suffering inflicted upon her ("Today I thought: Haya suffered much by me, possibly more than I have by her. Our friendship has been sealed by suffering and there is no way to resume it."[25]). Allegedly a closeted homosexual, Brenner had forewarned his fiancée in his letters of the suffering that would underlie their union:

> Surely you know that suffering awaits us when you come here [from Jaffa, where Haya stayed at the time, to Jerusalem, where Brenner resided]. There will not be emptiness: eating together, studying the Bible, reading Shofman, a trip to Abraham's Vineyard and Rachel's Tomb (if I do not fall ill). There will not be emptiness. If I have the strength, as I do these days, to kiss you as I desire, and to place you like a seal on my heart then emptiness will be filled to the brim. But there will be suffering.[26]

Presenting himself in these terms to his future wife, Brenner then bids her to bring with her to Jerusalem Tolstoy's *The Power of Darkness* (1886), a play that centers on a Russian villager who redeems his corrupt neighbors and son by repeatedly pleading with them to "attain a soul" and "follow God's laws," and whose Christian message of sin and repentance is universalized as the existential human condition. An avid reader and interpreter of Tolstoy and Dostoyevsky, Brenner writes of a similar world of suffering, redemption, and fellow-love. The suffering depicted in his works and letters is generalizable, not particularly rooted in a place or in the Jewish condition, and dramatized through allusions to and affinity with the Russian masters. And it is within this cultural framework that Haya Broyda answers him as well: "Yes, I have suffered much and am willing to suffer more, yet in my heart the hope that you will repent for everything in one grand moment has not died. Without intention, a scene from *Crime and Punishment* stands before me: that scene that comes at the end of the novel, where Raskolnikov kneels before Sonia."[27]

I'd like to end by tentatively arguing (and leaving the analysis of the implications of this argument to others) that as he transitions from Europe to Palestine, Brenner reads the face-off with native Palestinians through a similar lens of tragedy, guilt, suffering, and redemption. After immigrating to Palestine in 1909 and living there for more than a decade, Brenner wrote "From a Notebook" in 1921. It was his last piece of writing:

> I wandered in the darkness through the dusty trails of the orange groves at the edge of the City. All belonging to the sons of this land, to the Arabs. To them.—

I passed by one homeowner, a sort of little Effendi,[28] sitting in front of his home in the company of two elderly neighbors; a young man, adorned with his Kaffia,[29] was also seated among them. I greeted them. They did not answer me. I passed them, turned my head back, and saw that the lack of response was intentional, mean. The young man sat up erect and looked forward as if with a tinge of victory: We restrained ourselves from greeting a Yahud:

"That is what is to be done."

I thought to myself bitterly: even if the assumption that the natives of this land are part of our race is true and that in the farmers of Eretz Yisrael pulses the blood of the ancient Israelites—I want no part of them![30] Yet I don't have an option. I must pass by them whether they agree or not; but it's better to run into a Vaelikoros[31] in Tambov[32]—not to mention into a Lithuanian around Kovna—than into these Poles of the East.[33]

"Never ask for their well-being."

After a few footsteps, in the next trail, an Arab man dressed in rags of a European Tujurka[34] sprang behind me. "Hawaja!"[35]— He caught up with me. And I saw that he was not an adult Arab but a boy-laborer, probably thirteen or fourteen years old. He asked me something with a clear, somewhat loud voice, and in clear accentuated diction. I, to my determent, could not answer him, because I had not taught myself the Arabic tongue. I asked him one thing: from Salima? (I.e., are you from the nearby village Salima?) And he answered, shaking his head, no, from here; he works the boyar's land, and he kept on telling his story. Then I asked him, hinting with my finger: Effendi? (i.e., this boyar, for whom it appears that you work, is he the Effendi who was sitting there in his front yard?) He answered positively and continued talking: He, the boy, has no father and mother; both died during the war years, an orphan . . . This I understood from a few words and more so from his gestures and facial expressions. And he as well understood my question: "Kadeish?" (i.e., how much does he make a day?) And he answered with self-respect: "Tamnia Grash" (i.e., eight Grush [pennies]).—"Not good," I said, and he wondered for a moment, confused: what does it mean "not good"? Is it too little or too much? Then he explained to me at length that

there are those who get fifteen Grush a day and even twenty
. . . adult laborers . . . and he has young sisters . . . and needs
to eat, to make a living . . . and he gets eight . . . everything is
min Allah![36] . . .

At this moment I badly chastised myself for not having
taught myself the Arabic tongue. If it were possible . . . an
orphan-laborer . . . a younger brother! Whether the scholars'
hypothesis is right or not, whether you are blood kin to me
or not, the responsibility for you lies upon me. It is for me to
brighten your eyes, to give you a taste of human relations! . . .
No, not a hasty revolution in the East under orders from a
well-known committee and in the service of well-known Socialist politics—no, not politics! This, in fact, may not be our
role; we may practice it against our will, out of despair, when
we have no other options!—No, not that! . . . But the touch of
one soul to another . . . from this day . . . and for generations
. . . for many days . . . without a purpose . . . aside from that of
friend and brother . . .

—Farewell, sir!—the boy quit me when he saw, most likely,
that I am preoccupied and that the conversation had stopped.
But despite that, in his farewell greeting there was much contentment for having inadvertently snatched a decent conversation and for having spoken aptly, like an adult speaking to an
adult.

—Farewell to you, my dear, I whispered, and my heart
longed for him and me. I continued my wanderings in the
darkness. (1960:212)

Trying to negotiate, in the face of growing Arab hostility to Jewish
newcomers, a collectivist vision for both Jews and Palestinians, Brenner
considers the assumption of a single ethnic origin and the tenets of socialist politics as common glue, only to quickly shift to an ethic of unmediated fellow-love and sacrificial responsibility ("whether you are blood kin
to me or not, the responsibility for you lies upon me"). He thus avoids
facing the impending clash between the Zionist vision of political freedom and the fear and hostility of Palestinian landowners (for whom he
coins the term "the Poles of the East") by resorting to a quasi-Christian
message that annuls differences and resides in *feelings* of empathy, sacrifice, and redemption. It was the last piece Brenner published. Living in a
secluded orange grove in Jaffa, surrounded by Arab houses and ignoring

rumors of impending riots, he was murdered by Palestinians on May 1, 1921, along with all members of the family with whom he lodged. Earlier that day, a car was sent to collect him but he had refused, saying he wanted to stay back with the others, who could not all be evacuated. Hours later his body was found near his house. In an essay entitled "The Life of Hayyim Yosef Brenner," Y. Yaari writes of Brenner's longing for death, of his musings on his own death, sometimes at the hands of an Arab. An additional writer, Yaacov Fichman, likened Brenner to Jesus Christ, living an ascetic, otherworldly life already several days prior to his death.[37] As in Nietzsche's writings, Brenner's and other early Zionist writers' "Dionysian" affirmation of life was set not so much against but largely *within* the discourse of the crucified.

CHAPTER 8

Masculinity, Tragedy, and the Nation-State

We have traced, in the previous two chapters, the making of a tragic protagonist in prestatehood modern Hebrew literature. We have, that is, delineated the making of an emotional/political/aesthetic paradigm, a "structure of feeling" that was molded in the budding Zionist national community in Europe and was subsequently imported, with some changes, to the emergent national cultural scene in Palestine. In this final chapter I follow the evolution of tragedy into the foundation of the State of Israel half a century later. My overarching argument, I should say upfront, is that at least until 1967, images of Israeli soldiers continue to be fashioned along the tragic hero model set in Bialik's Kishinev poem and elsewhere, and that the tragic paradigm both affects as well as occludes representations of violent struggle in Israeli culture. Let us look, as a conclusion to this book, at a few examples.

He Walked the Fields

By far the most popular work of its time, Moshe Shamir's novel *Hu halakh ba-sadot* (*He Walked the Fields*) was first published in 1947, and was reprinted in numerous editions, eight of them between 1948 and 1951 alone. In 1948 the novel was recast as a stage play: the first original play to be performed in the independent State of Israel. Following the Six Day War of 1967, it was adapted into a film that featured Assi Dayan, the handsome son of then Defense Minister Moshe Dayan, as lead actor; it has since been the subject of numerous revivals. Scholars have noted considerable differences between the novel, the play, and the film, each reflecting its unique historical moment.[1] Unless stated otherwise, this analysis will focus on the play, which was performed at the Kameri Theater in Tel Aviv over three hundred times and remains to date the most powerful representation of post-state society in the immediate aftermath of the construction of the State of Israel (Spicehandler 1995).

The play is centered on the death of a young soldier, Uri Kahane, whose large portrait, framed in black, hangs in the back of the stage from the first scene on. All subsequent stage action that follows this scene is thus understood by the audience through the sign of Uri's death. The play begins with a generic display of the humdrum of daily kibbutz life: a man shaving, children being read a fairytale before bed at the "children's room," idle talk about the corruption of today's youth is heard. Behind the action on the stage, the portrait of the beautiful young man looms. References are made to the memorial service for the youth (na'ar), which is scheduled for that evening. There are no visible signs of shock, pain, or mourning. The dominant imagery is of the land and the seasons, the lives of elders and children, men and beasts. Within this context, Uri's memorial service is presented as an additional ritual. "He was twenty when he fell," a laconic kibbutz member announces. Such interludes by anonymous kibbutz members—an intermittent Greek chorus—periodically express common knowledge and the normative voice of kibbutz society.

From here, the events leading to Uri's death unfold on stage. Uri returns to the kibbutz after a long absence (having attended agricultural school). He searches for his parents among kibbutz residents who admire his physique ("we sent a child and he returned a man"[2]). He is told that his father Willy, barely back from a rescue mission of refugee Jewish children in Tehran, has decided to enlist in the British army and is due to leave tomorrow. Distraught, Uri finds his father in the cornfield, sharpening a large knife. "Have you forgotten my name?" he asks his father, who urges him to "be a man" and speaks of the duty to return to Europe and save European Jews.

With the looming image of the dead Uri, whom we later discover was the kibbutz's firstborn, juxtaposed so early in the play with the image of the father slowly sharpening the knife, the underlying myth of the play appears to be the Binding of Isaac, the Akedah, whose sacrificial imperative is now mandated by the state and not by God, a kind of test of a father's loyalty.

Uri, however, is more an Oedipus than an Isaac. He is the noble-born insider-outsider who has returned from afar into a degraded reality of sexual drama and ancestral sin. For no sooner than he meets his father, he encounters his mother's new lover, a foreigner to the kibbutz. The mother, now residing in a new abode adorned by several "luxuries" unheard of in the sparse kibbutz (an electric kettle), introduces her lover to Uri; his father, Uri discovers, has been usurped by this new man and is fleeing the kibbutz for war-torn Europe in a kind of suicide. Rutkeh, the mother, insists on "talking about" the situation and her new lover to Uri, but Uri, in what will become his modus operandi throughout the play, refuses to listen. "I don't want to know more," he storms out of her room, remaining adamantly blind and deaf to the complexities of the reality around him, including the details and precise justification for a deadly military assignment on which he is about to embark.

Feeling thrust out of his family of origin ("I have no one: mother, father, friends"), Uri turns to the flirtatious Mika, a recent émigré from Poland and a Holocaust survivor, who also harbors secrets of the sexual kind. Perhaps the mistress of a Polish doctor, perhaps an orphaned child prostitute (who may have even been involved with Uri's father when he came to fetch her from the refugee camp in Tehran), Mika with her sexual past ("Hayyim mufkarim" ["a promiscuous life"]) provokes rumors that circulate among kibbutz members: "What she has seen Uri will never see," they say (Shamir 1989:37). "You don't know what went on there," Mika tells Uri, to which he replies "I don't have to know" (37). Soon they are a couple, to the chagrin of Uri's mother, who warns Uri of the doomed match:

> Rutkeh: "[Mika] needs a mature man, who'll be able to slowly release her from her past."
> Uri: "I don't understand what you're talking about and have no desire to understand. Anyway, you should not bother. She is already my wife." (44)

Tragic Blindness

We have by now established blindness, passivity, and lack of consciousness to be properties of the tragic hero produced in and by early Zionist works. Miron, in his reading of Berdyczewski's "Between Two Camps," interprets this "lack of consciousness" as a symptom of the assimilation-aspiring young man, ruined by his overreliance on Enlightenment rationality and by his naive belief in individual self-fulfillment. It is this fundamental blindness, Miron claims, that leads the protagonist to "a psychological holocaust that befalls on [him] abruptly and all at once" (Miron 1987a:203; my translation) and which supposedly will subsequently push him beyond the limits of individual liberal aspirations and into the collectivist way. Yet as "national" Hebrew literature develops its first *Sabra* heroes like Uri, born and raised into a reality of national belonging, these heroes *continue to be characterized by blindness and lack of consciousness.* In both "Between Two Camps" and *He Walked the Fields,* it is the protagonist's blindness to the consequences of his own actions that enables a tragic ending: incest in "Between Two Camps," and semi-accidental death in *He Walked the Fields.* Uri in this sense is not a deviation or a correction to prenational masculinity but its direct continuation, his willed blindness and ignorance functioning in *He Walked the Fields* as the tragic hero's flaw. His blindness and inarticulateness are features of his tragic aura, but they also, as we soon witness, enable his sacrifice on behalf of the group.

Indeed Uri is not an Isaac. For to the extent that he follows a model of masculinity and male sacrifice created by turn-of-the-century Zionist works, that model is *not* of direct and explicit sacrifice of hapless young men under the clearly defined instructions of a biblical God (or an authoritarian state). The Bible, as Rene Girard (1986) stresses, is neither implicit nor ambiguous about its violent impetus: Isaac must die because God demands it. Greek tragedy, on the other hand, is disposed to concealment of the direct violence and absolute power of the Gods in multifaceted plots where the hero is only partly under their sway, and partly implicated by his own actions. Such is the structure of *He Walked the Fields* as well, where Uri, to a degree, is presented as the orchestrator of his own death.

Tragedy and Sacrifice

Paired with his mismatched bride, Uri sets out to secure a "family hut" in the kibbutz; yet no sooner is one made available, after much haggling, than a messenger carrying a letter arrives at the scene. "They want to take you," Mika cries, and rushes offstage (47).

> Chorus: And in the morning, the friend comes to get Uri. These were the days that ripped everyone's life apart. Taking him to the *Palmakh* [the prestate paramilitary brigades]. If there are no brigades, there will be no Kibbutz. (50)

Uri hesitates before leaving, then disappears with the messenger.

The play's second half, set in Uri's military compound, begins once more against the backdrop of his memorial portrait. In the forefront of the stage, Uri and his military unit are now stationed not far from the kibbutz. Two months have passed, the audience is told, and the soldiers appear tense and tired. They are getting ready for a mission; on the way there, Uri passes through a new settlement, where he now discovers both Mika and his mother. He is informed that Mika is pregnant and scared—an earlier abortion "back there" is alluded to vaguely (71)—but refuses to stay. In a brief encounter with Mika he tells her that a group of clandestine refugees is due to arrive that night in British-controlled Palestine and that he must immediately leave. His unit's mission is to distract the British occupier at a central port so that the refugees can board safely elsewhere. In the next scene, an argument about who will carry out the mission erupts among the soldiers. Uri declares that *he* will blow up a bridge, and leaves the stage; immediately after, a hurried messenger searches the kibbutz for Uri's parents, bearing news of his fatal wound.

Heroism or Escape?

He Walked the Fields, which enjoyed unprecedented success in all its versions, had for years been read by scholars as the most stereotypical and powerful representation of an early Zionist masculinist ethos of heroism and sacrifice, and an unabashed celebration of the *Sabra.*[3] More recent readings have exposed the plot's ambivalence, pointing not only to the problematic and unresolved question of Uri's death (heroic or suicidal?) but also to Uri's "weak" and irresolute character. The supposed embodiment of "stalwart" Zionist masculinity, Michael Gluzman writes, Uri appears on a closer read to be "a 'soft,' confused, flustered youth, with emotional and sexual difficulties, who cannot develop a distinct identity of his own" (2007:188).[4] More than heroic sacrifice, Gluzman argues, Shamir presented Uri's death as the escapist suicide of an immature boy or the mimetic act of a son who has not properly individuated from a demanding, towering father. "How is it possible," Gluzman asks, "that so many generations of readers ignored the subversive aspect of Shamir's text? How could it be that this novel, which radically disrupts the validity of the heroic sacrificial ritual, was viewed as a direct expression of the dominant ideology?" (2007:207).

It is possible, I think, precisely because the sacrificial plot in the play is structured as tragedy, which is neither ideological nor counterideological. It is possible because in veering between Uri's agency and his drive by forces beyond his control the play follows a model of "tragic responsibility," which was set by earlier Zionist works and with which audiences could deeply identify. Indeed, it is precisely those elements in the play that weaken Uri's character and occlude the precise reasons for his death that account, I think, for the play's effect on spectators and readers: the tragic death of the highborn yet blind hero (amply echoed in the film version by the real-life "royal" lineage of Assi Dayan).

Tragedy and Political Subjectivity

If fin-de-siècle European Zionist works like "Between Two Camps" enabled the "theoretical" passage into a new "national" political subjectivity, *He Walked the Fields* symbolizes the pivotal transformation of protonational subjectivity into actual citizenship. In this sense, we would expect post-state Israeli art to represent a rupture, a new political subjectivity associated with independence and autonomy. Etienne Balibar had located such a break, for example, in *The Declaration of the Rights of Man,* which he calls "an epistemic rupture in the psycho-political sphere where the citizen comes to occupy the position of the [sovereign] subject."[5] Yet to the extent that Uri represents the new "citizen," *He Walked the Fields* does *not* offer a vision of male citizenship as autonomy or sovereignty. Rather, it is Uri's tragic essence—his lack of consciousness, his instinctual actions unmarred by introspection, the flaw of his *radical ignorance* as contrasted with the knowledge of others (his parents, Mika), his adherence to his "destiny"—that makes him a citizen ideal and an object of identification and pity.

The fundamental question, of course, is how the revolutionary quality of citizenship, the elevation of man, of Jewish man, to the status of sovereign autonomous subject is to be reconciled with the nation's demand for absolute submission, particularly as the play is set on the eve of the 1948 war: in essence, the demand that Uri die for the sake of the nation and that his death be read by audiences as justified. This is at the heart of the problem of national sovereignty as *heteronomy:* the political subjection of the state, the opposite of autonomy. "At first glance," Gourgouris writes, "it would seem that the elevation of the people to the position of the sovereign (which is what warrants the new designation: citizen) grants them the space of unharnessed subjective action (autonomy)"; yet Uri must also become a *governed* subject, an obedient citizen, the executor of political power. This contradiction is solved by early post-statehood writers like Shamir by denying the male subject thought and subjectivity and portraying his "destiny" within the framework of the tragic. Like Oedipus, as we have seen, the long-absent Uri is both an insider and an outsider, the king's son (the kibbutz's firstborn) but also a pariah who neither fits back into the kibbutz nor is wanted by his parents. Like Oedipus, he is not a clean slate of innocence sacrificed to a demanding God, but a flawed, tragic hero who is both innocent and guilty. Like Oedipus, Uri is ruined because of his "sin"—the refusal to join the patriarchal order (by becoming a father)—but also because of his very identity.

And as in the Oedipal myth, Uri is fashioned as a scapegoat for his people, yet the fact of his violent sacrifice is obscured in the thickness and sexual drama of the "Oedipal" plot.

Scapegoat

Indeed, *He Walked the Fields* derives its dramatic effect from the tension between Uri's seemingly self-willed actions and his casting, from the very beginning of the play, as a *scapegoat* for the community. The scapegoat, as Girard defines it, is an a priori victim, an outsider bearing the physical sign of his difference: Oedipus's limp or, in the case of Uri, his extreme beauty, youth, and innocence. Uri, I argue, is marked as a sacrificial figure and a tragic scapegoat even before the events of his death are revealed. He is marked because though he is the representative *Sabra* and ultimate insider, he symbolizes difference from the rest of the "kibbutzniks": his beauty and ignorance, his youth and muscular body, his lack of experience and the taintlessness ("cleanliness," as Mika puts it) of his life: all these designate him as an otherworldly presence for the world-weary kibbutz community, as for the majority of audiences (including the Czech-born director, Yosef Millo) made up of largely foreign-born Jews. He is marked, most dramatically, because he appears from the play's very first scene as a dead icon.

Indeed, as Gluzman argues, Uri is constructed as a "soft," unformed youth; yet his "character" and the motivations and agency behind his actions are *deliberately* weakened in relation to other characters so that the structure of sacrifice can be seen and felt. With his character intentionally weakened, it is the chain of events presented in the first part of the play—the parents' betrayal, Mika's demands, his lack of place—that railroads Uri toward his death. For by the time he is summoned to the paramilitary brigades, we read him as having given up everything: a desire for any family (either old *or* new) and even a desire for heroism. And by the time of his death, we read Uri as an instrument whose fate was sealed by *destiny,* but one that he himself acts out. That his death is not explicitly presented as a consequence of his military duty does not interfere with its acceptance by the audience. Such direct representation of military sacrifice would in fact have been too direct a display of the state's unequivocal power, tarnishing the classical harmony (Girard 1986:104) of the play and tempering its dramatic effect.

Uri, in fact, is portrayed as participating in his own sacrifice. "There is only one person who is superfluous here," he declares already in scene 2, as he stands before the photo of his dead self. Raymond Williams deems this consent by the victim to be an integral part of the sacrificial plot: "It is not to the heroic will of the martyr that our response is directed, but to his subjugation of himself to his part of the pattern, and then to the fertilizing effect of his blood" (1966:191). By leaving the definitive reasons and the question of the legitimacy of Uri's self-sacrifice unanswered, Shamir not only emphasizes the tragic but also gives ample expression to the audience's modern ambivalence toward self-sacrifice. It is not that audiences "ignored" the subversive message of his work; it was that the play gave expression to their own felt conflicts. Audience guilt was triggered by Uri's death, but only to a degree; in its tragic outlook, the play did not demand that audiences bear *total* responsibility for Uri's violent death, and thus it evoked a general acceptance of Uri's blood.

The Scapegoat as Unifier

Moreover, in linking Uri's memorial service to the mundane rituals of kibbutz life and particularly to the image of the bustling "children's room" with which the play begins, death is linked in the play to the renewal of life. Whether the play begins with Uri's first or tenth memorial service, we do not know. What we do know is that as the events leading to Uri's death take place, the early national community in Palestine, represented by the kibbutz and particularly by Uri's divided parents, is portrayed as fragile and fractured: a group of hardened individuals weighted by weariness. Against this portrayal, Uri's sacrifice is read not merely as the family's and the kibbutz's redemption but also its conversion when, in the final scene, Uri's parents are united under the sign of grief, Mika decides to keep her child, and a reenergized kibbutz readies for the latest wave of refugees from the European hell. It is at the moment of its firstborn's ruin that the essence and value of both the kibbutz and the nation are revealed.

Shamir, who while writing *He Walked the Fields* was a member of an actual kibbutz (*Mishmar Ha-emek*) as well as a self-declared Marxist, fuses in Uri the Christian idea of redemption with the Marxist idea of history: a portrait of sacrifice for the sake of social change. In doing so he indicates, I think, that Uri and his actions are not meant to be separated out (as Gluzman does) for ethical approval or disapproval; they are the actions of a generation, not an individual. Rather, it is the effect of Uri's death on the national community that is the central feature of the play and the key to its success. Tragedy, Jaspers writes, "cleans[es] us of all that in our everyday experience is petty, bewildering and trivial" (1953:41). It is in this sense that Uri, the sacrificial youth, becomes a "redeemer" (Williams 1966:195) both within the context of the play and for audiences in the new state, propelling them to rise above narrow desire and to cohere and unite under the sign of grief.

The play, which was performed *after* the War of Independence and as large waves of new citizens were being absorbed into the country and a new war (the Sinai War of 1956) was being waged, undoubtedly contributed to shaping the role of male sacrifice in the new state. And yet the sacrificial demands of national independence are never *explicitly* revealed. Nor does the play portray directly the violence at the basis of the national project: Uri's death isn't acted on stage, and to the extent that it is attributed to violent conflict, it is in the context of a nostalgic allusion to the struggle against the British, who by then are long gone. By fashioning Uri's death as tragic destiny, rooted in part in personal and ancestral sin and partaking in a *pattern* of sacrifice, the play conceals not only the violence at the heart of national origins in general but the deep, unresolved, and horrifyingly violent struggle between Jews and Palestinian Arabs, which is barely mentioned in the work. As consumers of tragedy, Williams writes, "We fear but are not inspired to run away, shaken but not stirred" (1966:153). Thus, rather than for its accurate portrayal of post-state society, we should look for the play's performative function for this society. For this yet insecure and embattled national community, the staging of Uri's death as tragedy performed the politically valuable service of draining off an excess of the enfeebling emotions of fear and pity. *He Walked the Fields,* that is, owed much of its success to its cathartic effect, feeding audiences controlled doses of fear, pity, and guilt around the dead soldier's figure, while obscuring the gruesome violence at the heart of the national project.

The Spectacle of Dead Male Beauty

I began this book with Otto Weininger's famous description of women and Jews as *nonsubjects*—penetrable objects and passive matter, as contrasted with the active spirit of Man—and in various readings considered

Zionism's response to Weininger's popular paradigm. Yet as we arrive at post-statehood Hebrew literary production, and in contrast with Freud's dream of the "stalwart Jew," Eliot's dream of Deronda, or Herzl's dream of David Litvak, we discover that men, not women, are portrayed as sexualized, penetrable nonsubjects. Uri, as we have seen, has little character depth beyond the fantastical content with which he is invested internally by other characters and externally by audiences and readers. The novel's narrator describes him as "empty and completely hollow" (1966:9). Audiences were not gripped by Uri *despite* the feeble contours of his personality, but *because* they could project their desire onto his "emptiness." And in almost every case of artistic interrogation of post-state masculinity, this desire is also fueled by the spectacle of male beauty.

In both novel and play, Uri barely sees the reality around him yet is always *seen* by others. Often, as in the passage below, he is described through other characters' eyes for the enjoyment of readers and spectators. In a direct reversal to Weininger's assertions that "Woman is only and thoroughly sexual," lacking existence beyond her sexualization by Man, it is men, the "New Jews," who in early statehood works are invested most powerfully and exclusively with sexual appeal. And often, as in *He Walked the Fields*, it is the female gaze—the gaze of the sexually experienced Mika and her hyperdeveloped consciousness—that focuses audience attention on Uri's body:

> Now he was rather delightful. His shirt, hanging sloppily on his body, exposed to the sun a dark, self-confident triangle. All that she wished to hide he wished to display. His shirt was rolled up above his pants. When he stopped to pluck the fruit—it slipped and made room for the handsome waist and the back curves. This indifference of his clothes to his nudity, this leaning—was it chance or habit?—to strip with every single movement of the self assured body. (1966:66)

Indeed, while the (Diasporic) female body is associated with shame and cover,[6] the male body in both novel and play is displayed as spectacle and celebrated as such, especially as it is headed for tragic sacrifice or action. From this vision of Uri, to the heroes of the military bands' song lyrics, to the images of the actor Assi Dayan, to the misplaced portrayal of the young left-leaning writer Yaacov Shabtai on the rightist *Hatkhia* movement posters—the male body in early state culture is open and penetrable to the community's gaze.

Yet the handsomer they are, the more likely to be scapegoated: killed or maimed in various narratives. Uri was but one such figure; the title character of Yigal Mossinsohn's "Matityahu Schatz" is another.[7] Like Uri, Matityahu Schatz is an inherently vague character; like Uri, his life will end at its prime and under murky circumstances; and like him, Schatz will have been noted by his physical beauty: "Tall, exquisitely built, a man's man, who went and stuck a bullet in his head."[8] The more weakened, identity-less, beautiful, and sexualized these images are, the more they become associated with violent tragedy and a sacrificial plot that further heightens their magnetic appeal for the sentimental gaze and psychic investment of audiences.

For some time now, the critical practice of theorists of masculinities has focused on the Hollywood film hero, often the Westerner, acting as "serviceman for the culture" (Smith 1993:264). Much of this work has zeroed in on the ways in which the male figure—say that of Clint Eastwood in his numerous performances—is objectified and made an object of visual pleasure. Influenced by Laura Mulvey's seminal work on the objectification of the Hollywood-generated female body for the sadistic gaze of the male spectator, Steve Neale in his article "Masculinity as Spectacle" (1983) inaugurated a parallel argument for the heroic male figure, a figure both objectified and made spectacle through multifarious visual and narratological techniques, including, as the critic Paul Smith has shown, repeated shots from the waist up that cause the figure to loom large above the spectator's eye line.

It is, according to these theorists, the presence of the spectacle of male beauty in the vicinity of danger and its openness to violent attack or death that most powerfully triggers the spectator's feelings.

Such spectatorial relations, which characterize *He Walked the Fields* as well, date back to the early Zionist works we have been considering. Zionist ideology of the "New Jew" sought to create a morally and physically "healthy" Jew vis-à-vis images of Diasporic sickness, yet it also reveals a tremendous ambivalence around this figure. Tschernichowsky positions the admiring Jewish male poet at the heels of the statue of Apollo, "God of a generation of mighty ones and giants," who in turn is presented as a figure of identification for the reader. Yet the figure of Apollo is not *only* the embodiment of libratory, unchecked strength and vitality; from the early Zionist into the statehood period, the "new" Jewish male figure is never presented as fully wholesome, liberated, or free. On the contrary, it is an arrested, passive, or dead figure, driven by internal and external forces beyond its control. One recalls the final lines of "Before the Statue of Apollo," with their daunting image of a male God bound by "human corpses and the rotten seed of man," or Bialik's Kishinev poem, with its image of the poet/messenger bowing its head like an "ox before the altar," or Bialik's epic "Dead of the Wilderness," where giant muscular bodies lie dead on the hot sand dunes, or the figure of a live Uri standing before its dead portrait to grasp that the spectatorial relations around these figures are sadistic and tragic. It is the contrast between the wholesomeness of male beauty and strength and the instance of its demise that are most powerfully at work here.

This ambivalence around the male figure, which on the one hand glamorizes its beauty and on the other portrays its inevitable tragic hurt, continues to dominate Israeli culture, I argue, even after the 1967 Six Day War, when Israeli military power was definitively asserted. Hayyim Hefer's canonical post-1967 poem "The Parade of the Fallen" is a classic example:

> *They come from the mountains, from the lowlands, from the desert,*
> *They come—names, faces, eyes—and present themselves for the parade.*
> *They come with manly stride, strong and tanned*
> *They come out of the crashed planes and from the burnt tanks;*
> *They rise from behind rocks, beyond the dunes, and in the trenches,*
> *Brave as lions, strong as leopards, and swift as eagles,*
> *And they pass one by one between two rows of angels,*
> *Who feed them sweets and drape garlands around their necks;*
> *I look at them and they are happy.*
> *These are my brothers, these are my brothers.*
> *And they meet each other, brown eyes and blue and black,*
> *And they speak to each other of names, and weapons, and places,*
> *And they pour each other cups of coffee and tea*
> *And suddenly break out in shouts of "Hurrah!"*
> *And they meet in the great crowd, comrades and friends,*
> *Officers slap the backs of the privates and privates shake officers' hands,*
> *And they start singing and clapping*
> *And all those dwelling in heaven listen to them with amazement*
> *And the reunion goes on day and night, night and day.*
> *Because such a group has never been up there before!*
> *Then suddenly they hear familiar voices weeping,*
> *And they look towards home at father and mother, at the wives and*
>   *children and brothers,*
> *And their faces slacken and they stand in confusion,*
> *And then someone whispers: Forgive us, but we had to!*

We won the battles and now we are resting.
These are my brothers, these are my brothers.
And so they stand, with their faces in the light,
And only God himself walks among them,
With tears in His eyes He kisses their wounds
And He says with throbbing voice to his white angels:
These are my sons, these are my sons. (translation by Esther Raizen
  [1995:23])

Indeed, it is only in a self-assured post-1967 poem like "Parade of the Fallen" that we can read a direct fulfillment of the desire voiced by Tschernichowsky sixty years earlier for "a generation of mighty ones and giants, / conquering with their strength the bounds of Olympus, / an abode for their heroes, and adorning with garlands / of laurel-leaf the pride of their foreheads." To an even greater extent than in Shamir's Independence War play, male bodies in this 1967 poem are fetishized as strong, manly, tanned, a larger than life spectacle towering over the reader: "They rise from behind rocks, beyond the dunes, and in the trenches, / Brave as lions, strong as leopards."

Yet similarly to *He Walked the Fields,* the poem marries strength and innocence, beauty and ignorance: the innocence of tragic *dead* young men, servicemen for the people, whose agency and will are murky at best. Though death in the post-1967 poem is more conclusively associated with heroic victory in battle, it is still presented as inevitable destiny ("we had to") and diminished agency ("their faces slacken as they stand in confusion"). And as in *He Walked the Fields,* male figures appear across the veil of death: beautiful and strong yet arrested. Handsome, muscular, innocent Billy Budds, objects of pity and pathos, steeped in vitality. Male strength is hardly ever celebrated in Israeli war literature as such; the magnetism and symbolic power of the portrait of the male body lies in its depiction as muted, suffering, dead, or sacrificed.

Christ's image hovers over the male figures of "Parade of the Fallen," sons of God ("these are my sons, these are my sons") who have not only been memorialized in heaven but continue to appear among the living. "Before the Statue of Apollo," ending as it does with a crucified Jewish God, bound by the straps of the phylacteries; "The Parade of the Fallen," with its reference to "sons of God" and the Gospel of Matthew, its resurrection plot, its angels and flower garlands; a recent Israeli film on the subject of Zionist masculinities, which is explicitly titled *Walk on Water*: the image of Christ is written all over Israeli culture and particularly its war poetry and art. If modern culture, including modern Israeli culture, is highly ambivalent toward sacrifice in the traditional sense of the individual consciously and knowingly giving his life to the collective, sacrifice continues to resonate with Christianity. Like Jesus Christ, the living-dead soldiers are presented as sons of God, whose sacrifice remains in the domain of the divine, not the human. Seen in this light, tragic images of death in post-state culture do not exactly enact a renewal of collective life, but a renewal of collective *guilt,* an equally powerful cohesive force for the national community. In a seemingly continual cycle, works from the post-state mainstream, at least until the 1980s, do not reveal but rather reenact this mechanism, opening the artistic and political field to further reenactments.

Tragedy and Contemporary Culture

Since roughly the Lebanon War of 1982, the influx of post-Zionist critique and the general shift in Israeli culture toward greater reflection and introspection—by feminists, New Historians, and artists in general—have undoubtedly undermined the workings of the tragic paradigm in Israeli culture. In what can be loosely classified as "male awakening narratives," contemporary works, particularly in film, have taken to presenting plots in which the tragic hero undergoes a process in which he gradually and painfully gains access to the symbolic role he has been made to assume on behalf the group and works toward questioning, if not completely rejecting, this position. Interestingly, it is the awareness of the suffering caused *by* the tragic hero to an Other—the "enemy"—rather than to the self, which typically brings about this awareness and tentative refusal.

In Eytan Fox and Gal Uchovsky's *Walk on Water* (2004) and Steven Spielberg and Tony Kushner's *Munich* (2005),[9] tragic themes such as ancestral sin, destiny, heroism, and responsibility are so explicitly and exaggeratedly portrayed that the sacrificial ritual of the male hero is plainly exposed. *Munich,* which is set after the massacre of Israeli athletes at the Munich Olympics of 1972, features Avner (Eric Bana), a young Mossad agent who is chosen by the then Prime Minister Golda Meir to lead a team whose clandestine mission is to assassinate PLO operatives linked to the Olympics massacre. Avner is at first ambivalent and irresolute about his role; yet like Bialik's poet-witness, he is finally compelled to feeling and action through an act of witnessing—this time of the televised massacre of the Israeli athletes. "Will *they* ever stop?" sighs a weary Golda Meir (Lynn Cohen), drawing a direct line between the Russian mob of the 1903 pogrom and the Palestinian attackers of 1972.

Structurally, the events of *Munich* mirror Kishinev exactly: the humiliation of Jewish men, the failure of the "authorities" (German/Russian
police) in charge of protecting the Jews, the visual images of bloodied
Jewish bodies broadcast for the entire world to see. As in Bialik's poem,
the horror of these images is highlighted through quick imagistic shifts
between animate and inanimate objects—the dead breast and the healthy
sucking infant of Kishinev, or in *Munich*, the televised seconds that pass
between the image of anxious Israeli athletes huddled together on a van
and those same athletes shot and brutalized, their limp corpses piled
on top of one another in the very same van. These are the images that
Avner first witnesses, and which continue to haunt him throughout the
film to the very end when, having successfully completed his mission,
he becomes bitter and paranoid, eventually breaking from the national
community on behalf of which he has fought.

Munich consciously exposes the collapse of images of past and present
Jewish humiliation in the Israeli imagination; this exposure, embodied
by the exaggerated representation of Avner as a pawn tossed about by
his father and mother (war hero and Holocaust victim, respectively), the
circle of older, cunning generals who are his operators, and a shrewd,
weary Golda Meir, reveals the true underpinning of Avner's "destiny"
and tragic status and calls them into question from the very beginning.
The film also refuses to mask the violence that trails tragedy. At the beginning of *Munich*, Avner appears to be another "Uri"—handsome, inarticulate, doomed by his identity—but the violence done by and to him,
unlike the violence done by and to Uri, is in fact portrayed in graphic
detail. The film plays out Bialik's dream—the dream of a tragic hero who
avenges the blood of his people—to its logical conclusion, only to come
out on the other side: self-defense turned into unchecked aggression,
justice for the victims turned into blind revenge. Avner's killings breed
further Palestinian attacks and multiply the injury on all sides, triggering a growing level of paranoia even in the protagonist himself. That the
Jewish Hamlet has metamorphosed into a King Lear is, supposedly, the
film's cautionary moral message.

Yet we should also note that even while he is critiquing the dangers
of unchecked Dionysian-style violence, Spielberg makes the film's violence as appetizing as any other Hollywood war/gangster movie. Not
only does the group become increasingly more deceptive and violent,
but the degree of their attachment to their people grows accordingly.
As James Schamus (2007) observes, it is through this violence that the
men are inducted into the nation, as with each additional assassination
of a PLO operative, Avner and his gang become more visibly "Jewish,"

asserting their tribal loyalty over and against an initial alienation from it. In a peak moment we view Steve (Daniel Craig), a blond and blue-eyed South African member of the assassination team who initially expresses doubts about the mission, ecstatically shouting: "The only blood that matters to me is Jewish blood."

Yet it is not *Munich's* excessive violence that speaks to the popular imagination as much as its implementation by the quiet, unassuming, innocently beautiful Avner. In his reticence, boyish charm and anguished eyes, his middle-class *normality,* Avner makes an unlikely and therefore a fascinating killer. Spielberg makes a direct reference here to *The Godfather,* which draws its profound magnetism from the exact juxtaposition between the shaking hand of Al Pacino's Michael Corleone and the cold-blooded assassination that it triggers, between the quiet, handsome, civilized young man and his brutal savagery. Within the context of his team, Avner is also juxtaposed with the hotheaded Steve, a Sonny Corleone to Avner's Michael, a fanatic bully who serves to further glamorize the tragic grandeur of the saner, more violent other. As in *The Godfather,* Spielberg implicates the audience exactly by making the bearer and recipient of violence an arresting young man whom identity and destiny have thrust to the other side of the law. And as Avner's mission proceeds, it increasingly turns more glamorous and complex, grabbing the spectator for its own sake; Avner becomes invincible, we expect him to, and though he is presented by the end as disturbed and disillusioned, the spectator cannot fail to register his heroic growth—how much better dressed, more confident, more slick, and more attractive he is, his body the object of an increasing number of close-ups as the movie progresses. Spielberg draws on an existing affective field around the empowered, heroic male figure in popular culture, even as his sympathetic portrayal of the bombing victims presents a disturbing critique of Avner's enterprise.

That Avner is an Israeli Jew is everything in this context, for the film demands both in its underlying assumptions and its explicit story line that Avner's image and actions be read across the bar of a long Jewish history of helplessness and victimization. For this reason, and despite its critical message, the film continues to propagate—especially for mainstream Jewish audiences—a kind of pleasure associated with the joy of empowerment. By continuing to display Avner's beauty, strength, and charm and juxtaposing it with the unattractiveness of his "Diasporic-looking" deliverers (whose gaze often directs audience focus on his body), it further distributes the pleasure and allure of the tragic male spectacle. It is in this sense that the film's condemnation of the masculine Jewish national subject by Spielberg and Kushner, both American Jews, is inevitably also marked by an a priori desire that in spite of itself competes with and partially cancels the effect of the hero's narrative of self-awareness and the rejection of tragic violence.

A similar trajectory, yet with a homosexual spin, appears in *Walk on Water* (2004), a Hebrew language film by Israeli director Eytan Fox and writer Gal Uchovsky. The film portrays the psychological and moral downfall and potential healing of Eyal, another rugged and lovely Israeli Mossad agent (Lior Ashkenazi) who is also engaged in the latest round of state-licensed assassinations (in *Walk on Water*, Westernized PLO men have been superseded by bearded Hamas men); after a successful assassination, followed by the suicide of his wife, Eyal suffers a breakdown, unacknowledged by the protagonist, on account of which he is forced to take on a "lighter" assignment: to befriend and track the footsteps of the charming gay grandson of an escaped Nazi criminal, Axel (Knut Berger), who is on a visit to Israel. Like Avner, Eyal is conditioned for his role through repeated evocations of Jewish victimhood and a more specific allusion to his mother's torture at the hands of Axel's grandfather. Like Shamir's Uri, he is both beautiful and inarticulate, destined for tragic manipulation.

Yet the film, depicting the two men's relationship, is a narrative of male awakening. As the handsome Eyal poses as Axel's tour guide in Israel, a mirror is held to the Israeli/Palestinian landscape and bodyscape by Axel's casual, anti-Zionist leftist bourgeois eyes. Along the way there are scenes of Israeli-Palestinian altercations, which Axel witnesses and sharply criticizes and which eventually lead to the men's radical break from each other. And yet the film presents a "happy" ending: what begins as a hostile and homophobic encounter between Eyal and Axel ends in rapprochement at the palatial home of Axel's parents in Berlin; as Eyal lets down his ultra-masculinist, homophobic guard he becomes aware of the "role" he has been made to play and is no longer able to kill the aging Nazi. At the film's end, he has fathered a son with Axel's sister and is living as a farmer in a northern kibbutz. Through the encounter with both homosexuality and Germany—namely, the source of Jewish male trauma—tragic destiny, the film suggests, may alter its course and release its grip on the national imagination.

Tragedy and Homosexuality

I began this book with a quote from Proust in which homosexual and Jew are positioned in a metaphorical relationship to one another and serve as interchangeable tropes.[10] This parallel, though less explicitly, is also evident in the works of East European Jewish writers, where we may read, for example, an exorcism of excessive femininity in Bialik's brutal portrayal of Kishinev's Jewish men. "Parade of the Fallen" can in this respect be understood as an exaggerated, even parodic example of this masculinization. In its hyperbolic depictions of dead soldiers ("They come with manly stride, strong and tanned . . . Brave as lions, strong as leopards, and swift as an eagle") as in its prohibitive relationship to crying, suffering, or mourning, which are delegated to wives, mothers, and children ("I look at [the fallen men] and they are all happy"), the poem promotes images of manly men—albeit dead or wounded—as the opposite of popular images of effeminized, sentimental Diasporic Jewish men or homosexuals.

Yet as even Proust's narrator slyly acknowledges, Zionism is no more Diaspora's "other" than the openly homosexual man is "other" to the closeted one. And indeed, the sentimentality associated with the displayed male body in, for example, *The Picture of Dorian Gray*—sentimentality that, as Eve Sedgwick defines it, is "not a thematic or a particular subject matter, but a structure of relation, typically involving the author- or audience-relations of spectacle" (1990:143)—is, as we have seen, all over "Before the Statue of Apollo," *He Walked the Fields,* "Parade of the Fallen," and countless Israeli war poems and songs. The hyperbolic similes and the rugged male camaraderie evoked in "Parade," the extended, sexualized descriptions of Uri's body are displayed for an often male spectator and are legible within a heavily homosocial national and cultural realm, not entirely distinguishable from another homosexual closet.

Indeed, as I have demonstrated, the spectacle of the male body has been central to Zionist culture; and often the gaze at this spectacle was openly male: Eliot's Mordecai Cohen admiring Deronda, Herzl and his male protagonists, Nordau, Bialik, Tschernichowsky's Apollo—not to mention, as in *Munich,* Jewish-American writers, directors, and literary critics—Zionist culture, which posited the masculine figure at the center of its universe, created a space for the display and sentimentalization of the male body and afforded a climate through which this gaze was relatively unscrutinized and never formulated in gay terms.

Yet Fox, an openly gay auteur, leads the spectator's desire for his masculine hero through an *explicitly* homosexual gaze. In *Walk on Water,* he exposes the homophobic core at the center of Zionist masculinist institutions (the Mossad) and its servicemen (Eyal and his friends), suggesting that such exposure necessarily propels a parallel revelation and unraveling of the dominant ideology of male aggression and sacrifice. Indeed, as Eyal dispenses of his former life as a savior of the people, choosing instead the mundane life of a family man at a kibbutz, this exposure is presented by the film as a double liberation from both his tragic, fated destiny as from his homophobia.

Like *Munich,* nonetheless, the film cannot completely step outside the tragic paradigm. For in directly setting the critique of Israeli militant masculine ethos within the framework (literally, the screen's frame) of an admiring homosexual gaze, Fox, like Spielberg, further explores and celebrates the lure of the excessively masculine body (including several nude shots of Eyal) even while he is critiquing the masculinist Zionist ethos. Axel, who has become an anti-German, postnational cosmopolitan subject after discovering his grandfather's past and breaking with his indifferently racist parents, is a key figure in this regard. Though it is through his eyes that Eyal dispels his tragic heroism, it is also these same admiring eyes that constitute Eyal's rugged glamour. And it is also through Axel's gaze at Eyal's actions that heroism is finally validated and directed at a "proper" cause. This happens when in one of the film's last scenes, Eyal and Axel walk through a Berlin underground station, where Eyal has come in pursuit of the Nazi grandfather, and come across a gang of neo-Nazis who are attacking two cross-dressed men, acquaintances of Axel. Rushing to their rescue armed with his military prowess and his loaded gun, Eyal fights and scares the neo-Nazis away, thus winning cheers and forgiveness from both Axel and the film's audience.[11] "Why didn't you kill them?" mutters the panicked Axel, thus holding a mirror to the limits of European postwar pacifism, to the limits of modern suspicion of tragic heroism and even to the relativism of Western critique of Israeli aggression.

A Conclusion?

Indeed, while *Walk on Water* reveals and unravels the mythical underpinning of tragedy in Zionist culture, it also opens the space to explore the conditions under which sacrifice on behalf of others might be regarded as more than an instrument for narrow or reactionary national politics. The sacrificial metaphor underlying much of early and post-state Zionist culture is referenced, explicitly and sacrilegiously, in the title *Walk on Water,* and moreover placed in a gay context. This act of naming universalizes the metaphor's symbolic force and shifts it from a purely national sacrificial realm to one of cross-national social bonds. In this way, a scene in which Eyal crosses the Sea of Galilee to Axel's admiring eyes marks the end of his macho, isolationist outlook and the beginning of his renewed ties with the world at large.

Indeed tragedy is typically associated with reactionary politics and murderous national projects. Yet to reject tragic responsibility and sacrifice altogether is to naively reject the notion that there is real harm in the world and real reasons for sacrifice, a position that, as both Eagleton and Williams contend, is open only to those few Western millions whose lives are today unmarred by conflict or struggle. Both Eagleton and Williams have presented bold attempts to explore the possible deployment of tragedy in the realm of leftist politics, and Fox, as we have seen, interrogates and partially affirms this potential. Yet his film, like others that we may call post-Zionist or perhaps post-tragic, finds it difficult outlining how such a venue might be utilized for a progressive or at least a nondeadly solution to the Israeli-Palestinian conflict.

Nonetheless, in a subsequent film by Fox and Uchovsky, *The Bubble* (2006), tragedy is directly evoked in the Palestinian-Israeli context. Treating a love story between a young, handsome Israeli soldier, Noam (Ohad Knoller), and a young, handsome Palestinian, Ashraf (Yousef Sweid), who over the course of the film are continually joined and separated by political strife, *The Bubble* ends with the death of the two men in a suicide bombing spurred by the Palestinian. Indeed the tragic paradigm, which has loosened (though not abandoned) its grip on the Jewish national imagination, is ironically shifted to the Palestinian man, doomed to his sacrificial death by his identity and fate. It is an ironic though hardly progressive and decidedly unhopeful conclusion that nevertheless continues to glamorize the tragic dead male spectacle. In its final image of the two men rising in an embrace to the heavens, the film suggests that only a tragic deadlock is possible. And to the degree that tragedy is utilized in the service of a leftist politics and sensibility, and expanded to a non-Jewish realm, it remains expressive and retains its allure strictly in the domain of the masculine.

An Autobiographical Postlude: Woman, Tragedy, and the Making of the Universal Jew

When I was about seven or eight years old, I, and the rest of the country, was mad for the songs of the Israeli Army Bands. More often than not, the lyrics to these songs centered on the untimely, tragic death of young soldiers. At my aunt's wedding, a happy occasion by definition, my siblings and I sang two songs: "Anakhnu shneinu me-oto ha-kfar" ("We Are Both from the Same Village"), a tale of two boys raised together, and yet only one grows to be a man; and "Ballada la-khovesh" ("A Ballad for a Medic"), a song that I particularly adored and would listen to repeatedly:

They made their way slowly, it was quiet all round,
Across the river the reed was rattling
Sudden thunder roared: "I'm hit!" someone shouted.
"Coming!" the medic replied.
"We've stepped on a grenade!" the wounded cried.
"I'm right here with you" the medic replied.
A barrage of fire came down, heavy intermittent shelling
Across the river, the rattling reed
"Leave me here," the wounded said
"Leave off that talk," answered the medic
"Save yourself!" the wounded cried
"I'm staying with you," replied the medic
And the two of them stayed, and the field wide open
And the two of them stayed, under heavy fire
"We're lost," the wounded muttered
"Don't let go," the medic replied
"You've been hit too . . ." the wounded muttered
"Not so bad—forget it," the medic replied
The firing gets fiercer—pinned down, hard to move
(Don't give up, just don't give up—)
"I'll never forget you," the wounded promised

"Just don't fall!" the medic mumbled
"I am yours until you die" the wounded swore
"Die? that will be today . . . " answered the medic
Suddenly a cloud of dust, the wind is rising
And a shadow on the ground comes closer, rattling
"We are saved! They're coming!" cried the wounded
But didn't hear a word from the medic
"Brother, my brother!" cried the wounded then
Across the river, the reed is rattling
"Brother, my brother." (lyrics by Dan Almagor; music by Effi Netzer;
   my translation)

The heroic bond of the two young men under fire, the sacrificial commitment of one for the other, the dying yet still walking medic, the weight
of the live body atop the dead one, the sacrificial heroism of the medic, the
dissonance, dating back to Bialik's Kishinev poem, between the continuity of nation (the continual hymn of the rattling reed) and the finality of
death—all these powerfully affected my barely eight-year-old mind and
for a long time it was my absolutely favorite song. If the cultural arena of
the post-statehood years was largely male and largely homoerotic (as in
the lyrics above), as a young girl coming of age in somber post-1973 Israel I found these images of male innocence and male sacrifice strangely
satisfying. "The objectification and eroticization of the male body and
the registration on this body of a masochistic mark" (Smith 1993:80) accurately describes, I think, my earliest erotic attachments.

As the various readings of this book show, in Zionism's constitutive
moment at the late nineteenth century, Woman is cast as that which is
outside of the definition of a particular-universal Jewish national subject.
Woman is figured either as a warring antinationalist element (*Deronda,*
Frishman) or an inactive corrosive element. In Bialik's autobiographical poems, for example, the mother is associated with the poison that
saps the poet's strength ("Me-ayin nakhalti et shirati" ["From whence
did I inherit my poetry"])[1] and the prelinguistic moan (*anakha*) that
infiltrates the poet's body and threatens his poetic language as he eats the
mother's tear-soaked bread ("Shirati" ["My poetry"]).

Less than a conscious opponent of Zionism, Woman is imagined here
and elsewhere as its antithetical other, representing either a debilitating
unconscious presence or the locus of selfish private interests and anti-
sentimental resistance to innocent male bonding and sacrifice. In both
cases, whether she is actively or passively corrosive, Woman must either

be expelled or integrated for subjecthood and entrance into the universally construed symbolic order.

In many early Zionist works, it is female characters who voice a critique of sentimental nationalist bonds and represent assimilation. In *Daniel Deronda*, the Alcharisi is antisentimentality itself: "I did not wish you to be born. I parted with you willingly" (634), she tells Deronda, mocking his newly discovered commitment to Jewish nationalism. In Brenner's *Bakhoref*, the narrator recounts the sorry tale of his unrequited love for a blue-eyed, assimilated, critical girl whose only dream is to emigrate to Belgium. David Frishman, as we have seen, defends modern Hebrew literature against the imagined hostility of a worldly female interlocutor.

This critique is sometimes perpetuated in early statehood culture as a critique of military duty and commitment. Mika, in *He Walked the Fields*, negates Uri's call to duty, beckoning him to stay home; the same can be said in regards to Avner's wife in Spielberg's *Munich*. In *The Bubble*, women are explicitly cast as peace activists in the Israeli political left. Against the tragic love story between the two men—a Jewish soldier and a would-be Palestinian suicide bomber—they represent rationalist antisentimentality. Like Deronda's mother, they are figured as experienced, skeptical voices contrasted with male tragic innocence.

For conservative West European writers like Herzl, the problem and the solution to the question of Woman and Nation was linked to a conservative critique of decadence and its supposed effect on the sanctity of marriage at the fin de siècle. But this, for the most part, isn't true for the East European Hebrew writers whose works would become the basis of the Israeli canon. There is, as we have seen, at the heart of early Zionist discourse and beyond it, a strong, antidomestic streak that posits the male national subject as unwilling or unable to be inscribed within the familial order, marriage, and romantic love. At its center is the image of Apollo's statue; of Bialik's lone poet-messenger in the desert; of Uri, the quintessential young male hero of post-1948 culture, who is tragically killed or perhaps kills himself after learning he will soon father a child. "Forgive us, but we had to," the dead soldiers of "Parade of the Fallen" whisper to their wives and parents, as they leave them on earth for a heavenly world of male camaraderie ("And they meet each other, brown eyes and blue and black / And they speak to each other of names, and weapons, and places / And they pour each other cups of coffee and tea / . . . I look at them and they are happy"). As the poem makes clear, its erotic, political, and social energy and locus of its action is strictly among men.

Woman is not brought into the nationalistic fold in these works via
a plot of heterosexual love but through an identification with powerful
images of tragic male sacrifice that positions her as *guilty spectator*. Accordingly, the audience's/reader's gaze at the male body and its tragic demise is often directed, as in *He Walked the Fields*, by a female character.
And often, it is in the moment of demise or hurt to the male body that a
female character is inducted into the national cause. In Zionist tragedy,
as we have seen, men are assumed to be trapped by destiny, by circumstances over which they have no control; they are tied to the suffering,
humiliated "people" through a bond of tragic responsibility and tragic
guilt. Within this plot of male sacrifice, Woman is brought into the fold
precisely by displacing male guilt, and her own demand for an account-
ing from the warring men, with female guilt. Outrage and cynicism, in
other words, are turned into grieving.

Sometimes in early post-state works, the story of tragic male sacrifice
is narrated by a woman, even by a mother. In one of the most eerie canonical Hebrew poems—Nathan Alterman's "ha-em ha-shlisheet" ("The
Third Mother")—the young men who are both dead and alive are presented through the mother's eyes:

> *My son is tall and quiet.*
> *I am sewing a holiday shirt for my dear.*
> *He's walking in the fields. He will soon be here.*
> *And he holds in his heart a lead bullet.* (1978; translated by Robert
>   Friend[2])

The poem is narrated by three grieving mothers, each delivering a
lament for a dead son; whereas the first two mothers evoke a visual image of their living-dead sons, the third mother attests that she cannot
see him ("perhaps he is only resting"). Much of the dramatic impact of
the poem lies in the juxtaposition between seeing/not seeing, presence/
dissipation, antisentimentality and tears, as the poem evokes the spectacle of the *dead* young son seen by the mothers: "I see a tall ship in a
calm bay, and my son from the topmast hanging," sings the first mother;
here too the image of a crucified Billy Budd dominates.

It isn't an easy question, the relationship of Woman to Zionist nationalist masculinity, and it isn't entirely unique either. That women are
symbolically excluded from nationalist projects has long been an axiom
established by feminist scholars working on nationalisms. Yet Woman,
as Fanon had written, is not only absent from most national narratives
but cast as an explicit Other who must be conquered in the process of

establishing postminority independence and identity. This paradigm is apparent in many national literatures. Yukio Mishima's literally titled "Patriotism," for example, is a story in which a young Japanese military husband reflects approvingly on the trustworthiness of his wife, on the grounds of her willingness to accompany him in ritual suicide.[3] In *The Remasculinization of America: Gender and the Vietnam War* (1989), Susan Jeffords traces this structure in post-Vietnam era films, in which images of innocent masculinity and male bonding are juxtaposed with cynical female figures, often associated with the corrupt state.

Yet there is, as I have tried to show, a particularity to the Jewish national experience both in turn-of-the-century Europe and later in Israel, which produces this quandary and intensifies it. The tragic framework through which the Jewish experience is understood serves, as we have seen, multiple, evolving purposes. Not the least among these is the ambivalence toward violence and the deflection or masking of guilt and shame around the colonization of the land. The tragic "structure of feeling," which took hold in Europe and came to dominate the post-state national imaginary had, I think, to a degree substituted for a full recognition of and responsibility for the harsh reality around the colonization of the land. Female figures who are outside the cycle of combat and violence are thus often endowed with the reality masked by the tragic plot of inevitability; yet concurrently they are depicted as that which needs to be kept at bay lest an alternative reality be expressed.[4]

In *The Bubble*, whose politics are left-leaning, the articulate female peace activists who speak the language of political dissent are nonetheless juxtaposed with and largely overshadowed by images of emotional, handsome, and innocent men—Jewish and Palestinian. These coldly rational and nonsentimental peace activists are depicted as no less detached and heartless than *Munich*'s Golda Meir, who coldly sends Avner on his deadly and deadening mission. Within the context of the film (and in society at large) female peace activists are viewed as politically ineffective, unable to compete with audience identification with the tragic glamour of male sacrifice. They are ineffectual precisely because they are imagined as speaking from outside the dominant tragic discourse, in which the film invariably participates.

The Universal Jew

Like the question of Woman's relationship to nation, the question of Woman and militarism is no more easily answerable. To assume a pure dichotomy between female pacifism and male violent nationalism (as

Virginia Woolf did in *Three Guineas*) is not only to essentialize Woman but to divorce women from the material and imaginary conditions of their environment (which is essentially the sum of Susan Sontag's critique of Woolf[5]). Early Zionist culture had gendered its representative particular-universal national subject; yet the end result of Zionism—the creation of a majority subject, constituted in Hebrew, a subject at the center of its own universe—had applied to men *and* women. Women do not posses a greater capacity to remain outside the domain of a national imaginary; I, as my brief disclosure above reveals, certainly did not.

Yet if tragedy was one of the most dominant "structures of experience" to be articulated by early Zionist culture and to shape Israeli lived experience for something like its first thirty post-state years, if to a degree it retains some of its hold today (in popular more than in high culture, I think), then what I have been unpacking is the different subject positions assigned to men and woman in Zionist tragedy. More than a precise rendition of gender roles, early Zionist works depict the qualities, desires, and knowledge that are respectively distributed to representative figures of men and women at the nation-building moment, that is, as its image of a universal national subject is being formed.

That Zionism and the creation of the State of Israel had indeed created a particular-universal, modern, nonminority Jewish subject (for which Europe or the Gentile are *not* a majority Other) is undoubtedly true. I am that subject. Yet to the degree that this subject was constituted, at least in part, through the discourse of tragedy, early Zionist works also attest to the erosion and the demise of the autonomous subject as such. Indeed, in Brenner and Bialik especially, the subject—the romantic "I" at the center of its own universe—is erected dialectically: through its rise and fall, the constitution of a self and the loss (whether psychological or physical) of that self-identity. The tragic figure is universalized and aggrandized, yet it reaches the peak of its identity at the moment of loss. It is, moreover, a figure constituted by and for the national imagination; as such—especially in the case of post-state tragic figures like *He Walked the Fields*' Uri Kahana—its individual and singular subjecthood is never in fact asserted as such.

If for Weininger, Jew and Woman "do not exist" in the sense that they are heteronomous and dependent on the definition (or desire and affect) of others, the national subject constituted by Zionism "does not exist" either. Despite its declared efforts, Zionism does not create, in my view, a symmetrically antithetical definition of "Jew" to that of the anti-Semite; nor does it create an entirely antithetical definition to that afforded, for example, by Kafka's "minority" sensibility ("What have I in common with the Jews? I have hardly anything in common with myself and should stand very quietly in a corner, content that I can breathe"[6]). Rather, early Zionist works depict the *struggle* and the attendant failures of becoming an autonomous subject, and it is this perhaps more than any other attribute that marks it as a product of modernity.

Postmodern Israeli Works and the Question of Identity

In contemporary Israeli works, the gendered aspects of the struggle for subjecthood have been complicated and their depiction has been much more consciously politicized. *The Bubble,* as we have seen, perpetuates the tragic mode; yet it also stretches its definition and localizes it by representing tragedy as a meeting point between Jewish and Palestinian men. Leftist female activists, speaking from the vantage point of abstract universal moral criteria, are critiqued in the film precisely because they live in a "bubble"; that is, they are detached from the political and socioeconomic realities of the Middle East and aligned with the dominant leftist discourse outside Israel. In juxtaposing the local/tragic with the international/rational the film finally points to the inability of *either* discourse to sufficiently capture and potentially affect the present day realities of Israel/Palestine.

Several contemporary female Israeli writers offer a more greatly nuanced interrogation of these questions. In the novel *Sarah, Sarah* (2000)[7] by Ronit Matalon, the tragic persona is assumed by the character of a combatant female activist, Sarah, a photographer who periodically disappears into Gaza and emerges with photographs of sleeping Palestinian children. Sarah's smart, angry, destructive, elusive figure is contrasted with a passive and worn husband who represents the status quo; yet the novel's analysis does not end there but rather zigzags in a tense dialectic between the heroine's rigid moral/political position and a space besieged by trauma, hurt, and desire, which assaults not only the subject's political commitment but the subject's very subjecthood. Time and again, Sarah's rigid ideals of justice in Israel/Palestine are crushed not only against the paralysis of her family and friends but against economic realities, against conflicting power hierarchies, against her own depression, against life itself. Her affair with a fellow Palestinian activist ends in disaster that includes an abortion. Her incessant efforts to implicate the army in the death of a Palestinian girl are deflated when she discovers that in the middle of a strictly imposed curfew, the girl was sent to fetch cigarettes for her craving father. Matalon's politically committed novel exposes the discourse of Israeli male victimhood and tragedy as an empty shell, but it does not replace it with easy solutions. Rather, it depicts quite directly and brutally the dissolution of the Zionist subject and the limits of individual and national autonomy and links these directly, if not solely, to the unstable foundation of Israel. Indeed, a crucial difference between early and contemporary Hebrew literature is the conscious abandonment of the idea and ideal of the autonomous, bound, particular-universal subject. Whereas Bialik and Brenner depict a dialectic struggle between this ideal and its inattainability, Matalon and other postmodern Israeli writers take the erosion of the subject as a feature of subjecthood and subjectivity itself. They portray the subject as directly constituted by a national imaginary and as an effect of present and past traumas. And they link the instability of the subject both to a generalized postmodern condition *and* to a local reality where the nation itself is boundaryless, porous, and violent. It is a type of inquiry and art that aims not only at complexity but also at temporal and spatial precision.

In Orly Castel-Bloom's novel *Khalakim enoshiyim* (*Human Parts*),[8] published during the first intifada of 2000, the writer depicts a world in which death is continuous with life, where suicide bombings, lethal flu strains, poverty, and depression exist alongside TV talk shows and trips to Ikea. The stories of various "characters" are linked together through a uniform, monotonal, depersonalized third-person narration and a vocabulary derived mostly from Israeli slang and oversaturated linguistic tropes coined by the media.[9] This is the language through which both external events and internal thoughts and feelings are narrated; there is, Castel-Bloom suggests, no detached or purely private individual space outside traumatic reality and its representation in national fantasies from which even the most privileged witness can engage in a clearheaded analysis of its effects and causes. Thus, alongside the unrelenting assault of aggression, violence, and disease, the novel depicts their incessant reconfiguration and dramatization on the television, a bombardment of newscasts and talk shows in which those who have "not died yet"—doctors, meteorologists, and ordinary sufferers—are turned into overnight media stars. As in all her fiction, Castel-Bloom's protagonists are not "realistic" characters; rather, they are composite structures whose utterances, thoughts, and "interiority" consist of phrases coined mostly by Israeli media. One is either a victim of traumatic reality or its consumer on reality TV. And characters do not exist outside representation in language but are themselves the linguistic constructs of the national imaginary at a given time and place. In consciously composing them as such,

Castel-Bloom undermines all categories and pretentions of autonomous subjecthood, offering instead the vision of the human as "part": a transitory fragment constituted relationally and temporally. The fracturing of daily life and its fragile sense of autonomy and safety by Palestinian suicide bombings takes this condition of the subject to an extreme. Yet the implications of Castel-Bloom's technique are larger, undermining the very claim of the subject to autonomy, interiority, autonomous selfhood, and identity.

We see here, I think, a return to Kafka.

Or perhaps we see in the works of these two female writers (whose families, incidentally or not, both immigrated to Israel from Egypt) a kind of quiet revolution, the final infiltration of Bialik's mother's poisonous milk into the body politic. If Woman is imagined in early Zionist literature as an outsider and a menace to the nation-state, Matalon and Castel-Bloom both fulfill the threat and yet insert themselves as *the* mainstream national discourse. They reject tragedy, together with the patterns of desire and identification triggered by it, as an organizing structure for national feelings and discourse. Yet in doing so, they create a new concrete universal subject, a postmodern *nonsubject.* Indeed I view it as a return of sorts to Kafka's nonidentity, the complex subject position of the unrooted Jew that Eliot, Herzl, and others wholeheartedly reject at the turn of the nineteenth century. But distinct from that earlier position, it is a sensibility that has emerged from the detour in Jewish history into the autonomous majority identity that early Zionism struggled to create and to a degree succeeded, if only by virtue of the formation of a new, vigorous, Hebrew speaking cultural space. It is from a relative position of power, I think, that postmodern Israeli writers (like all postmodern writers) can interrogate powerlessness and subjectlessness, which are linked not to a minority identity but to identity as such.

In Matalon's surreal novella *Galu et pane'a* (*Uncover Her Face*) from 2006, where she is perhaps most indebted to Kafka, the writer interrogates the question of the subject directly in relationship to power, gender, and Israeli and Palestinian identities. The overarching plot is seemingly narrow: a first-person narrator's journey to burn down the house of her married lover. Along the way, gasoline and lighter fluid in tow, she encounters various persons and situations, including a ride and a conversation with a female Palestinian cab driver named Fauzia. "I haven't understood," the narrator asks Fauzia, "To be a victim, does that make one less of a person or more? After all, I wanted to live and could have lived under his [the married lover's] skin"[10] (15). As the two women drive through the Occupied Territories, Matalon draws parallels connecting the dependencies and power discrepancies between men and women and between occupier and occupied. In a hilarious passage about an extratight "explosive girdle," which Fauzia'a family presently manufactures for Hamas and for which she is the house model ("Because she was constantly gaining and losing weight she was a model to all sizes: small, medium, large, and extra-large" [13]) Matalon further conflates the states of oppression, dependence, and resistance of women and Palestinians. This alliance of victimhood is particularly aimed at Israeli mainstream bourgeois morality, represented in the novella by the abandoning lover:

> "What's the story," Fauzia asks the narrator, "Talk to me like they talk to taxi drivers:"
>
> "The strategy of last resort had imposed itself on me," I answer. "I wasted all the steps I had until this one. We loved like crazy, escaped like crazy, and at the end he didn't come because of the larger picture. I'm going to burn it down on him, so it doesn't come out as if our forces returned safely to their bases" . . .
>
> Fauzia lit a cigarette . . . and thought a little. "What closet is he in? What's the larger picture?" "A public figure and a moral authority," I said. She quietly whistled: "You went for the big money *ayouni*. What organization sent you?" (15–16)

The narrator and the Palestinian driver thus share a tenderly hilarious moment of female bonding, succinctly transmitted through media-generated vocabulary with which the narrator, the driver, and Matalon's readers are intimately acquainted. Not only is the phrase "our forces returned safely to their bases" ("khazru lebesisam beshalom") a standard phrase used in news casts of aerial bombings to indicate the absence of casualties (on the Israeli side), but it is also a euphemism, as *beshalom* means "in peace"—a darkly ironic phrase, especially when relayed to an interlocutor who is on the receiving end of the aerial bombings. Matalon thus both constructs and deconstructs the analogy between the Palestinian suicide bomber and the dejected female Israeli lover. When the two women "reach a large city" and must "lawfully register" with a "security officer," he, in a direct reference to Primo Levi's *Se questo è un uomo*? (*Is This a Man*?), casually wipes his glasses on Fauzia's shirttail. It is at this moment that Fauzia pays the narrator for the ride (yes!) and zooms off in her cab.[11]

Like Fauzia's constantly shifting body size (small, medium, large, and extra-large) identities and identifications in *Uncover Her Face* thus shrink and grow, merge and disjoin in time and space. Identities and identifications are formed in language, which can be at once a morally bankrupt euphemism ("returned to their bases in peace") and the basis of an intimacy shared by people—Jews and Palestinians, the two lovers—momentarily inhabiting overlapping cultural/spatial geographies. Matalon's language is porous, alluding directly and indirectly to various texts: Levi's *Is This a Man?;* Chekhov's "Lady with a Dog"; Kafka's *The Trial;* and George Steiner's *Errata,* a meditation on the dialectical relationship between love and hate recited by the narrator to her lover as her own words (without any reference to the original). These texts, Matalon implies, are not only metanarratives through which the narrator interprets her experience but are the very basis of the narrator's experience of love, power, dependence, and self-identity. It is a chain of endless dependencies and links that curtail the possibility of a truly autonomous individual and national identity. Like the lover, literary texts are posited as a kind of crutch for the narrator's "I"; and like the lover, who in his final encounter with the narrator "unscrews" Steiner's words from the narrator's written page and "puts them in his pocket one by one" (Matalon 2006:10) this crutch may lose its holding power at any given moment. No identity and will are autonomous and stable (the narrator herself defects from her original plan a number of times over the narrative) except at the moment of its own destruction and the destruction of the Other in what Matalon calls a "final disengagement" (burning down the lover's home).

Thus, and without masking over political inequalities, Matalon's work is a critique of any kind of identity politic that posits a stable, autonomous, universal subject. Her critique is aimed not only at the nationalist/Zionist subject but also at the kind of dogmatic antinationalist attack whose basis is a firm, fixed, and high moral ground. "We cannot be other than what we are at a given moment," Fauzia tells the narrator. "Go for it. Burn it. The purpose sanctifies the subjugated" ("hamatara mekadeshet et hanirtzaim") (Matalon 2006:15). (This again is a word play on *Hamatara mekadeshet et ha-emtzaim*—"the purpose sanctifies the means"—a logic shared by both Israelis and Palestinians.) Subjecthood may be momentarily achieved through love, hate, or desire for an Other (a lover, a text, a nation, an enemy) yet it is bound to be undone in the next moment. In this work, Matalon reclaims not only Kafka's complex position on identity—Jewish or otherwise—but also the irony that underlies his minority sensibility, and reconfigures it as her own.

Matalon's narrator's striving motion is thus portrayed as aimed not toward a self-conscious, positive identity but "*qua* void"; and the universality of her identity—Woman, Jew, and in essence all modern identities—lies precisely in this lack. It is, finally, a turning upside down of Weininger's dictum: the Jew and the Woman who for Weininger are nonsubjects, heteronomous entities, voids and projections of other's (Man/Christian) fantasies presented as the very essence of subjectivity. In doing so, Matalon effects here what Žižek has called "a Hegelian reflective reversal" (1994:104) of Weininger's theory, providing a kind of literary corollary to Lacan's model of the self as a lack negotiating between the Real and the Imaginary.

So the fantasy of a cohesive, autonomous individual and national subjecthood, both of which are at the ideological basis of the fin-de-siècle national dream, are consciously exposed in Matalon's novella as the work of the Imaginary. In its striving toward cohesive identity in the Imaginary, the self seeks crutches, mirrors, identifications, which is what Fauzia is to the narrator. "I alarmingly clung to her, tucking my hand under her shirt, seeking her soft, humongous breast," the narrator recounts (2006:16); yet the ease of lesbian, native, and nativist maternal comfort is, like all other fantasies, only momentarily fulfilled. "I never had that milk they talk about," Fauzia says (16), as she shakes the narrator off and starts her cab. Matalon thus depicts and condemns Israeli denial of Palestinian humanity (the wiping of the hand), but she does not fetishize a Palestinian, female, or lesbian identity any more than she does the mainstream Israeli male identity embodied in the selfish lover ("a public personality and moral authority"). The self and the nation are the "night," in the Hegelian sense—"an empty nothing that contains everything in its simplicity—an unending wealth of many representations, images, of which none belong to him"[12] Fauzia, whose real name is actually Laura, whose Ramallean family now makes explosive girdles for Hamas but in the past was selling bras and lingerie, is no more a locus of stable identity than the Israeli narrator, whose identity is made up mostly of (foreign language) texts.

The subject thus participates in the universal precisely insofar as its identity is felt as truncated and incomplete; this void is at the heart of destructive and violent politics (burning down the lover's house, suicide bombings, Gaza) but it can also, as Matalon's work suggests, potentially tentatively and momentarily be the ground for inclusionary politics and unpredictable human bonds.

Introduction

1. In his oft quoted words to the French National Assembly in 1789, Clermont-Tonnerre exclaimed that the Jews deserved everything as individuals, but nothing as a nation (Bauman 1991:176).

2. For an excellent summary of the good nation/bad nation distinction, see Gandhi (1998:102–10).

3. For a more detailed analysis and argument with Boyarin's view on the question of masculinity, see chapter 4.

4. For an interrogation of Freud's relationship to Herzl, Zionism, and Judaism, see Yosef Hayyim Yerushalmi's *Freud's Moses* (1991) and, more recently, Eliza Slavet's *Racial Fever: Freud and the Jewish Question* (2009).

5. As Yerushalmi (1991) and Slavet (2009) have shown, Freud's articulation of Moses as an Egyptian supports a vision of Jewish continuity that is not as removed from Ahad Ha'am's view as it initially seems.

6. In Jacqueline Rose's recent *The Question of Zion* (2005), which acknowledges early Zionists' fascination with the unconscious, the premise of her inquiry, which largely consists of literal readings of Zionist texts, suggests the possibility of deciphering the "question of Zion" through positivistic means.

7. Pinsker 1944:79.

8. Letter dated October 29, 1876 (Eliot 1908:211).

9. For a lengthy meditation on this topic, see Part III of this book.

10. Quoted in Le Rider (1993:59–60).

11. This how Tom Nairn (1977) reads the function of the nation at large.

12. For a detailed analysis, see chapter 2.

13. In "Zionism Reconsidered," 1944 (Arendt 1978:343–74). Later she sporadically expressed enthusiasm. See Pitterberg (2007).

Chapter One

1. In 1973, James Michie, editor at the Bodley Head Press, commissioned F. R. Leavis to finally execute what the latter had forcefully argued three decades earlier: to edit Daniel Deronda out of *Daniel Deronda* in order "to produce an extricated Gwendolen Harleth." Such amputation

was necessary, Leavis had argued, in order "to establish . . . that there is a major classic, which may be suitably called 'Gwendolen Harleth,' hidden from the general recognition it deserves in the voluminous mixed work that George Eliot published—a classic that it is incumbent on us to reclaim for English literature." Leavis then proceeded to edit the novel's "bad half": "Represented by Deronda himself, and by what may be called in general the Zionist inspiration," eliminating chapters 36 to 43 and smaller portions of other chapters. His proposed title for the project was "*Gwendolen Harleth* George Eliot's Superb Last Novel Liberated from *Daniel Deronda*" Leavis (1964:80). For the complete history of Leavis's suggested intervention in *Daniel Deronda*, see Johnson (2001:215). See also Storer (1995:40–49); and Leavis (1982:65–75). All references to *Daniel Deronda* are to the 1995 Penguin edition.

2. "That few dare being eccentric is a chief danger of the times. The tendency of the time is no excesses, increased regularity of conduct, desire nothing too strongly, instead of great energies guided by vigorous reason and strong feelings controlled by conscious will." Quoted in Bellamy (1992:28).

3. This was true particularly for Western European Zionists such as Herzl (see chapter 2). For the more complex relationship of Eastern European Jewish writers to decadence, see Hamutal Bar-Yosef (1997).

4. Quoted in Mosse (1993:172).

5. For a fuller discussion of Smiles's books, see ibid., 10.

6. For extensive discussion of Victorian character discourse, see Bellamy (1992:9–57).

7. This is how it is read by Cheyette (1993:48).

8. This unattributable review, circa 1876, is quoted in Lewis, *Gendering Orientalism* (1996:200).

9. For the history of *Deronda*'s reception in Britain, see Haight (1969: 486–88).

10. For an extensive discussion of late nineteenth-century images of Jews, see Gilman (1991).

11. Quoted in Hoberman (1995:141).

12. For an extended meditation on their ideas, see Gourgouris (1996: 14–46).

13. This stress on language is in itself a consequence of the new age of nationalism in the late nineteenth century (Hobsbawm 1990:102).

Chapter Two

1. See Shuttleworth (1984).

2. This is Radhakrishnan's (1992) recapitulation of Chatterjee's point.

3. See for example Phillip E. Wegner's discussion of the works of George Orwell in *Imaginary Communities: Utopia, the Nation and the Spatial Histories of Modernity* (2002:183–216).

4. For an analysis of the Indian example, see essays by Chatterjee (2001) and Radhakrishnan (1992).

5. Lazar (1900). Quoted in Menkin (2003).

6. For an analysis of Fanon's position on family, see McClintock, Mufti, and Shohat (1997).

7. For an analysis of motherhood and passing, see Elizabeth Abel, Barbara Christian, and Helene Moglen, eds., *Female Subjects in Black and White: Race, Psychoanalysis, Feminism* (1997).

8. Summarized by Judith Butler, *Bodies That Matter* (1993:43).

Chapter Three

1. Introduction to the Hebrew translation of *Daniel Deronda* (Eliot 1893).

2. It is ironic, since she argues in the "Modern Hep! Hep! Hep!" (Eliot 1879) against the tendency of studying foreign languages and cultures before one's own.

3. Some women did read Hebrew and actively sought Hebrew literature; their numbers, however, were disproportionate to the numbers of male readers. For a discussion of nineteenth-century female readers in Eastern Europe, see Parush (2004).

4. For a more detailed description of this group, see chapter 7.

5. Solomon (2005). For extensive research on this subject, see Parush (2004). See also Menkin (2003).

6. For a further discussion of women's education in traditional Jewish communities, see Parush (2004).

7. For further discussion, see Miron, *When Loners Come Together* (1987b).

8. There are also parallels, of course, to Eliot's own anxieties about the link of authorship and prostitution. See Gallagher (1986).

9. Frishman, "Introduction to *Daniel Deronda*" (1887:4; my emphasis).

10. Published by A. Y. Shapira in *ha-Asif* (1884). See Dekel (2007).

11. See Haight (1969:486–88).

12. For the complete history of the Guedella affair, see Versus (1980: 178).

13. Letter published in *ha-Tzfira* (1877), quoted ibid., 179.

14. Letter published in *ha-Levanon* (1876), quoted ibid.

15. Published in *ha-Levanon* (1876), quoted ibid. (my emphasis).

16. Quoted ibid., 180.

17. Shlomo Zemach, *Sipur hayay* (*The Story of My Life*), quoted in Dan Miron, *When Loners Come Together* (1987b:312).

18. Quoted in Johnson (2001:216).

19. Ahad Ha'am, "Hikuy ve-hitbolelut" (*Imitation and Assimilation*). In Ahad Ha'am (1970).

20. Like Leavis, Frishman was a strong advocate of realist fiction; he published numerous realist short stories himself. See Frishman, *Michtavim* (1968).

21. To date, the novel has not been fully translated into Hebrew. But a street has been named for George Eliot in the center of Tel Aviv.

Chapter Four

1. Details of Herzl's meetings and journeys are recorded in *The Diaries of Theodor Herzl* (Lowenthal 1956).

2. Herzl's travels and meetings are documented in detail in his extensive diaries (ibid.). It was his exclusive focus on conducting politics from above and his willingness to negotiate with imperial, fascist, and even anti-Semitic governments and leaders that constituted one of Arendt's main sources of criticism of Herzl. See Arendt, "Herzl and Lazare" (1978:125–30).

3. Theodor Herzl, preface to *Altneuland* (2000:vi).

4. Already more than a decade ago, Hamutal Bar-Yosef was writing about Zionism and decadence. More recently and comprehensively, Michael Stanislawski explored ideational links in *Zionism and the Fin de Siècle* (2001).

5. Ibid., 176–77 (my emphasis).

6. Vampire stories seem to have held and to continue holding a formidable place in culture. For a critical bibliography of these stories see Margaret L. Carter, ed., 1989. *The Vampire in Literature*. Ann Arbor, Michigan: UMI Research Press.

7. Carl Schorske, *Fin de Siècle Vienna* (1981:120).

8. Nordau wrote on behalf of Herzl in the Herzl/Ahad Ha'am debate. Ironically, he is also briefly mentioned in *Dracula:* Dracula's labeling as a "criminal type" according to Nordau's theory of criminology helps his pursuers "understand" him and thus leads to his demise!

9. Quoted in Schorske, *Fin de Siècle Vienna* (1981:164).

10. The survival of the Western bourgeois society certainly lies at the surface of *Dracula,* as the survival of the Jews lies at the surface of *Altneuland*. Yet even *Daniel Deronda* features the threat of extinction for England: a multiplicity of middle- and upper-class brides with no prospective husbands. I thank Nicholas Dames for this last insight.

11. Judith Butler, *Excitable Speech: A Politics of the Performative* (1997:3).

12. Bhabha, introduction to *Nation and Narration* (1990:3).

13. See de Vries and Weber (1997).

14. Those of Micah Josef Berdyczewski, for instance. Perhaps even of Bialik.

15. Renan (1881/1990).

16. Press (1997).

17. Herzl presents precisely Nordau's critique of fin-de-siècle marriage here. As Michael Stanislawski (2001) has shown, Nordau denounced the commercial character of the majority of marriages and called for marriages that are based on sexual attraction in order to enhance the "survival of the species." Needless to say, healthy, vigorous, heterosexual desire will be the basis for "New World" marriages in Palestine.

18. Herzl's vision of a secular, essentially non-Jewish state was the subject of harsh criticism by cultural Zionists, most forcefully by Ahad Ha'am.

19. Kingscourt's marriage had also ended in failure. It was in fact his young wife's adultery that propelled his desire to be removed from the civilized world.

20. See, for example, Eve Sedgwick's analysis of George Eliot's *Adam Bede* (1990:134–60).

21. Quoted in Lowenthal (1956:280–81).

22. Arendt, "On Violence." Discussed in Beatrice Hanssen, "On the Politics of Pure Means," in de Vries and Weber (1997:276).

23. *Altneuland,* 79.

Chapter Five

1. "Self-Criticism," in Brenner (1914/1975).

2. Kafka (1978:388). Quoted in Miron (2008).

Chapter Six

1. Nonetheless, Kishinev *was* the first pogrom to be extensively photographed, the first visually documented horror of the twentieth century, to be followed a decade later by the images of bloody battlefields and mutilated soldiers of the First World War. See Miron (2005).

2. All subsequent quotes from Bialik's poetry are taken from this edition.

3. Though Bialik held on to the notebooks containing the original testimonies, transferring them to Palestine when he emigrated there in

1924, he took great measures to avoid their publication. The testimonies were published only in 1991, nearly sixty years after Bialik's death and nearly a century after the Kishinev Pogrom. See Goren (1991).

4. "Emancipation remains a rich gift . . . willingly or unwillingly flung to the poor, humble beggars whom no one, however, cares to shelter, because a homeless, wandering beggar wins confidence or sympathy from none." Hertzberg (1997:187).

5. Gluzman (2005:13–36).

6. As the narrator tells us: "Despite all his glorious achievements Max Berlliant can't hide his Jewishness; not from us, the Jews, nor from them, the Gentiles. You can pick him out like a counterfeit coin in a handful of change, and in a crowd of Abels he stands like a Cain. At every twist and turn he is reminded who he is and what he is. In short, he's a sorry creature" (116).

7. Carl Schmitt's groundbreaking essays in *Political Theology* (1985) have spurred numerous analyses of political theology in various national contexts.

8. See Gluzman (2005:26–27).

9. See Miron (2000) as well as Klausner (1951:32).

10. See essays in *Ha-Zionut ve-hakhazara la-historia* (*Zionism and the Return to History: A Re-Assessment*), ed. Shmuel Noah Eisenstadt and Mosheh Lisak. Jerusalem (1999).

11. For a more detailed exploration of Tschernichowsky's poem as well as these ideas, see the previous chapter. See also Ahad Ha'am, "Nietzsche and the Jews" in Simon (1944) and, most recently, Golomb (2004).

12. Quoted in Hever (2005:37; translation mine).

Chapter Seven

1. See, for example, Jacob Golomb's *Nietzsche and Zion* (2004) and *Nietzsche ba-tarbut haivrit* (*Nietzsche in Hebrew Culture*) (2002); the latter book contains a (Hebrew) bibliography of the scores of works written on this subject from 1892 to 2001.

2. See most recently a special issue of *New Nietzsche Studies,* "Nietzsche and the Jews," ed. David Allison, Babette Babich, and Debra Bergoffen.

3. Brinker (2002:145).

4. *Ecce Homo,* sec. 4, p. 274.

5. Quoted in Parush (1992:33).

6. Quotes taken from Mendes-Flohr (1997:141, 237).

7. From "In Two Directions" (1900–1903) in Hertzberg (1997:295).

8. Ahad Ha'am, "Transvaluation of Values" in *Selected Essays* (1970).

9. My translation and my emphasis. Unless otherwise noted, all subsequent quotations from the story refer to this translation. An additional English translation by William Cutter was published in 2004 in Berdyczewski (2004:29–40).

10. I thank my friend and editor Lynn Dion for this point.

11. I owe my friend and colleague Nickolas Pappas thanks for explicating these distinctions.

12. Hertzberg (1997:256).

13. Sh. Y. Abramovitsh's *The Book of Beggars* (1869/1988) both exemplifies this trend and provides a wonderful analysis of the deficiencies of the Diasporic Jewish body politic and the bodies of Diasporic Jews. With its coarse and vivid descriptions of gluttony and sexuality, it sarcastically exposes the myth of Jewish spirituality. Yet it also critiques the instinctual, physical life as insufficient for community building. According to Mendele, only a "renewal" of emotional ties, in addition to the instinctual, will provide the glue needed for the renewal of the body politic.

14. For an analysis of the Yiddish bildungsroman, see Miron (1996).

15. Berdyczewski (1971:25–68; all translations of quoted passages are mine).

16. Ibid., 32.

17. Ibid., 50.

18. All subsequent quotes from *Bakhoref* are taken from Yosef Hayyim Brenner, *Ktavim* (*Collected Works*) (1978:95–267) and are translated by me.

19. Berdyczewski's doctoral dissertation (University of Bern, 1897). Published in Berdyczewski (1995:85–121, 121; translated from German by Alexander Barzel).

20. In his critique of Brenner's later works *Mikan u-mikan* (*From Here and There*) and *Atsabim* (*Nerves*), Boaz Arpali (1992) writes: "Paradoxically, the more Zionism is depicted in [Brenner's] literature as irrational and impractical and unrealizable, the more it is justified, because it is derived from the blind forces of life, those over which one has no control. Thus, Zionism's negation as a conscious-rational category is de facto its strength; Zionism reflects the hidden forces of life from which the most important aims are derived."

21. All translations from Hebrew throughout this chapter are mine, unless noted otherwise.

22. *The Birth of Tragedy* (1886), preface, sec 4. Also in *Twilight of the Idols* (1889:561–62).

23. More than the path to normative, heterosexual, patriarchal masculinity, the nationalist plot seems to me to be the road for shaking off this type of masculinity and its strenuous commitments. In the classic Zionist epic poem "Baruch me-Magentza" ("Baruch of Meintz") by turn-of-the-century Hebrew poet Saul Tschernichowsky, a bloody anti-Jewish pogrom leads the hero to burn down his entire village, wife and three daughters included. Only he remains, crazed *yet alone*.

24. Letter dated August 23, 1913. In *Makhbarot Brenner* (*Brenner's Notebooks*), (Brenner 1984:13). This and all subsequent translations of letters are mine.

25. Letter dated August 28, 1913. Ibid., 16.

26. Letter dated September 1, 1913. Ibid., 18.

27. August 28, 1913. Ibid., 17.

28. Used as a title of respect for men in Turkey, equivalent to sir (Turkish).

29. Arab headdress (Arabic).

30. A literal translation of the original is "it's neither they nor their bounty."

31. A native of central Russia.

32. A city in central Russia.

33. Brenner stresses the hostility of upper class Arabs toward the Jews: hostility even stronger than Polish anti-Semitism. He therefore sees prospects of change only in the lower classes, the workers.

34. A short overcoat (Russian).

35. Sir (Arabic).

36. From Allah.

37. Both writers are quoted in Guvrin (1991).

Chapter Eight

1. For an analysis of these differences, see Wilmer (2004:180–84).

2. All translations of *He Walked the Fields* are mine.

3. Native-born Israeli.

4. My translation.

5. Quoted in Stathis Gourgouris, *Dream Nation* (1996:21).

6. It was Gluzman (2007) who first noted these gendered implications.

7. For example: S. Yizhar, "Layla bli yeriyot" ("A Night with No Shooting") (1947); Yigal Mossinsohn, "Matityahu Schatz" (1989).

8. From Yigal Mossinsohn, *Aforim Ka-sak* (*Gray as a Sack: Stories and Plays*) (1989). My translation.

9. I am much indebted to James Schamus, whose fascinating article "Next Year in *Munich*: Zionism, Masculinity, and Diaspora in Spielberg's

Epic" (2007) made clear to me the links between early and late depictions of Zionist masculinity.

10. See Freedman (2001).

11. The film opened the 2005 Berlin Film Festival and received a long standing ovation.

An Autobiographical Postlude

1. "A withered breast bared to me by a mother wound in mourning clothes / And from it I sucked the poison cup. / Since then an adder nests in my heart / Courses its position in me and saps my strength . . ."—"Night Thoughts" (1895). Translated by Atar Hadari (Bialik 2000).

2. http://www.lorenz.com/Med/Pages/15_2596R.pdf.

3. I thank Lynn Dion for acquainting me with this story.

4. In Batia Gur's novel *Even takhat even* (*Stone for a Stone*) (1998), for example, a mother whose son was killed by friendly fire launches a legal battle against the army authorities and her own family in order to have her son's gravestone reflect the true circumstances of his death rather than the uniform, mandatory dedication "Fell in the line of duty."

5. In *Regarding the Pain of Others* (2003).

6. Taken from an entry in Kafka's diary dated January 8, 1914. I thank Vivian Liska's wonderful book *When Kafka Says We* (2009) for pointing me to this citation.

7. Published in English under the title *Bliss* (2003).

8. Published in English by David R. Godine Publishers, 2003.

9. "And so, suicide bombers took with them to the bosom of death people who had left their homes to go about their affairs . . . People . . . were blown to pieces in nearby streets . . . Others were mortally wounded. Some of them died of their wounds in the ambulance taking them to the hospital and others died later. Many others were severely wounded, or suffered moderate, moderate to light, or light wounds. The lightly wounded were usually those who afterward told the media what had happened. The description of the horror almost always began with the words: 'Suddenly I heard a boom'" (2003:6–7).

10. All quotes from *Galu et Pane'a* are translated by me.

11. In this scene, Primo Levi's capo supervisor, Alex, wipes *his* greasy palm on Levi's shirt. "He would be amazed," Levi writes, "the poor brute Alex, if someone told him that today, on the basis of this action, I judge him and Pannwitz and innumerable others like him, big and small, in Auschwitz and everywhere" (1996:108).

12. Quoted in Verene (1985:7).

SELECTED BIBLIOGRAPHY

Abel, Elizabeth, Barbara Christian, and Helene Moglen, eds. 1997. *Female Subjects in Black and White: Race, Psychoanalysis, Feminism*. Berkeley: University of California Press.

Aberbach, David. 1988. *Bialik*. London: Peter Halban Publishers.

Abrahams, Israel. 1981. *Jewish Life in the Middle Ages* (1898). New York: Atheneum.

Abramovitsh, Sholem (Mendele Mocher Sforim). 1869/1988. *Sefer ha-kabtsanim* (*The Book of Beggars*). Tel Aviv: Dvir.

Agnon, Shmuel Yosef. 1946. *Tmol Shilshom* (*Only Yesterday*). Tel Aviv: Schocken.

Ahad Ha'am (Asher Ginzburg). 1970. *Selected Essays of Ahad Ha'am*. Trans. and ed. Leon Simon. New York: Atheneum.

Allison, David. 2001. *Reading the New Nietzsche*. Lanham: Rowan and Littlefield.

Allison, David, Babette Babich, and Debra Bergoffen, eds. 2008. "Nietzsche and the Jews." Special issue, *New Nietzsche Studies* 7, no. 3–4 (Winter).

Alterman, Nathan. 1978. *Selected Poems: Bilingual Edition*. Trans. Robert Friend. Tel Aviv: Ha'kibbutz Ha'meuchad.

Anderson, Benedict. 1983. *Imagined Communities*. London: Verso.

Arendt, Hannah. 1958. *The Human Condition*. Chicago: University of Chicago Press.

———. 1978. *The Jew as Pariah: Jewish Identity and Politics in the Modern Age*. Ed. Ron H. Feldman. New York: Grove Press.

Armstrong, Nancy. 2005. *How Novels Think: The Limits of Individualism from 1719–1900*. New York: Columbia University Press.

Arpali, Boaz. 1992. *Ha-parshanut ha-chadasha la-romanim ha-rishonim shel Y. H. Brenner* (*New Criticism to Y. H. Brenner's Early Stories*). Tel Aviv: Open University of Israel Press.

Bar-Yosef, Hamutal. 1997. *Maga'im shel dekadens: Bialik, Berdychevsky, Brenner* (*Decadent Trends in Hebrew Literature*). Be'er Sheva: Ben Gurion University Press.

———. 1998. "Ahava, miniyut ve-musar yehudi be-shirat Bialik" ("Love, Sexuality and Jewish Morality in Bialik's Poetry"). *Bikoret u-parshanut*, vol. 33.

Bauman, Zygmunt. 1991. *Modernity and Ambivalence.* Cambridge: Polity Press.

Bellamy, Richard. 1992. *Liberalism and Modern Society.* University Park: Pennsylvania State University Press.

Benhabib, Seyla. 1999. "Sexual Difference and Collective Identities: The New Global Constellation." *Signs* 24, no. 2 (Winter): 335–61.

Benjamin, Walter. 1977. *The Origin of German Tragic Drama.* Trans. John Osborne. London: Verso.

———. 2000. "Psychologia pre-Freudianit bemifneh hameot" ("Pre-Freudian Psychopathology at the Turn of the Century"). In *Sadan: Research in Hebrew Literature,* vol. 4, ed. Avner Holtzman, 37–71. Tel Aviv: Tel Aviv University Press.

Berdyczewski, Micah Josef. 1971. "Ma'chanayim" ("Two Camps"). In *Romanim ktzarim (Short Novels),* 25–68. Tel Aviv: Bialik Institute.

———. 1996. *Ktavim (Collected Works).* 6 vols. Ed. Avner Holtzman. Tel Aviv: Ha'kibbutz ha'meuchad.

———. 1999. "On the Link Between Ethics and Aesthetics" (excerpts from Berdyczewski's doctoral dissertation submitted at the University of Bern in 1897). In *Ktavim (Writings),* vol. 4, ed. Avner Holtzman and Yizhak Kafkafi, 85–127. Tel Aviv: Ha'kibbutz ha'meuchad.

———. 2004. *Miriam and Other Stories.* Ed. Avner Holtzman. New York: Toby Press.

Berger, Maurice, ed. 1995. *Constructing Masculinity.* New York: Routledge.

Berkowitz, Michael. 1993. *Zionist Culture.* Chapel Hill: University of North Carolina Press.

Berlant, Lauren. 1991. *The Anatomy of National Fantasy: Hawthorne, Utopia, and Everyday Life.* Chicago: University of Chicago Press.

Berlin, Isaiah. 2000. "Two Concepts of Liberty" (1969). In *The Power of Ideas,* ed. Henry Hardy. Princeton, N.J.: Princeton University Press.

Bhabha, Homi, ed. 1990. *Nation and Narration.* London: Routledge.

———. 1994. *Location of Culture.* London: Routledge.

Bialik, Hayyim Nahman. 1983–90. *Shirim (Collected Poems).* 2 vols. Ed. Dan Miron. Tel Aviv: Dvir.

————. 2000. *Songs from Bialik: Selected Poems of Hayim Nahman Bialik.* Trans. Atar Hadari. Syracuse, N.Y.: Syracuse University Press.

Boyarin, Daniel. 1997. *Unheroic Conduct: The Rise of Heterosexuality and the Invention of the Jewish Man.* Berkeley: University of California Press.

Brenner, Yosef Hayyim. 1960. *Kol khitvei Y.H. Brenner (Complete Works of Y. H. Brenner).* Tel Aviv: Ha'kibbutz ha'meuchad.

————. 1975. "Self-Criticism" (1914). In *The Zionist Idea,* ed. Arthur Hertzberg, 307–12. New York: Atheneum.

————. 1978. *Ktavim (Writings).* Tel Aviv: Ha'kibbutz ha'meuchad.

————. 1984. *Makhbarot Brenner 3–4 (Brenner's Notebooks vols. 3–4).* Ed. Menakhem Dorman and Uzi Shavit. Tel Aviv: Ha'kibbutz ha'meuchad.

Brinker, Menachem. 2002. "Nietzsche ve-ha-sofrim ha-ivriyim: Nisayon le-reiya kolelet" ("Nietzsche and the Hebrew Writers: An Attempt at a General Overview"). In Golomb 2002, 131–60.

Butler, Judith. 1990. *Gender Trouble: Feminism and the Subversion of Identity.* New York: Routledge.

————. 1993. *Bodies That Matter.* New York: Routledge.

————. 1997. *Excitable Speech: A Politics of the Performative.* New York: Routledge.

Carey-Webb, Allen. 1998. *Making Subjects: Literature and the Emergence of National Identity.* New York: Garland Publishing.

Caruth, Cathy. 1993. "Past Recognition: Narrative Origins in Wordsworth and Freud." In *Romanticism,* ed. Cynthia Chase, 98–112. London and New York: Longman.

Castel-Bloom, Orly. 2003. *Human Parts.* Trans. Dalya Bilu. Jaffrey, N.H.: Godine Publisher.

Chase, Cynthia. 1978. "The Decomposition of Elephants: Double-Reading *Daniel Deronda.*" *PMLA* 93, no. 2 (March): 215–27.

Chatterjee, Partha. 2001. "The Nationalist Resolution of the Women's Question." In *Postcolonial Discourses,* ed. Gregory Castle, 151–66. Malden, Mass.: Blackwell.

Cheyette, Bryan. 1993. *Constructions of "The Jew" in English Literature and Society.* Cambridge: Cambridge University Press.

————, ed. 1996. *Between "Race" and Culture: Representations of "Race" and Culture in English and American Literature.* Stanford, Calif.: Stanford University Press.

Cheyette, Bryan, and Laura Marcus, eds. 1998. *Modernity, Culture and the Jew.* Stanford, Calif.: Stanford University Press.

Cross, John Walter, ed. 1885. *George Eliot's Life as Related in Her Letters and Journals.* 3 vols. Edinburgh: Blackwood.

De Beistegui, Miguel, and Simon Sparks, eds. 2000. *Philosophy and Tragedy.* London: Routledge.

Dekel, Mikhal. 2007. "'Who Taught This Foreign Woman About the Ways and Lives of the Jews?': George Eliot and the Hebrew Renaissance." *ELH* 74, no. 4 (Winter): 783–98.

———. 2008. "From the Mouth of the Raped Woman Rivka Schiff, 1903." In "Testimony." Special issue, *Women's Studies Quarterly,* Spring/Summer, 199–207.

Deleuze, Gilles. 1983. *Nietzsche and Philosophy.* Trans. Hugh Tomlinson. New York: Columbia University Press.

———. 2004. *Desert Islands and Other Texts, 1953–1974.* Trans. Michael Taormina. Cambridge, Mass.: MIT Press.

Deleuze, Gilles, and Felix Guattari. 1986. *Kafka: Toward a Minor Literature.* Minneapolis: University of Minnesota Press.

Derrida, Jacques. 1985. *Ear of the Other: Otobiography, Transference, Translation.* Trans. Peggy Kamuf. New York: Schocken.

De Vries, Hent, and Samuel Weber, eds. 1997. *Violence, Identity and Self-Determination.* Stanford, Calif.: Stanford University Press.

Diamant, Naomi. 1991. "Judaism, Homosexuality and Other Sign Systems in *A la recherche du temps perdu.*" *Romantic Review* 82, no. 2 (March): 179–92.

Eagleton, Terry. 2003. *Sweet Violence: The Idea of the Tragic.* Oxford: Blackwell Publishing.

Eagleton, Terry, Fredric Jameson, and Edward W. Said. 1990. *Nationalism, Irony and Commitment.* Minneapolis: University of Minnesota Press.

Easterling, P. E., ed. 1997. *The Cambridge Companion to Greek Tragedy.* Cambridge, Eng.: Cambridge University Press.

Eisenstadt, Shmuel Noah, and Moshe Lissak, eds. 1999. *Ha-Zionut ve-hakhazara la-historia* (*Zionism and the Return to History: A Re-Assessment*). Jerusalem: Yad Ben Zvi.

Eliot, George. 1856. "Silly Novels by Lady Novelists." *Westminster Review* 66 (October): 442–61.

———. 1893. *Daniel Deronda* (Hebrew). Trans. David Frishman. Warsaw: Achiasaf Publishers (microfilm).

———. 1908/1970. *The Writings of George Eliot.* New York: AMS Press.

———. 1985. *Adam Bede* (1869). New York: Penguin.

————. 1994. "The Modern Hep! Hep! Hep!" In *Impressions of Theophrastus Such* (1879). Ed. Nancy Henry. London: William Pickering.

————. 1995. *Daniel Deronda* (1876). New York: Penguin.

————. 1996. *Daniel Deronda Notebooks.* New York: Cambridge University Press.

Ellis-Fermor, Una. 1945. *The Frontiers of Drama.* London: Methuen.

Elon, Amos. 1977. *Herzl.* Tel Aviv: Am Oved.

Fanon, Frantz. 1963. *The Wretched of the Earth.* Trans. Constance Farrington. London: Penguin.

Feldman, Yael. 1999. *No Room of Their Own: Gender and Nation in Israeli Women's Fiction.* New York: Columbia University Press.

Flaubert, Gustave. 1972. *Première éducation sentimentale (First Sentimental Education).* Trans. Douglas Garman. Berkeley: University of California Press.

Foucault, Michel. 2001. *Madness and Civilization.* London: Routledge.

Freedman, Jonathan. 2001. "Coming Out of the Jewish Closet with Marcel Proust." *GLQ: A Journal of Lesbian and Gay Studies* 7 (4): 521–51.

Freud, Sigmund. 1965. *Interpretation of Dreams* (1900). New York: Avon Books.

Friedman, Thomas. 2002. "Crazier than Thou." *New York Times,* February 13, A31.

Frishman, David. 1887. "Ha-hakdama le-Daniel Deronda" ("Introduction to *Daniel Deronda*"). *Ben Ami* 1 (January).

————. 1968. *Michtavim al dvar ha-sifru. (Letters Pertaining to Literature: Book One).* Jerusalem: Newman, Inc.

Gallagher, Catherine. 1986. "George Eliot and *Daniel Deronda:* The Prostitute and the Jewish Question." In *Sex, Politics and Science in the Nineteenth Century Novel,* ed. Ruth Yeazell, 39–62. Baltimore: Johns Hopkins University Press.

Gandhi, Leela. 1998. *Postcolonial Theory.* New York: Columbia University Press.

Gay, Peter. 1988. *Freud: A Life for Our Time.* New York: Norton.

Gellner, Ernest. 1983. *Nations and Nationalism.* Ithaca, N.Y.: Cornell University Press.

Gilman, Sander. 1986. *Jewish Self-Hatred: Anti-Semitism and the Hidden Language of the Jews.* Baltimore: Johns Hopkins University Press.

————. 1991. *The Jew's Body.* New York: Routledge.

Girard, Rene. 1986. *The Scapegoat*. Baltimore: Johns Hopkins University Press.

Glover, David. 1996. *Vampires, Mummies and Liberals*. Durham, N.C.: Duke University Press.

Gluzman, Michael. 2005. "Khoser ko'akh: Ha-makhala ha-mavishah be-yoter" ("Lack of Strength: The Most Shameful Illness"). In *Be-ir Hahariga: Bikur Meuchar* (*In the City of Slaughter—a Visit at Twilight: Bialik's Poem a Century After*), ed. Dan Miron, 13–36. Tel Aviv: Resling Press.

———. 2007. *Ha-guf ha-Ziyyoni* (*The Zionist Body*). Tel Aviv: Ha'kibbutz ha'meuchad.

Gnessin, Uri Nisan. 1982. *Collected Works*. 2 Vols. Eds. Dan Miron and I. Zmora. Tel Aviv: Ha'kibbutz ha'meuchad.

Goggin, James, and Eileen Goggin. 2001. *Death of a Jewish Science*. West Lafayette, Ind.: Purdue University Press.

Golomb, Jacob, ed. 1996. *Nietzsche and Jewish Culture*. New York: Routledge.

———, ed. 2002. *Nietzsche ba-tarbut ha-ivrit* (*Nietzsche in Hebrew Culture*). Jerusalem: Hebrew University Press.

———. 2004. *Nietzsche and Zion*. Ithaca, N.Y.: Cornell University Press.

Goren, Jacob, ed. 1991. *Eduyot Nifgaei Kishinev, 1903* (*Testimony of Victims of the 1903 Kishinev Pogrom*). Tel Aviv: Ha'kibbutz ha'meuchad and Yad Tabenkin.

Gourgouris, Stathis. 1996. *Dream Nation: Enlightenment, Colonization and the Institution of Modern Greece*. Stanford, Calif.: Stanford University Press.

Greenberg, Jay R., and Stephen A. Mitchell. 1983. *Object Relations in Psychoanalytic Theory*. Cambridge, Mass.: Harvard University Press.

Gur, Batia. 1998. *Even takhat Even* (*Stone for Stone*). Tel Aviv: Am Oved.

Guvrin, Nurit. 1991. *Brenner*. Tel Aviv: Defense Ministry Publishing House.

Habermas, Jürgen. 1983. "Hannah Arendt on the Concept of Power." In *Philosophical-Political Profiles*, 171–88. Cambridge, Mass.: MIT Press.

———. 1991. *The Structural Transformation of the Public Sphere*. Trans. Thomas Burger. Cambridge, Mass.: MIT Press.

Haight, G. S. 1969. *George Eliot: A Biography*. Oxford: Oxford University Press.

Halliwell, Stephen. 1998. *Aristotle's Poetics*. Chicago: University of Chicago Press.

Hanssen, Beatrice. 1997. "On the Politics of Pure Means: Benjamin, Arendt, Foucault." In *Violence, Identity, and Self-Determination,* ed. Hent De Vries and Samuel Weber, 271–83. Stanford, Calif.: Stanford University Press.

Harrowitz, Nancy, and Barbara Hyams, eds. 1995. *Jews and Gender: Responses to Otto Weininger.* Philadelphia: Temple University Press.

Hegel, G. W. F. 1977. *The Phenomenology of the Spirit.* Oxford: Clarendon Press.

Hertzberg, Arthur. 1997. *The Zionist Idea.* New York: Meridian Books.

Herzl, Theodor. 1988. *The Jewish State.* New York: Dover Publications. (Orig. pub. *Judenstaat.* Leipzig: Wein M. Breitenstein, 1896.)

———. 2000. *Altneuland (Old New Land)* (1902). Ed. Jacques Kornberg. Trans. Lotta Levensohn. Princeton, N.J.: Markus Wiener.

Hever, Hannan. 2002. *Producing the Modern Hebrew Canon: Nation Building and Minority Discourse.* New York: New York University Press.

———. 2004. "The Beginning of Hebrew Poetry in *Eretz Yisrael*" (unpublished essay).

———. 2005. "Korbanot ha-zionut" ("Victims of Zionism"). In *Be-ir Hahariga: Bikur Meuchar (In the City of Slaughter—a Visit at Twilight: Bialik's Poem a Century After)*, ed. Dan Miron, 37–70. Tel Aviv: Resling Press.

———. 2007. *Ha-sipur ve-ha-le'om (The Narrative and the Nation).* Tel Aviv: Resling.

Hoberman, M. John. 1995. "Otto Weininger and the Critique of Jewish Masculinity." In Harrowitz and Hyams 1995, 141.

Hobsbawm, Eric. 1990. *Nations and Nationalisms Since 1780.* Cambridge: Cambridge University Press.

Hoffman, Anne Golomb. 2003. "The Red Heifer." In *Reading Hebrew Literature,* ed. Alan Mintz, 38–51. Hanover, N.H.: Brandeis University Press.

Hölderlin, Friedrich. 1988. *Essays and Letters on Theory.* Trans. Thomas Pfau. Albany, N.Y.: SUNY Press.

Honig, Bonnie, ed. 1995. *Feminist Interpretations of Hannah Arendt.* University Park: Pennsylvania State University Press.

Horkheimer, Max, and Theodor Adorno. 1972. *Dialectics of Enlightenment.* Trans. John Cumming. New York: Herder and Herder.

Howe, Irving, and Ruth R. Wisse, eds. 1979. *Best of Sholom Aleichem.* Washington, D.C.: New Republic Books.

Hume, David. 1985. *A Treatise of Human Nature.* London: Viking Penguin.

Jacobs, Steven L. 1987. *Shirot Bialik: A New and Annotated Translation of Chaim Nachman Bialik's Epic Poems.* Columbus, Ohio: Alpha Publishing Company.

Jaspers, Karl. 1953. *Tragedy Is Not Enough.* Trans. Harald A. T. Reiche, Harry T. Moore, and Karl W. Deutsch. London: V. Gollancz.

Jeffords, Susan. 1989. *The Remasculinization of America: Gender and the Vietnam War.* Bloomington: Indiana University Press.

Johnson, Barbara. 1998. *The Feminist Difference.* Cambridge, Mass.: Harvard University Press.

Johnson, Claudia L. 2001. "F. R. Leavis: The 'Great Tradition' of the English Novel and the Jewish Part." *Nineteenth Century Literature* 56, vol. 2 (September): 199–227.

Kadish, Sharman. 1992. *Bolsheviks and British Jews: The Anglo-Jewish Community, Britain, and the Russian Revolution.* London: Routledge.

Kafka, Franz. 1977. *Letters to Friends, Family and Editors.* Ed. Richard Winston. Trans. Richard and Clara Winston. New York: Schocken.

Kaplan, Carla. 1997. "Undesirable Desire: Citizenship and Romance in Modern American Fiction." *Modern Fiction Studies* 43, no. 1 (Spring): 144–69.

Kehde, Suzanne, and Jean Pickering, eds. 1997. *Narratives of Nostalgia, Gender and Nationalism.* New York: New York University Press.

Kierkegaard, Søren. 2006. *Fear and Trembling.* Trans. Stephen Evans and Sylvia Walsh. Cambridge: Cambridge University Press.

Kirk, Geoffrey Stephen. 1970. *Myth: Its Meanings and Functions in Ancient and Other Cultures.* Berkeley: University of California Press.

Klausner, Yosef. 1951. *Bialik ve-shirat hayav (Bialik and the Poetics of My Life).* Tel Aviv: Dvir.

Klein, Melanie. 1953. *Love, Hate and Reparation.* London: Hogarth Press.

Kornberg, Jacques, ed. 1983. *At the Crossroads: Essays on Ahad Ha'am.* Albany, NY: SUNY Press.

Kristeva, Julia. 1980. *Desire in Language.* New York: Columbia University Press.

Krook, Dorothea. 1969. *Elements of Tragedy.* New Haven, Conn.: Yale University Press.

Larsen, Nella. 1997. *Passing.* New York: Penguin Books.

Lazar, Shimon Menachem. 1900. "The Treacherous Daughters," *Hamagid,* March 1.

Leavis, F. R. 1964. *The Great Tradition: George Eliot, Henry James, Joseph Conrad.* New York: New York University Press.

———. 1982. *The Critic as Anti-Philosopher: Essays and Papers by F. R. Leavis.* Ed. G. Singh. London: Chatto and Windus.

Le Rider, Jacques. 1993. *Modernity and Crises of Identity.* Trans. Rosemary Morris. New York: Continuum.

Lerner, Lawrence. 1997. "Proust and the Profanation of the Jewish Mother." *Dissertation Abstracts* 58, no. 5 (November).

Levi, Primo. 1996. *Survival in Auschwitz (Se questo è un uomo?).* New York: Simon and Schuster.

Lewis, C. S. 1961. *Experiment in Criticism.* London: Cambridge University Press.

Lewis, Reina. 1996. *Gendering Orientalism: Race, Femininity and Representation.* New York: Routledge.

Liska, Vivian. 2009. *When Kafka Says We.* Bloomington: Indiana University Press.

Lloyd, David. 1997. "Nationalisms Against the State." In *The Politics of Culture in the Shadow of Capital.* Ed. Lisa Lowe and David Lloyd. Durham, N.C.: Duke University Press.

Lloyd, David, and Paul Thomas. eds. (with Abdul JanMohamed). 1991. *The Nature and Context of Minority Discourse.* Oxford: Oxford University Press.

———. 1998. *Culture and the State.* New York: Routledge.

Locke, John. 1988. *Two Treatises of Government.* New York: Cambridge University Press.

Lowenthal, Marvin, ed. and trans. 1956. *The Diaries of Theodor Herzl.* New York: Dial Press.

Lukács, Georg. 1971. *The Theory of the Novel.* Trans. Anna Bostock. Cambridge, Mass.: MIT Press.

———. 1974. *Soul and Form.* Trans. Anna Bostock. Cambridge, Mass.: MIT Press.

Matalon, Ronit. 2003. *Bliss.* New York: Metropolitan. (Orig. pub. *Sarah, Sarah.* Tel Aviv: Am Oved, 2000.)

———. 2006. *Galu et panea (Uncover Her Face).* Tel Aviv: Am Oved.

McClintock, Anne. 1997. "No Longer in a Future Heaven: Gender, Race and Nationalism." In McClintock, Mufti, and Shohat 1997, 89–112.

McClintock, Anne, Aamir Mufti, and Ella Shohat, eds. 1997. *Dangerous Liaisons: Gender, Nation, and Postcolonial Perspectives.* Minneapolis: University of Minnesota Press.

McGann, Jerome. 1983. *The Romantic Ideology*. Chicago: University of Chicago Press.

McGuire, William, ed. 1974. *The Freud/Jung Letters*. Princeton, N.J.: Bollingen Series.

Melville, Herman. 1969. "Billy Budd, Sailor." *Great Short Works of Herman Melville*, 429–505. New York: Harper and Row.

Mendelsohn, Daniel. 2006. *The Lost: A Search for Six of Six Million*. New York: HarperCollins Publishers.

Mendes-Flohr, Paul. 1997. "Zarathustra's Apostle: Martin Buber and the Jewish Renaissance." In *Nietzsche and Jewish Culture*, ed. Jacob Golomb, 233–41. London: Routledge.

Menkin, Rachel. 2003. "Tehila's Daughter and Mikhlina Aratin, That Damned Convert." *Haaretz* 6, no. 27.

Meyer, Susan. 1996. *Imperialism at Home: Race and Victorian Women's Fiction*. Ithaca, N.Y.: Cornell University Press.

Mill, John Stuart. 1955. *On Liberty*. New York: Gateway.

Miller, Arthur. 1949. "Tragedy and the Common Man." *New York Times*, February 27.

Mintz, Alan. 1989. *"Banished from Their Father's Table": Loss of Faith and Hebrew Autobiography*. Bloomington: Indiana University Press.

Miron, Dan. 1980. *Ha-preda min ha-ani ha-ani (Taking Leave of the Impoverished Self: Ch. N. Bialik's Early Poetry 1891–1901)*. Tel Aviv: Ha-universita Ha-ptucha.

———. 1987a. *Bo'ah, laylah: Ha-sifrut ha-Ivrit ben higayon le-i-gayon be-mifneh ha-me'ah ha-estrim: 'Iyunim bi-yetsirot H. N. Bialik u-M. Y. Berdyczewski (Come Night: Hebrew Literature Between the Rational and the Irrational at the Turn of the Twentieth Century)*. Tel Aviv: Dvir.

———. 1987b. *Bodedim be'moadam (When Loners Come Together)*. Tel Aviv: Am Oved.

———. 1990–91. "Without References: An 'Innocent' Introduction to Bialik's Poetry," Pt. 1, *Moznaim* 65, no. 2 (October 1990): 40–47; Pt. 2, *Moznaim* 65, no. 3 (November/December 1990): 7–14; Pt. 3, *Moznaim* 65, no. 5 (February/March 1991): 57–64.

———. 1996. *A Traveler Disguised: The Rise of Yiddish Fiction in the Nineteenth Century*. Syracuse, N.Y.: Syracuse University Press.

———. 2000. *H. N. Bialik and the Prophetic Mode in Modern Hebrew Poetry*. Syracuse, N.Y.: Syracuse University Press.

———. 2005. "Me'ir ha-hariga ve-hal'a." ("From the 'City of Slaughter' Onward"). In *Be-ir Hahariga: Bikur Meuchar (In the City of*

Slaughter—a Visit at Twilight: Bialik's Poem a Century After), ed. Dan Miron, 71–154. Tel Aviv: Resling.

———. 2008. "Sadness in Palestine?" *Haaretz*, December 10.

Morell, Roy. 1965. "The Psychology of Tragic Pleasure." *Essays in Criticism*, vol. 6.

Moretti, Franco. 1987. *The Way of the World: The Bildungsroman in European Culture*. London: Verso.

———. 2005. *Signs Taken for Wonders*. London: Verso.

Mosse, George L. 1985. *Nationalism and Sexuality*. Madison: University of Wisconsin Press.

———. 1993. *Confronting the Nation: Jewish and Western Nationalism*. Hanover, N.H.: Brandeis University Press.

———. 1996. *The Image of Man: The Creation of Modern Masculinity*. New York: Oxford University Press.

Mossinsohn, Yigal. 1989. "Matityahu Schatz" in *Aforim ka-sak: Sipurim u-machazot* (*Gray as Sack: Stories and Plays*). Jerusalem: Bialik Institute.

Nairn, Tom. 1977. *The Break-Up of Britain: Crisis and Neo-Nationalism*. London: New Left Books.

Neale, Steve. 1983. "Masculinity as Spectacle." *Screen* 24: 2–17.

Nietzsche, Friedrich. 1955. *Beyond Good and Evil*. Chicago: Gateway.

———. 1961. *Thus Spoke Zarathustra*. London: Penguin.

———. 1962. *Philosophy in the Tragic Age of the Greeks*. Trans. Marianne Cowan. Chicago: Regnery.

———. 1989. *On the Genealogy of Morals*. Trans. and ed. Walter Kaufmann. New York: Vintage.

———. 1886/1995. *The Birth of Tragedy*. Trans. Clifton P. Fadiman. New York: Dover.

Nochlin, Linda, and Tamar Garb, eds. 1995. *The Jew in the Text: Modernity and the Construction of Identity*. London: Thames and Hudson.

Nordau, Max. 1993. *Degeneration* (1895). Lincoln: University of Nebraska Press.

Nurbhai, Saleel, and K. M. Newton. 2002. *George Eliot, Judaism and the Novels: Jewish Myth and Mysticism*. New York: Palgrave.

Pappas, Nickolas. 2005. *The Nietzsche Disappointment*. New York: Rowan and Littlefield.

Parker, Andrew, Mary Russon, and Doris Sommer, eds. 1992. *Nationalisms and Sexualities*. New York: Routledge.

Parush, Iris. 1992. *Kanon sifruti ve-ide'ologyah le'umit* (*National Ideology and Literary Canon*). Jerusalem: Bialik Institute.

——. 2004. *Reading Jewish Women: Marginalization and Moderniza-tion in 19th Century Eastern European Jewish Society.* Trans. Saadya Sternberg. Boston: Brandeis University Press.

Pinsker, Leo. 1944. *Autoemancipation* (1882). In *Road to Freedom: Writ-ings and Addresses by Leo Pinsker,* ed. Ben-Zion Netanyahu, 82–113. New York: Scopus Publishing.

Pitterberg, Gabriel. 2007. "Zion's Rebel Daughter." *New Left Review,* November/December. http://www.newleftreview.org.

Press, Jacob. 1997. "Same-Sex Unions in Modern Europe: *Daniel De-ronda, Altneuland,* and the Homoerotics of Jewish Nationalism." In *Novel Gazing: Queer Reading in Fiction,* ed. Eve Kosofsky Sedgwick, 299–329. Durham, N.C.: Duke University Press.

Proust, Marcel. 1982. *In Search of Lost Time (A la recherche du temps perdu)* (1913–27). New York: Vintage.

Radhakrishnan, Rajagopalan. 1992. "Nationalism, Gender, and the Narrative of Identity." In *Nationalisms and Sexualities,* ed. An-drew Parker, Mary Russo, and Doris Sommer, 77–95. London: Routledge.

Ragussis, Michael. 1995. *Figures of Conversion: "The Jewish Question" and English National Identity.* Durham, N.C.: Duke University Press.

Raizen, Esther R., trans. 1980. *No Rattling of Sabers: An Anthology of Israeli War Poetry.* Austin: Center for Middle Eastern Studies, University of Texas at Austin.

Raz-Karkotzkin, Amnon. 1999. "Ha-shiva el ha-historia shel ha-geula" ("The Return to the History of Redemption"). In *Ha-Zionut ve-hakhazara la-historia (Zionism and the Return to History: A New Assessment),* ed. Shmuel Noah Eisenstadt and Moshe Lis-sak, 238–60. Jerusalem: Yad Ben Zvi.

Reiss, Timothy. 1980. *Tragedy and Truth.* New Haven, Conn.: Yale Uni-versity Press.

Renan, Ernest. 1881/1990. "What Is a Nation?" Trans. Martin Thom. In *Na-tion and Narration,* ed. Homi Bhabha, 8–22. London: Routledge.

Riesman, David. 1955. *Lonely Crowd.* New Haven, Conn.: Yale Univer-sity Press.

Rose, Jacqueline. 2005. *The Question of Zion.* Princeton, N.J.: Princeton University Press.

Roselli, John. 1980. "The Self-Image of Effectness: Physical Education and Nationalism in Nineteenth Century Bengal." *Past and Pres-ent* 86: 121–48.

Roskies, David G., ed. 1989. *The Literature of Destruction: Jewish Responses to Catastrophe.* Philadelphia: Jewish Publication Society.

Rousseau, Jean-Jacques. 1987. *Basic Political Writings.* Indianapolis: Hackett.

Scarry, Elaine. 1985. *The Body in Pain.* New York: Oxford University Press.

———. 1988. *Literature and the Body: Essays on Populations and Persons.* Baltimore: Johns Hopkins University Press.

Schapiro, Barbara A. 1983. *The Romantic Mother.* Baltimore and London: Johns Hopkins University Press.

Schamus, James. 2007. "Next Year in *Munich:* Zionism, Masculinity, and Diaspora in Spielberg's Epic." *Representations* 100, no. 1 (Fall): 53–66.

Schmitt, Carl. 1985. *Political Theology: Four Essays on the Concept of Sovereignty.* Cambridge, Mass.: MIT Press.

Schopenhauer, Arthur. 1999. *Prize Essay on the Freedom of the Will.* Cambridge: Cambridge University Press.

Schorske, Carl E. 1981. *Fin-De-Siècle Vienna: Politics and Culture.* New York: Vintage Books.

Scott, Joan, and Debra Keats. 2004. *Going Public: Feminism and the Shifting Boundaries of the Private Sphere.* Urbana and Champaign: University of Illinois Press.

Sedgwick, Eve. 1985. *Between Men: English Literature and Male Homosexual Desire.* New York: Columbia University Press.

———. 1990. *Epistemology of the Closet.* Berkeley: University of California Press.

Shamir, Moshe. 1966. *Hu halakh ba-sadot (He Walked the Fields).* Tel Aviv: Sifriyat ha'poalim.

———.1989. *Hu halakh ba-sadot: ma'khazeh beshney khalakim (He Walked the Field: A Play in Two Parts).* Tel Aviv: Or-Am.

Shamir, Ziva. 1985. "The Battle of the Young Tel-Aviv Modernists with the Literary Establishment and Its Traces in Bialik's Later Works." *Proceedings of the Ninth World Zionist Congress of Jewish Studies,* ed. Moshe Goshen-Gottstein, 357–63. Jerusalem: Publications of the Perry Foundation for Biblical Research in the Hebrew University of Jerusalem.

Shapira, Anita. 1990. "Herzl, Ahad Ha'am, and Berdichevsky: Comments on Their Nationalist Concepts." *Jewish History* 4, no. 2 (Fall).

————. 2002. "Ha-mitos shel ha-yehudi ha-khadash" ("The Myth of the New Jew"). In Golomb 2002, 113–30.

Shoham, Reuven. 1995. "The Archetypal Birth Narrative and Its Rhetorical Meaning in the New Hebrew Literature: Bialik, Grinberg, Shlonsky." *Alei Siach* 36: 19–30.

Sholom Aleichem (Sholem Rabinowitz). "Two Anti-Semites." Trans. Miriam Waddington. In *Best of Sholom Aleichem,* ed. Irving Howe and Ruth R. Wisse, 115–21. Washington, D.C.: New Republic Books.

Showalter, Elaine, ed. 1990. *Sexual Anarchy: Gender and Culture at the Fin de siècle.* New York: Viking.

Shuttleworth, Sally. 1984. *George Eliot and Nineteenth-Century Science: The Make-Believe of a Beginning.* Cambridge: Cambridge University Press.

Silberschlag, Eisig. 1968. *Saul Tschernichowsky: Poet of Revolt.* Ithaca, N.Y.: Cornell University Press.

Simon, Leon, ed. and trans. 1944. *Essays, Letters, Memoirs of Ahad Ha'am.* Oxford: East and West Library.

Slavet, Eliza. 2009. *Racial Fever: Freud and the Jewish Question.* New York: Fordham University Press.

Smith, Paul. 1993. *Clint Eastwood: A Cultural Production.* Minneapolis: University of Minnesota Press.

Smith, Steven B. 1997. *Spinoza, Liberalism, and the Question of Jewish Identity.* New Haven, Conn.: Yale University Press.

Solomon, Esther. 2005. "The Light Brigades." *Haaretz* (Engl.), June 27.

Sommers, Doris. 1991. *Foundational Fictions.* Berkeley: University of California Press.

Sontag, Susan. 2003. *Regarding the Pain of Others.* New York: Farrar, Strauss and Giroux.

Sophocles. 1994. *Oedipus Rex.* Trans. H. D. F. Kitto. New York: Oxford University Press.

Spicehandler, Ezra. 1995. "The Fiction of 'The Generation in the Land.'" In *Israel: The First Decade,* ed. Ilan Troen, 313–30. Albany: SUNY Press.

Spivak, Gayatri. 1988. *In Other Worlds: Essays in Cultural Politics.* New York: Routledge.

Stanislawski, Michael. 2001. *Zionism and the Fin de Siècle.* Berkeley: University of California Press.

Stecopoulos, Harry, and Michael Uebel, eds. 1997. *Race and the Subject of Masculinities.* Durham, N.C.: Duke University Press.

Steiner, George. 1980. *Death of Tragedy.* New Haven, Conn.: Yale University Press.

Stendhal. 1981. *Le Rouge et le noir (The Red and the Black).* Trans. Lloyd C. Parks. New York: New American Library.

Stoker, Bram. 1993. *Dracula.* London: Wordsworth Classics.

Storer, Richard. 1995. "Leavis and 'Gwendolen Harleth.'" In *F. R. Leavis: Essay and Documents,* ed. Ian MacKillop and Richard Storer, 40–49. Sheffield: Sheffield Academic Press.

Tosh, John. 1994. "What Should Historians Do with Masculinity? Reflections on Nineteenth Century Britain." *History Workshop Journal,* vol. 38.

Tucker, Irene. 2000. *A Probable State: The Novel, the Contract, and the Jews.* Chicago: University of Chicago Press.

Verene, Donald Phillip. 1985. *Hegel's Recollections.* Albany, N.Y.: SUNY Press.

Vernant, Jean-Pierre, and Pierre Vidal-Naquet. 1988. *Myth and Tragedy in Ancient Greece.* Trans. Janet Lloyd. New York: Zone Books.

Versus, Shmuel. 1980. "*Daniel Deronda* ba'itonut ve-hasifrut ha-ivrit" ("*Daniel Deronda* in Hebrew Journals and Literature"). *Molad* 39–40: 176–88.

Waller, Margaret. 1993. *The Male Malady.* New Brunswick, N.J.: Rutgers University Press.

Walzer, Michael. 1986. *Exodus and Revolution.* New York: Basic Books.

Wegner, Phillip E. 2002. *Imaginary Communities: Utopia, the Nation, and the Spatial Histories of Modernity.* Berkeley: University of California Press.

Weininger, Otto. 1906. *Sex and Character.* London: Heinemann.

Williams, Raymond. 1983. *Culture and Society (1780–1950).* New York: Columbia University Press.

———. 2006. *Modern Tragedy* (1966). Ed. Pamela McCallum. Toronto: Broadview Encore Editions.

Wilmer, S. E. 2004. *Writing and Rewriting National Theatre Histories.* Iowa City: University of Iowa Press, 2004.

Wordsworth, William. 1981. *The Prelude.* London: Oxford University Press.

Yerushalmi, Yosef Hayyim. 1991. *Freud's Moses.* New Haven, Conn.: Yale University Press.

Yizhar, S. 1947. "Layla bli yeriyot" (Night Without Stars) in *Ha-chorsha ba-giv'a* (*The Forest on the Hill*). Merchavia: Sifriyat Ha'poalim.

————. 1971. *Shiv'a sipurim* (*Seven Stories*). Tel Aviv: Ha'kibbutz ha'meuchad.

Zeitlin, Froma. 1986. "Configurations of Rape in Greek Myth." In *Rape*, ed. Sylvana Tomaselli and Roy Porter, 122–51. Oxford and New York: Basil Blackwell.

Zemach, Adi. 1988. "Two Poles in Bialik's Love Poetry." In *Ha-lavi hamistater* (*The Cloaked Lion*), 34–55. Jerusalem: Kiryat Sefer.

Zipperstein, Steven. 1993. *Elusive Prophet: Ahad Ha'am and the Origins of Zionism*. Berkeley: University of California Press.

Žižek, Slavoj. 1994. "Otto Weininger, or 'Woman Doesn't Exist.'" *New Formations* 23: 97–113.

INDEX

Ahad Ha'am. *See* Ginzburg, Asher

Alcharisi, the, 31, 41, 63–67, 227; as enemy of Zion, 31–32; lack of identity, 65; motherhood, refusal of, 72–76; negative liberty, 67, 72; parallels to Eliot, 67, 73; and passing, 74; and secular culture, 81

alienism, 52, 54; as detachment from origins, 58; Jewish alienism, 46, 52–53, 54; as symptom of modernity, 54

Allison, David, 196

allosemitism, 9

Almagor, Dan, and Effi Netzer ("A Ballad for a Medic/Balada la-khovesh"), 225–26

Alterman, Nathan ("The Third Mother/ Ha-em ha-shlisheet"), 228

Altneuland: and assimilated intellectuals, 104; as bildungsroman, 97; and *Dracula,* 100; and homoerotic male bond, 105; as imagined community, 102; and male communal bond, 103; masculinity, ideal model of, 97; national subject, formation of, 111; progressive society portrayed in, 97; public/private and gender, 120–22; as response to decadence, 102; stereotypes as performative in, 107; submission and nonviolent debate in, 125–29; as utopian novel, 99; and will to action, 100. See also *Old New Land*

Anderson, Benedict, 5; antinationalism, Western, 24; nation as family, 15–16; "permanent present" of nations, 22

anti-Semitism, political, 95

Arab, as Other, 34

Arendt, Hannah: anti-Semitism, political, 96; city-state and public life, 119; Eichmann trial, 35; Herzl, criticism of, 240n2; *selbstdenken,* 35; and Six Day War, 35

Armstrong, Nancy, 186, 191, 196

Aryan culture: Herzl and, 108–9; as masculine identity, 8, 15

assimilation, 44

Athens and democratic age, 136, 161

Austin, J. L., 108

Autoemancipation, 3, 9, 22, 26–27, 45, 183; as constitutive of nation, 23; and Enlightenment ideals, 28; and national consciousness, 15; and the tragic, 26–27

autogenesis, male, 76–77

Ba-khoref. See "In Winter"

Balibar, Etienne, 186, 191, 210

Bar-Yosef, Hamutal, 182

Bauman, Zygmunt, 9; Christian imagination, Jews in, 25; "living fossil," Jews as, 22

Be-ir ha-hariga. *See under* Bialik, Hayyim Nahman

Benjamin, Walter (*The Origin of German Tragic Drama*), 154; modernity as rediscovery of tragedy, 155

Ben Yehuda, Eliezer, 86

Berdyczewski, Micah Josef, 134, 135, 165, 175, 186, 196; "Between Two Camps" (Makhanayim), 189–91, 195, 207; biography, 169–70; and Hasidic Judaism, 188; and Nietzsche, 172; "On the Relationship Between Ethics and Aesthetics" (dissertation), 169, 194, 198; "The Question of Culture," 185; "Red Heifer," 166, 176–78, 183–84, 185, 187–88, 198

Berlant, Lauren, 5, 16, 171

Berlin, Isaiah, 41

Bialik, Hayyim Nahman, 135, 139–40, 161, 186, 230; autobiographical poems, 226, 245n1; Be-ir ha-hariga ("In the City of Killing"), 135, 157, 159, 205, 216; "Dead of the Wilderness," 216; and discourse of tragedy, 165; extended excerpts from poem, 141, 146–47, 149, 150–51, 153, 154, 155; image of raped nation, 154; "On the Slaughter," 140; witness as male subject, 154

bildungsroman, 31, 39; as failed erotic relationship, 34; fin-de-siècle Hebrew, 135; Hebrew language, 28, 135 (defined); interiority and individuality in, 39–40,